STEPHEN KING

Recent Titles in Greenwood Biographies

STEPHEN KING

A Biography

Albert Rolls

GREENWOOD BIOGRAPHIES

GREENWOOD PRESS
WESTPORT, CONNECTICUT • LONDON

Library of Congress Cataloging-in-Publication Data

Rolls, Albert.
   Stephen King : a biography / Albert Rolls.
       p. cm. — (Greenwood biographies, ISSN 1540–4900)
   Includes bibliographical references and index.
   ISBN 978–0–313–34572–2 (alk. paper)
   1. King, Stephen, 1947– 2. Novelists, American—20th century—
Biography. 3. Horror tales–Authorship. 4. Authorship. I. Title.
   PS3561.I483Z855 2009
   813'.54—dc22
   [B]   2008036702

British Library Cataloguing in Publication Data is available.

Library of Congress Catalog Card Number: 2008036702
ISBN: 978–0–313–34572–2
ISSN: 1540–4900

First published in 2009

Greenwood Press, 88 Post Road West, Westport, CT 06881
An imprint of Greenwood Publishing Group, Inc.
www.greenwood.com

Printed in the United States of America

The paper used in this book complies with the
Permanent Paper Standard issued by the National
Information Standards Organization (Z39.48–1984).

10 9 8 7 6 5 4 3 2 1

CONTENTS

Photo essay follows page 104

SERIES FOREWORD

In response to high school and public library needs, Greenwood developed this distinguished series of full-length biographies specifically for student use. Prepared by field experts and professionals, these engaging biographies are tailored for high school students who need challenging yet accessible biographies. Ideal for secondary school assignments, the length, format and subject areas are designed to meet educators' requirements and students' interests.

Greenwood offers an extensive selection of biographies spanning all curriculum-related subject areas including social studies, the sciences, literature and the arts, history and politics, as well as popular culture, covering public figures and famous personalities from all time periods and backgrounds, both historic and contemporary, who have made an impact on American and/or world culture. Greenwood biographies were chosen based on comprehensive feedback from librarians and educators. Consideration was given to both curriculum relevance and inherent interest. The result is an intriguing mix of the well known and the unexpected, the saints and sinners from long-ago history and contemporary pop culture. Readers will find a wide array of subject choices from fascinating crime figures like Al Capone to inspiring pioneers like Margaret Mead, from the greatest minds of our time like Stephen Hawking to the most amazing success stories of our day like J.K. Rowling.

While the emphasis is on fact, not glorification, the books are meant to be fun to read. Each volume provides in-depth information about the subject's life from birth through childhood, the teen years, and adulthood.

A thorough account relates family background and education, traces personal and professional influences, and explores struggles, accomplishments, and contributions. A timeline highlights the most significant life events against a historical perspective. Bibliographies supplement the reference value of each volume.

PREFACE

Stephen King, who is primarily known as a writer of horror fiction, has become, with more than 50 books published since 1974, one of the best-selling authors ever to put pen to paper. His sales figures, however, have not always brought him the respect of the literary establishment, and in 2003, when he was awarded a medal for his distinguished contribution to American Letters by the National Book Foundation, he called attention to the ambiguous place he holds in the literary marketplace. He observed in his acceptance speech that the foundation's board had taken "a huge risk in giving this award to a man many people see as a rich hack." King went on to say:

> For far too long the so-called popular writers of this country and the so-called literary writers have stared at each other with animosity and a willful lack of understanding. This is the way it has always been. . . . But giving an award like this to a guy like me suggests that in the future things don't have to be the way they've always been. Bridges can be built between the so-called popular fiction and the so-called literary fiction.[1]

The distinction between popular and literary fiction that King refers to, and attempts to dismiss here, has haunted him since well before he began publishing books. As early as high school his creative work, as well as his reading interests, was discounted as trash by his school's arbiters of taste, even as he was creating outlets for his writing and finding fans among his peers. As a college student he fought against academic tastes in literature

and convinced his college's English department to offer a seminar in popular fiction.

Since the appearance of his first novel, *Carrie,* in 1974, King has wa-
vered between accepting his position as a mere popular writer, whose
work shouldn't be categorized as serious fiction, and lamenting the small-
mindedness of those who discount the value of a book simply because it
sells well. In his afterword to *Different Seasons* (1982), for example, he
observed that most of his novels and stories "have been plain fiction for
plain folks, the literary equivalent of a Big Mac and a large fries from
McDonald's."[2] Elsewhere, he has shown a desire to garner the respect
accorded to other literary figures, telling *Publisher's Weekly* in the early
1990s, "I'd like to win the National Book Award, the Pulitzer Prize, the
Nobel Prize; I'd like to have someone write a *New York Times Book Review*
piece that says, 'Hey, wait a minute guys, we made a mistake—this guy is
one of the great writers of the 20th century.'"[3] King went on to note
that he would be unlikely to earn any of the abovementioned awards or
read such an admission in the *New York Times Book Review.* "It's clear in
the critical stance; I hear it in the voice of people from literary journals
where somebody will start by saying, 'I don't read Stephen King,' and they
are really saying, 'I don't lower myself.'"[4]

The critical response to King has not always been as bad as he suggests. The eminent literary critic Harold Bloom might have attacked the
National Book Foundation for honoring King with a medal, arguing that
the decision to do so was "another low in the shocking process of dumbing down our cultural life."[5] Others, however, have been more supportive.
Critic Susan Bolotin, writing for the *New York Times,* clearly placed King
among the literati of his day, commenting: "Stephen King's fiction, at its
best, is equivalent to the post-Expressionist art found in the tiny galleries
of Manhattan's East Village, where painters, sculptors and collagists often
turn to the aggressive headlines of tabloid newspapers for inspiration."[6]
In fact, King's work has long distinguished itself from that of other popular writers by inspiring a critical body of work, which runs the spectrum
from popular celebration to academic high seriousness. King, regardless of
what some arbiters of taste may think, has become a literary figure in his
own right—one who is as concerned as Bloom about the dumbing down
of American culture. "I can find out where you live. I have my resources,"
King said at a commencement speech at the University of Maine in 2005.
"And if I show up at your house 10 years from now, and find nothing in
your living room but *Reader's Digests,* nothing in your bedroom but the
latest Dan Brown novel, and nothing in your bathroom but *Jokes for the
John,* I will chase you down to the end of your driveway and back shouting,

'Where are the damn books?... Why are you living the mental equivalent of a Kraft Macaroni & Cheese life?' "[7]

NOTES

1. Stephen King, National Book Awards Acceptance Speeches, http://www.nationalbook.org/nbaacceptspeech_sking.html.

2. Stephen King, *Different Seasons* (New York: Signet, 1983 [1982]), p. 504.

3. Quoted in Linnea Lannon, "Stephen King: Too Many Books, Not Enough Awards?" *Oregonian* (June 19, 1991), p. D5, http://www.lexis-nexis.com/.

4. Ibid.

5. Harold Bloom, "Dumbing Down American Readers," *Boston Globe* (September 24, 2003), http://www.boston.com/news/globe/editorial_opinion/oped/articles/2003/09/24/dumbing_down_american_readers.

6. Susan Bolotin, "Don't Turn Your Back on This Book," *New York Times* (June 9, 1985), sec. 7, p. 11, http://www.lexis-nexis.com/.

7. Judy Harrison, "King to UM Grads: Please Stay in Maine," *Bangor Daily News* (May 9, 2005), p. A1, http://www.lexis-nexis.com/.

TIMELINE: EVENTS IN THE
LIFE OF STEPHEN KING

1947	September 21: Stephen Edwin King is born to Donald Edwin King and Nellie Ruth Pillsbury King, in Portland, Maine
1949	Donald Edwin King walks out on his family
1953 or 1954	Stephen King writes his first stories, first copying *Combat Casey* comics and then creating his own, which featured the character Mr. Rabbit Trick
1958	After moving from town to town in the Midwest and the Northeast for nine years, King's family settles in Durham, Maine, where Ruth King begins to care for her parents, Guy and Nellie Pillsbury, in whose house the Kings begin to live
1959	Begins writing for his older brother's newspaper *Dave's Rag*
1959 or 1960	Discovers a box of his father's books, among them H. P. Lovecraft's *The Lurking Fear and Other Stories*
1962	Enters Lisbon High School, located in Lisbon Falls, a town near Durham
1963–1964	Begins writing for the sports pages of the Lisbon *Weekly Enterprise*, a local newspaper
1965	Publishes his first story, "I Was a Teenage Grave Robber," in Mike Garrett's *Comics Review*
1966	Graduates from Lisbon High School and enters the University of Maine, at Orono (UMO)

1967   Makes his first short-story sale, getting $35 for "The Glass Floor" from *Startling Mystery Stories*, edited by Robert A.W. Lowndes

1969   Begins writing a weekly column, King's Garbage Truck, for the *Maine Campus*, UMO's student newspaper; meets and falls in love with Tabitha Jane Spruce

1970   Graduates from UMO and takes a job pumping gas; later gets a job pressing sheets at New Franklin Laundry in Bangor

1971   January 2: Marries Tabitha Spruce

1971   Daughter Naomi King is born

1971   September: Takes a teaching job at Hampden Academy, where he had done his student teaching

1972   First son, Joe, is born

1973   March: First novel, *Carrie*, is bought by Doubleday for $2,500

1973   May: The paperback rights for *Carrie* are bought for $400,000; King quits teaching

1974   February: Nellie Ruth Pillsbury King dies

1974   *Carrie* appears in bookstores; King moves to Boulder, Colorado

1975   *'Salem's Lot* is published; King moves back to Maine and buys a home in Bridgton, Maine

1976   First film based on a King novel, Brian De Palma's *Carrie*, is released in theaters; King meets Kirby McCauley, who becomes his agent

1977   Second son, Owen, is born; King publishes *The Shining* and, under the pseudonym Richard Bachman, *Rage*

1978   Publishes *Night Shift*, a collection of short stories, and *The Stand*; leaves Doubleday

1979   Publishes *The Dead Zone* and, under the Bachman pseudonym, *The Long Walk*; the miniseries based on King's novel *'Salem's Lot* appears on CBS

1980   Publishes *Firestarter*; Stanley Kubrick's *The Shining* appears in theaters; moves to Bangor

1981   Publishes *Cujo*, *Danse Macabre*, and, under the Bachman pseudonym, *Roadwork*; receives Career Alumni award from UMO

1982   Publishes, under the Bachman pseudonym, *Running Man*; *Different Seasons*, a collection of novellas; *Creepshow*, a collection of graphic stories, which served as a tie-in to the movie of the same name; *The Dark Tower: The Gunslinger*; and privately issues the first part of *The Plant*; the film *Creepshows*, in which King plays the title character in the segment "The Lonesome Death of Jordy Verrill," is released; wins the nonfiction Hugo Award and Locus Award for *Danse Macabre* and a World Fantasy Award for the short story "Do the Dead Sing?"

1983 Publishes *Christine*, *Pet Sematary*, and *Cycle of the Werewolf*; buys WZON, a radio station in Bangor. The movies *Christine*, *Cujo*, and *The Dead Zone* are released

1984 Publishes *The Talisman*, with Peter Straub, and *Thinner*, under the Bachman pseudonym; Privately issues *The Eyes of the Dragon*. The movies *Children of the Corn* and *Firestarter* are released

1985 Publicly acknowledges that he is Richard Bachman; publishes *Skeleton Crew*, a collection of short stories, and *The Bachman Books*, a collection containing the first four Bachman novels; adapts his short story "Word Processor of the Gods" for *Tales from the Darkside*; the movies *Cat's Eye* and *Silver Bullet* are released

1986 Publishes *It*. The movies *Maximum Overdrive*, which King directed himself, and *Stand By Me* are released. Wins a Locus Award for the collection *Skeleton Crew*

1987 Publishes *Misery*, *The Dark Tower II: The Drawing of the Three*, and *The Tommyknockers*; releases *The Eyes of the Dragon* for general audiences. The movies *Creepshow II* and *The Running Man* are released. Wins a Bram Stoker Award in the best novel category for *Misery*

1988 Publishes, with the Whitney Museum, a limited edition of the story "My Pretty Pony"

1989 Publishes *The Dark Half* and a limited edition of the short story "Dolan's Cadillac"; the movie *Pet Sematary* is released

1990 Reissues *The Stand: The Complete & Uncut Edition*; publishes *Four Past Midnight*, a collection of novellas. The movies *Graveyard Shift* and *Misery* are released; the miniseries *It* airs on television; wins a Bram Stoker Award for best collection for *Four Past Midnight*

1991 Publishes *Needful Things* and *The Dark Tower III: The Waste Lands*; *Stephen King's Golden Years*, a TV series, and the movie *Sometimes They Come Back* appear on CBS

1992 Publishes *Gerald's Game* and *Dolores Claiborne*; the movie *Sleepwalkers* appears

1993 Publishes *Nightmares & Dreamscapes*, a collection of short stories; the miniseries *The Tommyknockers* appears on television; the movies *Needful Things* and *The Dark Half* are released

1994 Publishes *Insomnia*; the miniseries *The Stand* airs on television; the movie *The Shawshank Redemption* is released

1995 Publishes *Rose Madder*; the movies *Dolores Claiborne* and *The Mangler* are released; the miniseries *The Langoliers* airs on ABC; wins a World Fantasy Award for the short story "The Man in the

Black Suit" and wins a Bram Stoker Award for best long fiction for "Lunch at the Gotham Café"

1996   Publishes *The Green Mile* as a monthly serial consisting of six parts—"The Two Dead Girls," "The Mouse on the Mile," "Coffey's Hands," "The Bad Death of Eduard Delacroix," "Night Journey," and "Coffey on the Mile"—*Desperation*, and, under the Bachman pseudonym, *The Regulators*; the movie *Thinner* is released; wins an O. Henry Award for "The Man in the Black Suit" and wins a Bram Stoker Award in the best novel category for *The Green Mile*

1997   Publishes *The Dark Tower IV: Wizard and Glass* and privately issues *Six Stories*; the movies *Quicksilver Highway*, *Trucks*, and the miniseries *The Shining* appear on TV. The movie *The Night Flier* is released; wins a Locus Award and a best novel award from the Horror Guild for *Desperation*

1998   Publishes *Bag of Bones*; co-writes script for an episode of *The X-Files*; the movie *Apt Pupil* is released; wins a Bram Stoker Award for best novel for *Bag of Bones*

1999   Publishes *The Girl Who Loved Tom Gordon*

1999   June 19: King is severely injured when he is struck by a van

1999   Publishes *Hearts in Atlantis* and the audio book *Blood and Smoke*. The movie *The Green Mile* is released. *Storm of the Century* appears on television. Wins a Locus Award for *Bag of Bones*

2000   Releases "Riding the Bullet" on the Internet with the aid of his publisher; electronically releases six parts of *The Plant* on his own Web site; publishes *On Writing: A Memoir of the Craft* and *Secret Windows: Essays and Fiction on the Craft of Writing*; wins a Bram Stoker Award for nonfiction for *On Writing*

2001   Publishes *Dreamcatcher* and *Black House*, with Straub; the movie *Hearts in Atlantis* appears; wins a Locus Award for *On Writing* and the award for best nonfiction for *On Writing* and the award for best long fiction for "Riding the Bullet" from the Horror Guild

2002   Publishes *From a Buick 8* and *Everything's Eventual: 14 Dark Tales*; the miniseries *Rose Red* appears on television; wins an award, with Straub, for best novel for *Black House* from the Horror Guild

2003   Publishes a revised edition of *The Dark Tower I: The Gunslinger* and *The Dark Tower V: Wolves of the Calla*; the movie *Dreamcatcher* is released; receives The National Book Foundation Medal for Distinguished Contribution to American Letters and a Lifetime Achievement Award from Horror Writers Association; wins an award for best novel for *From A Buick 8* and an award for best collection for *Everything's Eventual* from the Horror Guild

2004 Publishes *The Dark Tower VI: Song of Susannah*, *The Dark Tower VII: The Dark Tower*, and *Faithful: Two Diehard Boston Red Sox Fans Chronicle the Historic 2004 Season*, with Stewart O'Nan; the TV series *Kingdom Hospital* and a remake of the miniseries *Salem's Lot* appear on television; the movies *Riding the Bullet* and *Secret Window* are released; receives Lifetime Achievement World Fantasy Award

2005 Publishes *The Colorado Kid*; the movie *Desperation* airs on television

2006 Publishes *Cell*, *Lisey's Story*, and *The Secretary of Dreams*, a collection of short stories

2007 Publishes, under the Bachman pseudonym, *Blaze*; the movie *The Mist* is released

2008 Publishes *Duma Key* and *Just after Sunset*, a collection of short stories

Chapter 1

TAKING UP THE PEN

Stephen Edwin King was born in Portland, Maine, on September 21, 1947, to Donald Edwin King, whose original family name was Spansky, and Nellie Ruth Pillsbury King. Donald King had been a captain in the Merchant Marines but had become a door-to-door salesman for Electrolux, a vacuum company, in Scarborough, a town about eight miles outside Portland. Something of a philanderer and not above breaking the law, he was apparently unhappy about being a family man, and after telling his wife—a little more than two years after Stephen was born—that he needed a pack of cigarettes, he went out and never returned. Thereafter, Ruth King, who claimed to have come "from the same family that produced the Pillsburys who now make cake mixes and flour,"[1] was left to raise Stephen and his older brother, David—who had been adopted in 1945—by herself. "After my father took off," King recalled, "my mother landed on her feet, scrambling. My brother and I didn't see a great deal of her over the next nine years. She worked at a succession of low-paying jobs: presser in a laundry, doughnut-maker on the night shift at a bakery, store clerk, housekeeper.... We never had a car (nor a TV set until 1956), but we never missed any meals."[2]

King's mother not only changed jobs often during those nine years, but she also moved quite a lot, going first to Fort Wayne, Indiana, where Donald King's family lived. She may have been hoping to find her husband. If that were the case, she was disappointed. Donald King was never heard from again, though what he left behind him did contribute, as we will see, to King's development. From Fort Wayne the Kings moved to De Pere, Wisconsin, where Carolyn, one of Ruth's four sisters, lived. It was probably at the end of his time in Illinois that Stephen had his first encounter with horror, both real and fictitious. When he was four, his mother later told him—though he has no memory of the event—he came home one day very pale and would not speak. She later discovered that he had witnessed a friend being run over by a train. During that same year an adaptation of Ray Bradbury's "Mars is Heaven" (1948) was broadcast on the radio. King begged his mother to allow him to listen to the show, but she, believing he would be scared by it, forbade him to do so. He disobeyed, listening to the radio from the door of his bedroom. As his mother had predicted, King was too frightened to sleep that night and remained awake in the spot from which he had heard the broadcast, keeping the light in the hallway in view.

Other stops on the family's itinerary included Chicago, Illinois; Malden, Massachusetts (the setting of the novel *Cell* [2006]), where his aunt Molly lived; and Stratford, Connecticut, where his aunt Lois lived. King began school and a love affair with the movies in Stratford. The first movie he can recall seeing, at a drive-in theater, was *The Creature from the Black Lagoon*, which was first released in 3-D in 1954 (though King does not remember having to wear 3-D glasses, so the version he saw may have been released later). Another formative experience of King's early years was his mother's introducing him, when he was seven, to Robert Louis Stevenson's *The Strange Case of Dr. Jekyll and Mr. Hyde* (1886). She had brought the book home from the library, and King, assuring her that it would not be too scary for him, convinced her to read it to him. "I lived and died with that story, with Mr. Utterson and with poor Dr. Jekyll, and particularly with Dr. Jekyll's other side, which was every vestige of pretense of civilization thrown away. I can remember lying in bed, wakeful after that night's reading was done, and what I usually thought of was how Mr. Hyde walked over the little girl, back and forth, breaking her bones; and it was such a terrible image and I thought, *I have to do that; but I have to do that worse*," King recalled.[3]

The family settled in Durham, Maine, when King was 11, moving into the house of his grandparents, Guy and Nellie Pillsbury, which was located in a section of the town known as Methodist Corners. (Methodists themselves, the Kings attended the nearby West Durham Methodist Church.) Guy and Nellie were no longer able to care for themselves, so King's mother took on that responsibility on a full-time basis. King has written little of his grandparents, though he does remember listening to radio plays "with my grandfather when I was growing up (and he was growing old)."[4] The Kings continued living in the house after Guy and Nellie died, when Ruth took a job at Pineland, a home for the mentally disabled.

King attended Durham Elementary, a one-room schoolhouse that would grow to four rooms by the time he graduated in 1962. More important to his development at this point was the fact that reading became, at his grandparents', a household activity. The family had a subscription to the *Saturday Evening Post*, which published fiction in serial form—a new episode of a larger story appeared each week—as nineteenth-century publications had done with the novels of Charles Dickens, among other authors. King looked forward to receiving the episodes of these stories, but "[b]est of all," he recalled in the foreword to *The Green Mile* (1996), "in my house we often read them aloud—my brother, David, one night, myself the next, my mother taking a turn on the third, then back to my brother again. It was a rare chance to enjoy a written work as we enjoyed the movies we went to and the TV programs (*Rawhide, Bonanza, Route 66*) that we watched together; they were a family event."[5]

In Durham King began to be identified as a writer, although he had begun writing a few years before arriving there, taking it up while he was homebound during an extended illness—measles followed by ear infections—that kept him away from school and the first grade for about nine months. His first efforts were pure imitation: he copied *Combat Casey* comics verbatim, though he sometimes provided extra descriptions. His mother was proud but cajoled King into admitting that he had mostly copied from his comic books. "Write one of your own, Stevie," she told him. "Those *Combat Casey* funny-books are just junk—he's always knocking someone's teeth out. I bet you could do better."[6] Soon afterward he followed her advice, writing a four-page story about animals who, led by Mr. Rabbit Trick, went around in a car and helped small children. His mom, having been assured by King that he had not copied another's work that time, told him that the story was good enough to be published. He produced four more stories using the same characters; his mother paid him twenty-five cents for each piece. "That was the first buck I made in this business."[7]

King has not recorded most of what he wrote between those early stories and January 1959, when his older brother, the source of many of King's childhood adventures, came up with the idea of publishing a newspaper, which was called *Dave's Rag*. King, however, had already been writing fairly regularly, as is evidenced by his receiving, in 1958, a Royal typewriter for Christmas. His stories, at that point, included one about dinosaurs that terrorize a small town but are defeated after the townspeople discover that the dinosaurs are allergic to leather and another called "Jhonathan and the Witches" (1956; published in Paul Mandelbaum's *First Words* in 1993), which tells the story of a poor cobbler who gets employed by his king to kill three witches. Dave asked his younger brother to write for *Dave's Rag,* and as well as writing some features, including television commentary, King wrote "Jumper," a story that was released in three parts starting in 1959, and "Rush Call," a story that came out in 1960. (These stories were later published in *Secret Windows* [2000].) Forthcoming King books, such as "Land of 100 Thousand Years Ago," were also advertised in the paper's pages. First printed with a hectograph, a device that consisted "of a film of reusable gelatin in an 8 ½ by 11 inch tray" that was used to create copies one page at a time,[8] the paper began with a circulation of five but grew to 50 or 60 copies an issue, when friends and their relatives joined King's own family in buying it. Dave, too impatient to print the issues a page at a time, bought a drum printing press, or mimeograph, and could complete what the hectograph took a week to produce in a couple of days.

Around the time that the paper began to appear—he is unsure whether the event should be dated in the fall of 1959 or 1960—King stumbled on a box of his father's books in the attic over his aunt Ethelyn's garage, which was "a kind of family museum."[9] A 1947 edition of H. P. Lovecraft's *The Lurking Fear and Other Stories* was among the books, as well as a number of other horror titles. That Lovecraft collection provided King with his "first encounter with serious fantasy-horror fiction.... So that book, courtesy of my departed father, was my first taste of a world that went deeper than the B-pictures which played at the movies on Saturday afternoon or the boys' fiction of Carl Carmer and Roy Rockwell."[10] Those B-movies had a formative importance for King, as his childhood friend Chris Chesley recalled, telling author George Beahm, "King, in effect, learned *how* to write from what he saw on the screen at the Ritz—the place where parents sent their kids on Saturdays." Lovecraft helped King see that he could localize the horror genre, or, as Chesley put it to Beahm, "What Steve learned from Lovecraft was the possibility of taking the New England atmosphere and using that as a springboard. Lovecraft showed him a milieu that was definitely New England horror. *Dracula* could be moved to Durham, basically."[11]

King thereafter pursued his three passions: watching movies, which meant hitchhiking 14 miles to the Ritz in Lisbon almost every Saturday between 1958 and 1966; writing, both fiction and nonfiction; and reading, usually pulp novels and magazines, as well as comic books. Most thought he was wasting his life, as he noted, "My interest in horror and the fantastic wasn't looked upon with any approval whatsoever—there went young Steve King, his nose either in a lurid issue of *Tales from the Vault* or an even more lurid paper of some sort or other."[12] King ignored such disapproval, beginning, even before entering Lisbon High School in the nearby town of Lisbon Falls, to attempt to find places for his own stories other than his brother's newspaper. He sent one, for example, to Forrest J. Ackerman's magazine *Spaceman* sometime in 1960. The story was rejected, but King was undeterred and continued to submit stories for publication to a number of fiction magazines. Those he submitted included "Happy Stamps," a story about Roger, a counterfeiter, who begins forging Green Stamps instead of money. King regards that story idea as his first good one; three weeks after sending it to *Alfred Hitchcock's Mystery Magazine*, a rejection slip arrived in the mail, and King placed it on a nail on a wall in his room. By the time he entered high school, the nail was too full to hold his rejection slips. He replaced it with a spike and continued writing. Two more years passed before he received a positive response. He was 16, and the editor of *Fantasy and Science Fiction*, to whom King had sent a story called "The Night of the Tiger," wrote on a rejection slip, "This is good. Not for us, but good. You have talent. Submit again."[13]

King, in the meantime, had continued publishing privately. As an eighth grader, in 1961, he saw Richard Matheson's *The Pit and the Pendulum*, wrote an eight-page novelization of it, and printed it on his brother's mimeograph. It "turned out to be my first bestseller," King wrote. "I took the entire print-run to school in my book-bag...and by noon that day I had sold two dozen. By the end of lunch hour, when word had gotten around about the lady buried in the wall...I had sold three dozen. I had nine dollars in change weighing down the bottom of my book-bag...and was walking around in a kind of dream, unable to believe my sudden ascension to previously unsuspected realms of wealth. It all seemed too good to be true. It was."[14] The school's principal forced him to return all the money he had made.

In the summer before entering high school, King wrote and self-published "The Invasion of the Star-Creatures," selling about three and a half dozen copies, and in 1962 he released "People, Places, and Things: Volume I," a collection of 18 one-page short stories written by him and Chesley. King had contributed such stories as "Hotel at the End of the Road," "I've Got to Get Away!," "The Dimension Warp," "The Thing at the Bottom of the Well," "The Stranger," "I'm Falling," "The Cursed Expedition," and "The Other Side of the Fog."

Then, in 1963, King tried his hand at a full-length book, writing a 50,000–word novel called "The Aftermath" that was set in a post-nuclear apocalyptic world. That same year he was talked into taking up the editorship of his high-school newspaper, *The Drum*. The position bored both him and his co-editor, and they only put out one issue during the

1963–1964 academic year. During that period King did produce a magazine, *The Village Vomit*; it satirized the faculty of his school and was popular with students. The faculty members were not so amused, especially the shorthand and typing teacher Miss Margitan, who was described in the *Vomit* as "Miss Margitan, known affectionately to Lisbonians everywhere as Maggot."[15] Two years later Miss Margitan, in her capacity as the advisor of the National Honor Society, would prevent King from gaining a place in that society, asserting that "his type"[16] was not needed. The school's response to the *Vomit* was to get King a job at the local newspaper, the Lisbon *Weekly Enterprise*, under the editorial direction of John Gould.

At the paper King earned half a cent a word for articles about local sports, a subject King knew something about, as he played the left-tackle position on his school's football team and followed baseball as "a recreational Red Sox user."[17] (He would become an obsessive fan, "a full-blown junkie,"[18] during the 1967 season, when Boston came close to winning the World Series.) King learned more about writing in his first week with the paper than he had in any of his English classes in high school or would later learn in college. Gould taught him the importance of concision, taking King's first articles, crossing out all the unnecessary adjectives and purple passages, and telling him: "When you write a story, you're telling yourself the story. When you rewrite, your main job is taking out all the things that are *not* the story."

> Gould said something else that was interesting on the day I turned in my first two pieces: write with the door closed, rewrite with the door open. Your stuff starts out being just for you, in other words, but then it goes out. Once you know what the story is and get it right—as right as you can, anyway—it belongs to anyone who wants to read it. Or criticize it. If you're very lucky (this is my idea, not John Gould's, but I believe he would have subscribed to the notion), more will want to do the former than the latter.[19]

Not satisfied with publishing newspaper pieces, King continued printing his stories, self-publishing "The Star Invaders," a 3,000-word piece, in 1964. Then, in 1965, he got his first story accepted for publication in *Comics Review*, a 12-page horror fanzine published by Mike Garrett out of Birmingham, Alabama. Garrett agreed to print "I Was a Teenage Graverobber," although he altered the title to "In a Half-World of Terror," a title King still regards as inferior. In the fall of 1965, he also published in the high-school newspaper "Codename Mousetrap," a story in which the main character, Kelly, breaks into a supermarket and finds himself being pursued by product displays, beefsteaks, and a mousetrap. In the end he jumps through a window to escape and a parking meter catches him. In the spring semester of King's senior year, the paper published "The 43rd Dream," a story about a boy who tells of his strange dream.

In 1966 King graduated high school—where he had, besides making a name for himself as a writer, fostered his interest in popular music (which began when his mother brought home an Elvis single in the mid-1950s) by helping form a rock band, The Mune Spinners, and playing rhythm guitar—and headed off to college. Because his family lacked the money, he had turned down a place at Drew University in New Jersey and accepted a full scholarship at the University of Maine, the school his brother, a certified genius with an I.Q. of 150, graduated from in 1966. The summer in between high school and college, King went to work at Worumbo Mills and Weaving, which he later compared to "a workhouse in a Charles Dickens novel,"[20] and began a full-length novel. Called "Getting It On" the story is about a high-school kid who returns to his school after he has been expelled and kills a teacher and a number of students. King would not finish the manuscript that summer, but he did eventually complete the book, publishing it as *Rage* under the pseudonym Richard Bachman in 1977.

NOTES

1. Stephen King, *Danse Macabre* (New York: Berkley Books, 1983 [1981]), p. 92.

2. Ibid., p. 93. King dated the appearance of a television in his home in 1958 in *On Writing: A Memoir of the Craft* (New York: Scribners, 2000), see p. 34.

3. Quoted in George Beahm, *The Stephen King Story: A Literary Profile* (Kansas City, MO: Andrews and McMeel, 1992), p. 17.

4. Stephen King, "Introduction: Practicing the Almost Lost Art," *Everything's Eventual: 14 Dark Tales* (New York: Pocket Books: 2007 [2002]), p. xiii.

5. Stephen King, *The Green Mile* (New York: Scribner, 2000 [1996]), p. 17.

6. Stephen King, *On Writing: A Memoir of the Craft* (New York: Scribner, 2000), p. 28.

7. Ibid., p. 29.

8. D. Brett King and Michael Wertheimer, *Max Wertheimer and Gestalt Theory* (New Brunswick, NJ: Transaction Publishers, 2005), p. 228.

9. King, *Danse Macabre*, p. 94.

10. Ibid., p. 96.

11. Quoted in George Beahm, *Stephen King: America's Best-Loved Boogeyman* (Kansas City, MO: Andrews and McMeel, 1998), pp. 3, 5.

12. Stephen King, "The Importance of Being Forry," in *Mr. Monster's Movie Gold,* ed. Forrest J. Ackerman (Norfolk, VA: Donning Company, 1982), p. 9.

13. King, *On Writing,* p. 41.

14. Ibid., pp. 48–49.

15. Ibid., p. 53.

16. Ibid., p. 54.

17. Stewart O'Nan and Stephen King, *Faithful: Two Diehard Boston Red Sox Fans Chronicle the Historic 2004 Season* (New York: Scribner, 2004), p. 31.

18. Ibid., p. 31.

19. King, *On Writing,* pp. 57–58.

20. Ibid., p. 58.

Chapter 2

BECOMING A WRITER

When King moved into his dormitory on the campus of the University of Maine, at Orono (UMO), a college town north of Bangor, in the fall of 1966, he was a clean-cut, socially conservative young man, unsure about how he was going to fit into his new environment. Over the next four years, he would find a place for himself and shed his conservative, small-town perspective, getting caught up in the social movement of the 1960s and embracing the liberal ideals that went along with it. The change in his politics didn't come immediately; he clung to his conservatism for some time, voting for Republican Richard Nixon in the 1968 presidential election, for example. That vote, however, may have hinted toward the radicalism that he would soon embrace. As he wrote years later, "My Wife still delights in telling people that her husband cast his first Presidential ballot, at the tender age of twenty-one, for Richard Nixon. 'Nixon said he had a plan to get us out of Vietnam,' she says, usually with a gleeful gleam in her eye, *'and Steve believed him!'*"[1]

Finding a niche for himself wasn't very difficult. What King lacked in social confidence, he made up for with his belief in himself as a writer. Even during his first year, "he saw himself as a famous writer and he thought he could make money at it," Jim Bishop, his freshman composition teacher, recalled. "Steve was writing continuously, industriously, and diligently. He was amiable, resilient, and created his own world."[2] Indeed, he religiously plied away at his craft, experimenting with fiction, drama, and poetry and earning the respect of both his peers and his professors. Perhaps the one detour along the way was that he put down the manuscript of "Getting It On" to focus on his course work when he first began classes. Before his freshman year had ended, however, he had begun and finished a different novel, the idea for which came to him while he was hitchhiking to Durham to see his mom.

Called *The Long Walk* (1979) and partially inspired by President Kennedy's call for Americans to take part in walkathons,[3] the novel was set in a future, totalitarian United States and was about a contest in which 100 male adolescents, starting in Maine, walk south along the eastern coast, competing to be the last boy standing. Those boys who fail to maintain a pace of four miles an hour or faster are warned to speed up. Each is allowed to receive three warnings, though a contestant is able to get a warning removed if he can avoid being warned for an hour, but a fourth infraction leads to a ticket, which, it is eventually revealed, is a euphemism for being shot to death. The last boy standing receives "The Prize," which is anything he wants for the rest of his life. Exploring the psychological as well as physical struggle that the competitors go through, King had the final two contestants, as Carroll F. Terrell recalls, discover that "their heart's desire was not for a billion dollars, or some Shangri-La, or the most beautiful woman in the world. The heart's desire of each one was to give up his own life so that his friend could realize his heart's desire."[4]

After finishing the novel King turned to a story, writing, in the summer of 1967, "The Glass Floor," which is about a man, Charles Wharton, who wants to see where his sister, Janine, died—a room that her widower, Anthony Reynard, has had sealed. When Charles finally gains entrance to it, he finds that the room has a glass floor and ceiling; he then loses his balance and dies himself. "I remember getting the idea for the story, and it just came as the ideas come now—casually, with no flourish of trumpets. I was walking down a dirt road to see a friend, and for no reason at all I began to wonder what it would be like to stand in a room whose floor was a mirror. The image was so intriguing that writing the story became a necessity. It wasn't written for money; it was written so I could see better."[5] He then submitted it to Robert A. W. Lowndes, an editor of two magazines that published horror fiction. He had sent Lowndes work before but had merely managed to add to his collection of rejection slips. "The Glass Floor" turned out to be different, partly because it was better than most of the earlier stories King had submitted and partly because it fit Lowndes's needs. Lowndes placed it in the fall issue of his *Startling Mystery Stories*, a pulp journal that was published from 1966 to 1971, commenting in an introductory note that, of the stories King had submitted to him before, "we returned one of them most reluctantly, since it would be far too long before we could use it, due to its length."[6] King recalled in an introductory note for a reprint of the story in the fall 1990 issue of *Weird Tales*, "That first check was for thirty-five dollars. I've cashed many bigger ones since then, but none gave me more satisfaction; someone had finally paid me some real money for something I had found in my head!"[7]

Perhaps buoyed up by his success, King, who moved into an apartment off UMO's campus in the fall semester of 1967, took *The Long Walk* out of his trunk of unpublished manuscripts and began showing it to English professors, who mostly responded positively. Burton Hatlen, a professor with whom King was taking an American Literature course, as well as his wife, found the story compelling, feeling that King had already developed a strong narrative sense. Others in the English department agreed, although Terrell, who found it remarkable as a whole, saw problems: he felt that "the design of the book made the action repetitive and got him [King] into a kind of 'another Indian bit the dust' trap.... Steve's reaction to this was precise," Terrell goes on to write, "and (as I eventually came to see) correct. He said, in effect, that the sameness and the routine were deliberate and part of the point. On the road of life few people become distinguished from the mass: they just stagger along until they conk out."[8] King also submitted the manuscript to the Bennett Cerf/Random House first novel competition and got a less positive response. It was returned without comment, probably because it wasn't what the judges were looking for rather than because it showed a lack of maturity. Indeed, it would be published pseudonymously in 1979, and when it was re-released in 1985, with three other pseudonymous King novels in *The Bachman Books*, Arthur Ellis would describe it as the "one winner" among the four novels.[9] Though Ellis complained, "Reasons and rules for the [walking competition] are hazy," he went on to note, in a comment that seemed to address Terrell's criticism two decades earlier, "King manages to build vivid descriptions and characterizations into what is essentially a repetitive, process-of-elimination tale."

For some time, after showing Terrell *The Long Walk*, King would look to Terrell for informal instruction, bringing him chapters of a manuscript that came to be called *Sword in the Darkness* and that dealt with racial issues, since Terrell had suggested that King write something that was topical. "Mostly I'd have only praise as he went along," Terrell wrote. "Once in a while I'd object to what I'd call a false note in dialogue: that is, given the way the guy was *feeling* at the time, he wouldn't say what Steve had given him to say. Each time, Steve would bridle and say something like: 'But you forget. Back here in Chapter II see, he sees Joe, out of the corner of his eye. And a couple of pages later, he has this double take, and wonders what he was doing there. He can't figure it out, so he becomes wary and suspicious. The formality in what he says to him here reflects this doubt.' Each time

Steve would be right."[10] What impressed Terrell the most during these sessions was that each scene in the story took into account the collective experiences of the characters within it. Having finished a number of chapters, King tried to get a publisher interested in buying it; he was gently rejected and put the manuscript in his trunk, incomplete.

King wrote and published a number of other short stories during his college years, mostly in UMO's literary student magazine, *Ubris*, a publication with which he became involved during his sophomore year. "Here There be Tygers" and "Cain Rose Up" appeared in the spring 1968 issue. The first of these stories, the title of which comes from the phrase medieval cartographers placed on maps over unexplored and thus potentially dangerous regions, concerned a boy who believes that a tiger, which devours teachers, lurks in his grade school's bathroom. The second returns to the theme of "Getting It On" but drew its immediate inspiration from the case of Charles Whitman, a former marine and a student at the University of Texas who in 1966 positioned himself within the University of Texas Tower in Austin, the tallest building on the campus, and began shooting people. In King's tale the Whitman character, Curt Garrish, holes up in his dorm room and kills people with a .352 magnum. The gesture was one with which King himself identified, he would later say. "I might very well have ended up there in the Texas tower with Charlie Whitman, working out my demons with a high-powered telescopic rifle instead of a word processor. I mean, I know that guy Whitman. My writing has kept me out of that tower."[11]

King continued publishing in *Ubris*, placing "Strawberry Spring," another story of mayhem on a college campus, in the journal's fall 1968 issue. The events of the story—which involve a killing spree at New Sharon Teachers' College—take place during the false spring, or strawberry spring, of 1968, and are told from the perspective of a narrator who is possibly the killer, seven or eight years later, during another killing spree that is being carried out by a figure, who may also be the narrator and whom the press has taken to calling Springheel Jack. King also published, in that issue of *Ubris*, the free-verse, popular-culture inspired poem, "Harrison State Park '68." That poem was likely written as a result of King's taking Bishop and Hatlen's Contemporary Poetry, a seminar limited to 12 students, each of whom was accepted on a case-by-case basis, and that involved, Hatlen recalled, a "very intense discussion about poetics, how you write poetry, and so on."[12] A number of students who had not thought about doing so before began writing poetry. King was one of them. He wrote approximately 50 poems during the seminar, which officially ended in January 1969, and during the informal meetings that followed. King claims that these poems came to nothing, but one, "The Dark Man," which appeared in the fall 1969 issue of *Ubris*, did provide him with the character of Randall Flagg, who appears in a number of King's novels. The poem, as King recalled, "came to me out of nowhere, this guy in cowboy boots who moved around on the roads, mostly hitchhiking at night, always wore jeans and a denim jacket. I wrote this poem, and it was basically just a page long. I was in the college restaurant.... I wrote the poem on the back of a placemat. It was published, as a matter of fact, but that idea of the guy never left my mind. The thing about him that really attracted me was the idea of the villain as somebody who was always on the outside looking in and hated people who had good fellowship and good conversation and friends."[13]

King then took up writing for a newspaper again, this time on his own terms. In February 1969 he began doing a weekly column, King's Garbage Truck, for the college newspaper, the *Maine Campus*. (The last column appeared on May 21, 1970.) David Bright, the editor, "remembers King coming to him and saying he'd like to write a column. 'Steve named it "Garbage Truck" because you never know what you're going to find in a garbage truck.'"[14] Allowed to write anything that he wanted, King appeared in the paper's office each week as his deadline was approaching, put a piece of paper in the typewriter, and pounded out a column, which contained reviews of television shows, movies, and rock albums as well as discussions of such subjects as the California grape boycott, girl-watching, and the courses that he was taking. Terrell recalls one that began "After listening to another boring lecture by professor Terrell, I went...."[15] While King was usually in class, he wasn't too thrilled by what was being taught. He had always had a problem with the school's English curriculum, particularly because it contained classics but no popular literature. Thus, when the English faculty held a meeting with students to discuss its curriculum, King complained about the absence of courses with popular novels, the value of which he defended, and proposed a seminar on popular American fiction. The consequence was that UMO held a seminar in the spring term of 1969 called Popular Literature and Culture, which was officially conducted by Graham Adams but unofficially taught by King, who knew the subject better than anyone in the school.[16]

During the summer between his junior and senior year, King met Tabitha Jane Spruce, a history major who was also an aspiring writer. Both were working at the university's library on a work-study program. "I fell in love with her during a poetry workshop in the fall of 1969 [the unofficial continuation of Bishop and Hatlen's Contemporary Poetry], when I was a senior and Tabby was a junior," King wrote. "I fell in love with her partly because I understood what she was doing with her work. I fell because *she* understood what she was doing with it. I also fell because she was wearing a sexy black dress and silk stockings, the kind that hook with garters."[17] The two would remain a couple thereafter.

The following fall "Night Surf" and "Stud City" appeared in *Ubris*. King would incorporate the latter story into "The Body," one of the novellas published in *Different Seasons* (1982), where it was recast as an early work by the novel's narrator, Gordon LaChance. LaChance will belittle the effort, observing "It ought to have THIS IS A PRODUCT OF AN UNDER-GRADUATE CREATIVE WRITING WORKSHOP stamped on every page...because that's just what it was, at least up to a certain point. It seems both painfully derivative and painfully sophomoric to me now; style by Hemingway...theme by Faulkner."[18] During that same period, King would take further steps toward becoming a professional writer, earning another $35 when Lowndes placed "The Reaper's Image," a ghost story concerning an Elizabethan mirror in which an image of the Grim Reaper appears and causes all those who see it to disappear, in the fall issue of *Startling Mystery Stories* (1969). King was also paid $250 for "The Float" by a magazine called *Adam*, either late in 1969 or in the Spring of 1970, although he never saw the story in print and can only assume it was published.

The money from *Adam* would come at a propitious time, as King revealed in the notes to *Skeleton Crew* (1985), the collection in which he published a version of the story that was, in 1981, reconstructed from memory and retitled "The Raft." Coming home after a night of drinking, King had driven over a number traffic cones. After one loosened his muffler, he "was immediately suffused with the sort of towering, righteous rage which only drunk undergraduates can feel. I decided to circle the town of Orono, picking up traffic cones."[19] After grabbing about 150 cones, by his count, he was arrested, charged with petty larceny, and fined $250. He had seven days to pay the fine or face 30 days in jail. Three days after learning of his punishment, a check, the total of which was just enough to pay his fine, arrived for "The Float." "It was like having someone send you a *real* Get Out of Jail Free card."[20]

During his last semester King took a position as a student teacher, a requirement for the teaching certificate that he was working to get, at Hampden Academy, a school located south of Bangor. To take the position King was required to cut his hair and shave his beard, both of which he had grown as his politics were radicalized during his junior year. "Can you imagine," he wrote for his February 20, 1970, Garbage Truck column, "a country supposedly based on freedom of expression telling people that they can't grow hair on their head or their face? Since when have we descended to the point where we care more about what people look like than what they think like?"[21] King, needing to get his teaching certificate, would not let anger get the better of him and cut his hair. Having long hair, after all, was not of major importance. His thoughts were primarily focused on establishing himself as a writer. With that in mind he completed *Sword in the Darkness*, which grew to 150,000 words, and managed to get an agent, Patricia Shartle Myrer of McIntosh and Otis, to show it to a number of publishers. None bought it, and it remained completely unpublished until 2006, when *Weekend Australian* released a portion of it with the following note that King asked to have accompany it: "'Readers should know I was only 20 when I wrote this story. I was just a kid and should not be held responsible!' He asked that it be noted he said this with a smile."[22] The only work, other than his columns in the *Maine Campus*, that he would see into print during his final term were two poems—"Donovan's Brain" and "Silence," both of which appeared in *Moth*, a literary journal associated with the Contemporary Poetry seminar.

As he was preparing for graduation, King wrote in one of his final columns, "This boy has shown evidences of some talent, although at this point it is impossible to tell if he is just a flash in the pan or if he has real possibilities...he does not feel very bright-eyed by this time."[23] King, who now had a degree in English and a teaching certificate, remained tied to the environment in which he had come to feel comfortable. "A draft board examination immediately post-graduation found him 4-F on grounds of high blood pressure, limited vision, flat feet, and punctured eardrums."[24] He thus avoided Vietnam, and during the summer he continued to contribute work to the school paper, publishing "Slade," a 6,500-word Western that was serialized in eight installments from June to August and that would eventually become *The Gunslinger* (1982). More significantly, his relationship with Tabitha Spruce, who wouldn't complete her history degree for another year, had become serious, so King wanted to remain near the university, which meant that he had to take any job that he could get. His first job as a college graduate was pumping gas in Brewer, not too far from Orono, for $1.25 an hour.

NOTES

1. Stephen King, "Introduction: Myth, Belief, Faith, and *Ripley's Believe It or Not*," *Nightmares & Dreamscapes* (New York: Signet, 1994 [1993]), p. 1.

2. Quoted in Sanford Phippin, "The Student King: The Master of Modern Horror at Maine," *The Stephen King Companion*, ed. George Beahm (Kansas City, MO: Andrews and McMeel, 1995), p. 22.

3. See George Beahm, *Stephen King: America's Best-Loved Boogeyman* (Kansas City, MO: Andrews and McMeel, 1998), p. 14.

4. Carroll F. Terrell, *Stephen King: Man and Artist* (Orono, ME: Northern Lights, 1991), p. 31.

5. Quoted at http://www.kingclub.ru/e-books/shortstories/rares/eng/htm/Glass-Floor-htm.htm.

6. Quoted in George Beahm, *Stephen King from A to Z: An Encyclopedia of His Life and Work* (Kansas City, MO: Andrews McMeel, 1988), p. 83.

7. Quoted at http://www.kingclub.ru/e-books/shortstories/rares/eng/htm/Glass-Floor-htm.htm.

8. Terrell, *Stephen King*, p. 31.

9. Arthur Ellis, "Only for Hardy Fans of Stephen King," *Toronto Star* (December 29, 1985), p. E10, http://www.lexis-nexis.com/.

10. Terrell, *Stephen King*, pp. 33–34.

11. Eric Norden, "*Playboy* Interview," in *Bare Bones: Conversations on Terror with Stephen King*, ed. Tim Underwood and Chuck Miller (New York: McGraw-Hill, 1988), p. 44.

12. Phippin, "The Student King," p. 21.

13. Trudy Wyss, "Interview: Stephen King's Favored Child: The Dark Tower Series is Finally Finished," Borders Web site, http://www.bordersstores.com/features/feature.jsp?file=stephenking.

14. Quoted in Phippin, "The Student King," p. 25; King would claim in his introduction to a 1999 paperback edition of *Carrie* that the editor-in-chief made up the name. See *Carrie* (New York: Pocket Books, 1999 [1974]), p. ix.

15. Terrell, *Stephen King*, p. 36.

16. See George Beahm, *The Stephen King Story* (Kansas City, MO: Andrews and McMeel, 1992), p. 44.

17. Stephen King, *On Writing: A Memoir of the Craft* (New York: Scribner, 2000), p. 62.

18. Stephen King, *Different Seasons* (New York: Viking, 1982), p. 322.

19. Stephen King, *Skeleton Crew* (New York: Signet, 1986 [1985]), p. 570.

20. Ibid., p. 571.

21. Quoted in Beahm, *Stephen King: America's Best Loved Boogeyman*, p. 20.

22. "Stephen King—*Sword in the Darkness*—World First Publication," *Weekend Australian* (January 14, 2006), Review, p. 1, http://www.lexis-nexis.com/.

23. Quoted in Beahm, *Stephen King: America's Best Loved Boogeyman*, p. 21.

24. Stephen King.com: The Official Web Site, http://www.stephenking.com/biography.php.

Chapter 3

FINDING A PUBLISHER

King's second job out of college was pressing sheets at New Franklin Laundry in Bangor. He earned $1.60 an hour, plus all the overtime that he could get, but his focus remained on writing. As the summer came to an end, he was determined to find professional outlets for his work, realizing that writing for student publications would get him nowhere. He therefore sent "Graveyard Shift," a story he had written in the office of the *Maine Campus* that drew on his experience working at Worumbo Mills and Weaving in the summer of 1966, to the men's magazine *Cavalier*, which published it in October 1970. King would develop a relationship with that publication throughout the 1970s, later explaining, "I have a particular warmth for *Cavalier*, because they published my own first marketable horror stories. Both Doug Allen and Nye Willden are warm and helpful, and if your story is good, they'll publish it. They report in four to six weeks and pay from $200 to $300 depending on the length and previous number of stories published."[1]

The publication in *Cavalier* gave him hope, but he did not completely abandon submitting stories to UMO publications. He gave "Toothy Trauma" to the *Maine Campus*, as well as some pieces to *Onan*, UMO's literary journal, as opposed to the student-run *Ubris*, making it a professional, if unpaid, outlet for his work. Money was a major issue, however. Tabitha had gotten pregnant, and she and King wed on January 2, 1971. Five days later the *Maine Campus* released "Toothy Trauma," and later that month the story "The Blue Air Compressor" and a poem, "In The Key Chords of Dawn," appeared in *Onan*. These would be the last pieces, until he had become something of a success, that King would submit to university publications. He would place "It Grows on You"—a story set in the town of Castle Rock, the fictional small town, loosely based on Durham, that became a major setting for King's stories and novels—in the UMO literary journal *Marshroots* in the fall of 1975, after he had seen his first two novels published.[2]

For the moment publishing was a way to supplement his income, so King focused on those magazines that paid their writers, crafting his stories for the editors to whom he sent them. In March 1971 *Cavalier* published a second King story, "I am the Doorway," which featured an astronaut, Arthur, who returns from Venus and discovers that eyes, the doorway through which a malevolent alien intelligence gains access into our world, have appeared on his hands. Eventually, the intelligence is able to take control of Arthur's body and go on a killing spree. The occasional money that King received from *Cavalier* for such stories was barely enough, nor could Tabitha get a decent job after graduating, in the Spring of 1971, with a history degree. She took a job at a Dunkin' Donuts.

After the Kings' first child, Naomi Rachel, was born, money became even more important, and King thought he might earn a lot more if he could sell a novel. He thus finished, in the summer of 1971, "Getting It On," which he found "moldering away in an old box in the cellar of the house where I'd grown up—this rediscovery was in 1970,"[3] and sent a query to an editor at Doubleday, because, as he explained to Edwin McDowell, "Most of the books I liked seemed to carry the Doubleday imprint. I particularly liked one of their novels, *The Parallax View* by Loren Singer, so when I finally had a manuscript ready, I addressed [my query] to 'The Editor of the Parallax View.'"[4] That editor had left Doubleday, and King's letter went to William G. Thompson, who encouraged King to send a complete manuscript. Thompson liked what he read, recalling that the story "was a masterful study in character and suspense, but it was quiet, deliberately claustrophobic and it proved a tough sell within the house. I'd asked Stephen…for changes which he willingly and promptly made, but even so I couldn't glean sufficient support and reluctantly returned it."[5] King would send the other manuscripts that he had lying around to Thompson, only to have them rejected, but certain that King would eventually write a sellable novel, Thompson kept in touch with him.

King improved his income in the fall of 1971, when he started teaching English at Hampden Academy. His salary was $6,400 a year, more than double what he had been earning in the laundry, but his income remained too small to support his family, especially after Tabitha got pregnant with their second child, Joseph Hillstrom, who was born in 1972. King thus continued working at the laundry in the summers, and the

Kings soon moved to Hermon, taking up residence in a trailer, the furnace room of which King turned into an office, where he wrote after he got home from school. Having a little extra space, King rented a room to his childhood friend Chesley. While money remained very tight, it did not seem the most important issue, at least for Tabitha, who made sure that King had enough time to write, even if it meant turning down paying work. As King recalled in his acceptance speech at the National Book Awards, in 2003, "the subject of moonlighting did come up once. The head of the English department where I taught told me that the debate club was going to need a new faculty advisor and he put me up for the job if I wanted. It would pay $300 per school year which doesn't sound like much but...equaled ten weeks worth of groceries. The English department head told me he'd need my decision by the end of the week. When I told Tabby about the opening, she asked if I'd still have time to write. I told her not as much. Her response to that was unequivocal, 'Well then, you can't take it.'"[6]

King wasn't as sure of himself as Tabitha seemed to be. "I'd lie awake at night seeing myself at fifty, my hair graying, my jowls thickening, a network of whiskey-ruptured capillaries spiderwebbing across my nose—'drinker's tattoos,' we call them in Maine—with a dusty trunkful of unpublished novels rotting in the basement, teaching high school English for the rest of my life and getting off what few literary rocks I had left by advising the student newspaper or maybe teaching a creative-writing course."[7] The doubt was slightly alleviated by the editors at *Cavalier*, who accepted four of King's stories in 1972: "Suffer the Little Children" in February; "The Fifth Quarter," which King published under the name John Swithen, in April; "Battleground" in September; and "The Mangler" in December. Uncertainty, however, continued to plague him, leading him to drink heavily and to throw money away on poker and bumper pool. "You know the scene: It's Friday night and you cash your pay check in the bar and start knocking them down, and before you know what's happened, you've pissed away half the food budget for that week."[8]

Such uncertainty led King to throw away his first attempt at writing *Carrie*—which he thought, when he began to write it, was going to make another *Cavalier* story. He started it after Chesley questioned his commitment to his writing, complaining about the macho nature of the stories that King had been publishing and challenging him to write something more feminine. King, while noting that the magazines that were paying him for the stories were men's magazines, accepted the challenge, sitting down to write a tale, the idea for which he first had come up with in high school, about an adolescent girl who uses her telekinetic powers to take revenge on the classmates who have bullied her. He found he lacked an understanding of the situations about which he had obliged himself to write. "The opening scene revolves around the unexpected (and late) arrival of Carrie White's first menstrual period, and as I arrived at this—on page two—I suddenly realized that I (1) had never been a girl, (2) had never had a menstrual cramp or a menstrual period, (3) had absolutely no idea how I'd react to one."[9] The impasse led him to conclude that Chesley had been correct, and he threw the pages he had typed into the trash, where Tabitha found them.

Tabitha listened to King's doubts about the story but convinced him to continue working on it, promising to help with the parts that he felt incapable of imagining. Another problem arose about a week later. The story was growing too large for a short story and ended up, at least in the first draft, to be too small for a novel. Indeed, King recalled, "I persisted, not out of any noble motivation, not out of any glimmers into the future, not even because my wife had asked me to, but because I was dry and had no better ideas."[10] He finished a first draft that was 198 single-spaced pages and, as King saw it, "the world's all-time loser."[11] He nevertheless picked up the manuscript again in December 1972, expanding it into a short novel. That same month Thompson sent him a country-music calendar for Christmas and, at the beginning of January, King responded with his manuscript and a note asking Thompson to look at it.

Thompson read *Carrie* almost immediately, getting back to King in about three weeks, cautiously suggesting that it might be the book to get him a Doubleday contract but asking him to revise the last quarter of it. King remained skeptical about *Carrie*'s chances, later recalling that he returned to it because he continued to be short on ideas. He found, however, that Thompson's suggestions worked well and resubmitted the manuscript in February. Thomson responded to the rewrite more positively, asking King to meet him. Borrowing $75 from his wife's grandmother, King traveled to New York, meeting Thompson for lunch at the end of February and, despite getting a little too drunk, went home feeling good. Thomson, after all, had said King had a better chance than not of getting a contract.

In March 1973 *Cavalier* published King's "The Boogeyman," a ghost story in which Lester Billings is terrorized by a boogeyman, and Doubleday sent King, who could not afford a telephone, a telegram accepting *Carrie* and offering him a $2,500 advance, a respectable sum for a first novel at the time. Expecting to earn little more from the book, since first novels are often greeted with indifference, King planned to buy another car and continue teaching, believing that even if another publisher bought the paperback rights from Doubleday, he could not afford to become a fulltime writer for more than a few years. Something unexpected happened, however. Two months after King received the telegram, New America Library (NAL) offered $400,000 for the paperback rights. King received half under the terms of the standard Doubleday contract and was able to quit teaching. "It was a great feeling of liberation, because at last I was free to quit teaching and fulfill what I believe is my only function in life: to write books. Good, bad, or indifferent books, that's for others to decide; it's enough to *write*."[12]

For the next six months, ideas again began to flow. King wrote, in little more than a month, *Blaze*, a suspense novel that remained unpublished until 2007, when he released it, after considerable revision, as a Richard Bachman novel. He also worked on a vampire novel. Tentatively titled "Second Coming," he had begun it—before *Carrie* had been accepted—after a conversation with Tabitha and Chesley about bringing Dracula to Maine. King was teaching Bram Stoker's *Dracula* (1897) at school, as well as Thornton Wilder's *Our Town* (1938), and the idea occurred to him that he could place a Dracula story in an *Our Town*–like environment. King, in fact, had already developed the location, a fictional Maine town named "Jerusalem's Lot" that he had created for a short story of the same name while he was a sophomore in college. Set in the 1850s, the piece was later published in the short-story collection *Night Shift* (1978).

In June 1973 *Cavalier* published "Trucks," a story in which King, for the first time, played with the idea of machines coming to life and rebelling against their human masters. With a novel about to be released and his stories being regularly accepted, it seemed as if nothing could go wrong. Then, in August, King's mother was diagnosed with uterine cancer, which was too far advanced to treat. King and his family moved closer to Durham, settling in North Windham, near Sebago Lake, so that he could help care for his mother. While his personal life may have seemed on hold during the fall of 1973, his career continued to gain momentum. As Doubleday prepared to release *Carrie*, *Cavalier*, in October 1973, published yet another story, "Gray Matter," a Bangor tale about Richie Grenadine, who drinks a bad beer and is metamorphosed into a grey blob-like creature that eats cats and eventually people.

King's mother would never see King's books on the shelves of a bookstore or a library, but she lived long enough to know that her son had achieved his dream. "She was old-fashioned about *Carrie*. She didn't like the sex parts. But she recognized that a lot of *Carrie* had to do with bullying. If there's a moral in the book it is 'Don't mess around with people. You never know whom you may be tangling with.' Ah, if my mother had lived, she'd have been the Queen of Durham by now."[13] She died in February 1974, at the age of 59. Her last day began with both her sons by her side:

> Dave woke me at 6:15 in the morning, calling softly through the door that he thought she was going. When I got into the master bedroom he was sitting beside her on the bed and holding a Kool for her to smoke. This she did between harsh gasps for breath. She was only semiconscious, her eyes going from Dave to me and then back to Dave again. I sat next to Dave, took the cigarette, and held it to her mouth. Her lips stretched out to clamp on the filter. Beside her bed, reflected over and over again in a cluster of glasses, was an early bound galley of *Carrie*.[14]

NOTES

1. Stephen King, "The Horror Writer and the Ten Bears," in *Kingdom of Fear: The World of Stephen King,* ed. Tim Underwood and Chuck Miller (New York: Signet, 1987), p. 16.

2. King would return to "It Grows on You" numerous times, revising it significantly and republishing it in *Whispers* and in an anthology called *Death* in 1982 and revising it again in 1991 for the summer 1991 issue of *Weird Tales.* Two years later he again made major revisions and placed it in *Nightmares & Dreamscapes.*

3. Stephen King, "Why I was Bachman," *The Bachman Books: Four Early Novels* (New York: New American Library, 1985), p. vi.

4. Edwin McDowell, "Behind the Best Sellers," *New York Times* (September 27, 1981), sec. 7, p. 40, http://www.lexis-nexis.com/.

5. Bill Thompson, "A Girl Named Carrie," in *Kingdom of Fear,* p. 31.

6. Stephen King, National Book Awards Acceptance Speeches, http://www.nationalbook.org/nbaacceptspeech_sking.html.

7. Eric Norden, "*Playboy* Interview," in *Bare Bones: Conversations on Terror with Stephen King,* ed. Tim Underwood and Chuck Miller (New York: McGraw-Hill, 1988), p. 32.

8. Ibid., pp. 31–32.

9. Stephen King, "On Becoming a Brand Name," *Secret Windows: Essays and Fiction on the Craft of Writing* (New York: Book of the Month Club, 2000), p. 45.

10. Ibid., p. 47.

11. Ibid., p. 48.

12. Norden, "*Playboy* Interview," p. 33.

13. Mel Allen, "The Man Who Writes Nightmares," in *Bare Bones,* p. 66.

14. Stephen King, *On Writing: A Memoir of the Craft* (New York: Scribner, 2000), p. 93.

Chapter 4

BEGINNING TO ESTABLISH
THE NAME STEPHEN KING

Carrie appeared in May 1974—two months after *Cavalier* published King's "Sometimes They Come Back," a tale for which King had received a $500 check the previous year, at a time when he was still broke and needed money to buy medicine for his daughter. The story featured Jim Norman, a high-school teacher who at the age of nine had witnessed his brother's murder at the hands of three bullies, whose ghosts have returned and are now threatening him. Such publications were still necessary to him to establish himself in his field, for the novel, as King had anticipated, did not immediately thrust him into the limelight. It sold about 13,000 of the 30,000 copies that were printed, and it received little mainstream critical attention. "It didn't get within hailing distance of anyone's bestseller list, it wasn't announced with trumpet flourishes from the first three pages of any critical magazine, and as far as *Playboy, The New Yorker, The Saturday Review, Time,* and *Newsweek* were concerned, it didn't exist at all,"[1] King would later complain. Some, however, did take notice: *Publisher's Weekly* found it to be a "sheer horror for all concerned," and went on to observe, "King's talent lies in his making Carrie always more pitiable than evil."[2] The *Library Journal* complained that it was perhaps "the bloodiest book of the year" and concluding "*Carrie* will provide a vicarious thrill for some, but cannot honestly be recommended."[3]

Having sold the paperback rights, Doubleday had earned more than it probably expected it would from the book. Hollywood had also shown interest in buying the movie rights to the story, although the money that had been offered was small. Both King and Doubleday, therefore, decided to see how the book would sell before accepting any offers. Despite the low sales of the hardcover, Hollywood remained interested, and the movie rights were sold by the end of the summer of 1974. King would later recall, "We didn't do wonderfully well out of it, but I got a piece of the action, so the money end of it was all right."[4]

Doubleday was also interested in publishing another King novel and had been looking at a manuscript even before *Carrie* had been released. Thompson had called King to find out about the next book, and King discussed the two books that he had written in the months after he first sent *Carrie* to Thomson: *Blaze* and the vampire tale that King was still calling "Second Coming." Thompson thought the vampire book would make the better follow up to *Carrie* but expressed concerns that King would get "'a reputation as a spook writer,'" King recalled. "My own response to that was that reputation follows function as much as form does; I would write the things I had it in me to write and leave it to the critics to figure out labels."[5] After reading the manuscript Thompson asked King to make revisions, and he spent the winter of 1974 in North Windham redrafting "Second Coming" in his garage. By the time Doubleday accepted it, finalizing the contract in April 1974, he had changed the title to "Jerusalem's Lot," a title that would be shortened to *'Salem's Lot* by the time the novel was issued. NAL again bought the paperback rights, this time for $500,000, half of which went to King.

King was now working on *Roadwork*. The project, King would reveal, "was an effort to write a 'straight' [or serious] novel....I think it was also an effort to make some sense of my mother's death....Following this death I was left both grieving and shaken by the apparent senselessness of it all."[6] Telling the story of Barton Dawes, who, after his son dies of cancer, loses everything when he attempts to fight the city council's plans to tear down his house and make way for a highway, the novel was left unpublished until 1981, when it was released as a Bachman book. King would say that it was "the worst of the [Bachman books] simply because it tries so hard to be good and to find some answers to the conundrum of human pain,"[7] after he was obliged to acknowledge that he was Bachman. In the mid-1990s, however, he called it "my favorite of the early Bachman books,"[8] echoing a comment that he had made to Stephen P. Brown, when Bachman's identity was first revealed.[9] The critics echoed King's own negative assessment. Arthur Ellis described it for the *Toronto Star* as "one humdrum exercise in pseudo-psychology"[10]; Ben Field was more kind but equally dismissive, simply commenting that it was "the slowest of the Bachman books."[11]

The summer after he had completed *Roadwork*, King—whose books and stories, published as well as unpublished, had all been set in Maine, where he had lived continuously since he had arrived in Durham at the age of 11—determined that he needed to expand the range of his fictional geography. Arbitrarily picking a destination King headed off to Boulder, Colorado with his family. During his first months in Boulder, he began "Darkshine," a novel set in an amusement park about a child with psychic powers. The story would not come together, but King continued struggling with it for a while. In the meantime he published, in August, "Night Surf" in *Cavalier*. The story, which proved to be a precursor to *The Stand* (1978), was built around the attempt of rural Maine teenagers—Bernie, Corey, Joan, Kelly, Susie, and Needles—to survive a super flu that is referred to as Captain Trips, after the Grateful Dead's Jerry Garcia's nickname.

Still getting nowhere with "Darkshine," King put the manuscript away, and on the day before Halloween, he and Tabitha headed off to Estes Park for a stay at The Stanley Hotel. It was closing down for the season, and except for the hotel staff, the place was empty. During his first night King "stayed at the bar [after dinner]...and had a few beers, and Tabby went upstairs to read. When I went up later, I got lost. It was just a warren of corridors and doorways, with everything shut tight and dark and the wind howling outside. The carpet was ominous, with jungly things woven into a black-and-gold background. There were these old-fashioned fire extinguishers along the walls that were thick and serpentine. I thought, 'There's got to be a story in here somewhere.'"[12] The story turned out to be a different version of the novel he was working on. Transplanting the setting of "Darkshine" to a hotel, one very much like The Stanley, King was able to continue the story. He changed the book's title to "The Shine," which "had been suggested by a John Lennon song, 'Instant Karma,' the chorus of which goes, 'We all shine on...like the moon and the stars and the sun.'"[13]

Over the next two months, King worked on "The Shine." It came together quickly, and by January 1975 King had almost completed the first draft and was already thinking about it as his third novel. When he went to New York that month to meet Thompson and check the proofs of *'Salem's Lot*, King discussed the new book with him, summarizing the plot over beers. Thompson, as King recalls, was not very enthusiastic, once again worrying over King's being labeled a horror novelist, but this time as a friend rather than an editor: "the part of Bill that was the company man liked the idea of a third horror novel...but the part that was just Steve King's friend seemed to think that I might be hurting myself, and maybe my future."[14] Thompson, however, would change his attitude once he looked at the actual manuscript, which he regarded as the best written of King's books. Warner Brothers, who bought the film rights, objected to the title, fearing "shine" would call to mind the pre–World War II use of the word as a pejorative term for African Americans, especially because Dick Hallorann, one of the main characters, is African American. The book was thus given the title *The Shining* (1977), despite King's misgivings. The origin of King's title, nonetheless, is alluded to in the dedication to his son, "This is for Joe Hill King, who shines on."[15]

That dedication also called attention to one of the motivating forces behind the writing. As King later elaborated:

> One of the things I was really horrified to find out as a young father was that not all my feelings were the sort of things I'd seen on *Leave it to Beaver* and *Father Knows Best*. I was encountering fatherhood from my end and I'd never experienced it from the other end—that is, being a child and having a father, and going on fishing trips and all the rest of the stuff. So I was really surprised to find that there were times when I felt like I wanted to kick some kid's butt, and I'm saying, "Jeez, Robert Young never would have felt this way." In a sense, I wrote *The Shining* out of just trying to understand my own feelings.[16]

For the moment King, unconcerned with Thompson's unease, returned to Colorado, wrote the novella "Apt Pupil," which was collected in *Different Seasons*, over a two-week period, and, in February, began working on another novel, "The House on Value Street," a fictionalized version of the story of Patty Hearst, who was kidnapped by the Symbionese Liberation Army and then joined its cause. He had done some research for the idea the previous year and now wanted to get a draft on paper. "It seemed to me to be a highly potent subject, and while I was aware that lots of nonfiction books were sure to be written on the subject, it seemed to me that only a novel might really succeed in explaining all the contradictions. The novelist is, after all, God's liar, and if he does his job well...he can sometimes find the truth that lives at the center of the lie."[17] After six weeks, unable to get the story to work, King put it down.

The next idea was already beginning to percolate in his mind. King had seen a story in the paper about "an accidental CBW [chemical/biological weapons] spill in Utah. All the bad nasty bugs got out of the canister and killed a bunch of sheep. But... if the wind had been blowing the other way, the good people of Salt Lake City might have gotten a nasty surprise."[18] The story reminded him of George R. Stewart's novel *Earth Abides* (1949), which is about a plague that the protagonist is protected from because a snakebite has rendered him immune, and of a radio preacher he had heard sermonizing on the biblical text "Once in every generation the plague will fall among them." The biblical passage, King's memories of Stewart's novel, and the story of the CBW leak, along with the Patty Hearst story, converged in his mind to suggest the novel that would become *The Stand* and that would introduce Randall Flagg to King's fiction. King would work on that novel—which he later said was his attempt to recast the United States in the image of J.R.R. Tolkien's Middle-earth—for the next two or three years; it grew to become a 1,200-page manuscript. "It got to the point where I began describing it to friends as my own little Vietnam, because I was telling myself that in another hundred pages or so I would begin to see light at the end of the tunnel."[19] Despite the struggle to bring the story to a conclusion, King thoroughly enjoyed the challenge, and no matter what was going on in his life, he looked forward to sitting down in the morning to work on it.

King's life would change significantly while he was writing *The Stand*. The paperback edition of *Carrie* appeared in April 1975—six months before *'Salem's Lot* was to be released in hardcover—and was a phenomenal success, selling 1.33 million copies in nine months. Such success did not translate into hardcover sales for *'Salem's Lot*, which was released the day before Halloween, in 1975, nor did Doubleday seem to have expected any paperback sales to help contribute to the hardcover's success: it had printed only 20,000 copies, and *'Salem's Lot*, like its predecessor, failed to reach any bestseller lists as a hardcover. King, nonetheless, was now, thanks to the paperback of *Carrie*, a household name, and after he returned to Maine in the summer of 1975, buying a house in Bridgton, in the Lakes Region of western Maine, in the fall, his writing schedule would come to be disrupted by fans looking to meet him. The problem would grow worse as his success increased, but King always remained more interested in being a writer than in embracing his public. His focus on writing, rather than on his celebrity status, was perhaps best illustrated by his continuing to publish short stories in small magazines, even though he no longer needed the extra money such publications had provided him earlier in the decade: "The Lawnmower Man"—an odd story in which a man from a landscaping service, Pastoral Greenery and Outdoor Services, comes to cut Harold Parkette's grass, strips, and proceeds to crawl behind the lawnmower, devouring the grass as it is cut—appeared in *Cavalier* in May; "The Revenge of Lard Ass Hogan"—which is reminiscent of *Carrie* in that it deals with the revenge of a teenager, Hogan, whose obesity has left him open to bullying—was published in the *Maine Review* in July; and a revised version of "Strawberry Spring" came out in *Cavalier* in November. King also put the finishing touches on *The Shining* over the summer, continued to work on *The Stand*, and began, but didn't get too far into, a number of other books, two that were never finished—"Welcome to

Clearwater" and "The Corner"—and two that would be successful—*The Dead Zone* (1979) and *Firestarter* (1980).

NOTES

1. Quoted in George Beahm, *The Stephen King Story* (Kansas City, MO: Andrews and McMeel, 1992), p. 67.

2. Ibid., p. 66.

3. Ibid.

4. Stephen Jones, *Creepshows: The Illustrated Stephen King Movie Guide* (New York: Billboard Books, 2002), p. 177.

5. Stephen King, "On Becoming a Brand Name," *Secret Windows: Essays and Fiction on the Craft of Writing* (New York: Book of the Month Club, 2000), p. 57.

6. Stephen King, "Why I was Bachman," in *The Bachman Books: Four Early Novels* (New York: New American Library, 1985), pp. ix–x. King says his mother died the year before he began *Roadwork*, which was written, according to King, in 1974—between *'Salem's Lot* and *The Shining*—in his Bachman essay, seeming to confirm Beahm's assertion that Ruth King died in December 1973; King, however, dates her death in February 1974 in *On Writing: A Memoir of the Craft*, see p. 93.

7. King, "Why I was Bachman," p. x.

8. Quoted in Stanley Wiater, et al., *The Stephen King Universe: A Guide to the Worlds of the King of Horror* (New York: Renaissance Books, 2006), p. 431.

9. "Yeah, *Roadwork*'s my favorite" he told Stephen P. Brown. See Brown, "The Life and Death of Richard Bachman," in *Kingdom of Fear: The World of Stephen King*, ed. Tim Underwood and Chuck Miller (New York: Signet, 1987), p. 139.

10. Arthur Ellis, "Only for Hardy Fans of Stephen King," *Toronto Star* (December 29, 1985), p. E10, http://www.lexis-nexis.com/.

11. Ben Field, "Book Reviews," United Press International (October 18, 1985), http://www.lexis-nexis.com/.

12. Mel Allen, "The Man Who Writes Nightmares," in *Bare Bones: Conversations on Terror with Stephen King*, ed. Tim Underwood and Chuck Miller (New York: McGraw-Hill, 1988), p. 67.

13. King, "On Becoming a Brand Name," p. 67.

14. Ibid., p. 63.

15. Stephen King, *The Shining* (New York: Doubleday, 1978 [1977]).

16. Quoted in Richard Helm, "Stephen King Taking Another Run at *Shining*," *Toronto Star* (February 8, 1997), p. M4, http://www.lexis-nexis.com/.

17. Stephen King, *Danse Macabre* (New York: Berkley Books, 1983 [1981]), p. 397.

18. Ibid., p. 398.

19. Ibid., p. 399.

Chapter 5

BECOMING THE KING

King signed a multi-book deal with Doubleday after the release of 'Salem's Lot, and he would publish three more books with that publisher, The Shining (1977), Night Shift (1978), and The Stand (1978). His advances for his first five books totaled $77,500, a small sum considering the substantial profit that Doubleday had made through selling the paperback and movie rights to King's first two books. King would later observe, "A writer who is his own agent has a fool for a client,"[1] but at the time he would need to be convinced that signing with an agent was a good idea. In fact, one had to approach him before he even began to consider letting someone handle the business side of his professional life. The meeting would take place in 1976, the year before the Kings' last child, Owen, was born. While the last two of the three remaining books that King had contracted to publish with Doubleday were making their way toward the bookstore, his future books were being shopped to other publishers. King, it turned out, would not have to look far to find one willing to pay him the money he deserved.

The agent King would meet was Kirby McCauley, a fan of horror fiction who had been serving as an agent for other horror writers and had edited the story collections Night Chills (1975), Beyond Midnight (1976), and Frights (1976), which would be released after the meeting with King. Having heard of King but not actually having read any of his work, Kirby got a hold of 'Salem's Lot when he learned he would have a chance to meet him and Tabitha at a literary party. Kirby loved the book, and at the party he and King struck up a conversation about the horror field, rather than joining those who were interested in meeting James Baldwin, who was also in attendance. Finding that their tastes jived, the two corresponded after-wards, and Kirby soon offered his services as King's agent. King was cautious, asking Kirby to place some stories in mainstream magazines to test his abilities but sending out the story "Weeds" to *Cavalier,* which placed the piece in its May 1976 issue. That story is about a farmer who finds a meteor on his property and, when he touches it, is infected by a spore that causes green weeds to grow on everything he touches, as well as his body.

McCauley succeeded in getting "The Ledge" in *Penthouse* in July 1976. The story is about Stan Norris, a former professional tennis player. He is having an affair with Marcia Cresner, the wife of a crime lord, who makes Norris walk around on a five-inch-wide ledge that surrounded his pent-house. McCauley then got "I Know What You Need," a story that is set on a college campus and is about Ed Hamner, who uses voodoo to win the heart of Liz Rogan and kill her boyfriend, in *Cosmopolitan* in September 1976. McCauley was also collecting stories for another horror collection, *Dark Forces,* which would not be published until 1980. He pursued King for a story "with doggedness, determination . . . and a kind of gentle diplomacy,"[2] and King agreed to submit one, writing "The Mist," the idea for which was inspired by a storm that was so wild that King asked his family to stay with him downstairs and a trip to the grocery store the following day, when the image of a "prehistoric bird flapping its way toward the meat counter"[3] came to him. Before he had left the store, he was constructing the story about David Drayton, who goes to the supermarket the day after a powerful storm that has knocked down power lines to get supplies and finds himself trapped. A mist rolls in, and the supermarket is surrounded by prehistoric animal. The manuscript was initially 70 pages in length, but the story grew: when it was finally ready for publication, it was around 145 pages, edging toward the territory of a novel. King would revise it for inclusion in the collection *Skeleton Crew,* where he remarked in a note that he had never really liked it until the revision.

In the meantime work began in the spring on the *Carrie* movie. With a budget of under $2 million, it was directed by Brian De Palma, who was just beginning to make a name for himself, and its cast was composed of relative newcomers. Sissy Spacek, who had had some secondary parts in films and had made appearances on episodes of a few television series, took the lead role. Other characters were played by Amy Irving, Nancy Allen, and William Katt. Besides the one known quantity, Piper Laurie, who played Carrie's fundamentalist Christian mother, John Travolta was perhaps the most well-known personality in the cast, as he was playing Vinnie Barbarino on the television sitcom *Welcome Back Kotter* (1975–1979). *Carrie* was filmed over the summer and released in November, three months after the appearance of the paperback of 'Salem's Lot, which was selling well. Carrie's success would push up the sales of the Lot, and it would sell over two million copies in a 12-month period. The Shining appeared in January 1977; NAL had again bought the paperback rights, but it turned out to be different from King's other books, selling 50,000 copies in hardcover, enough to get King's name on the New York Times hardcover bestseller list for the first time, and the paperback edition went on to sell over two million copies.

King was still under contract to do two more books for Doubleday, both of which would be released in 1978. Night Shift, King's first book of short stories, appeared in February. The collection contained 16 stories that had been published previously in magazines and journals and four—"Quitters, Inc.," "The Last Rung on the Ladder," "The Woman in the Room," and "Jerusalem's Lot"—that had never been published. Selling 24,000 copies, the hardcover did not succeed in becoming a bestseller but did extraordinary well for a story collection, something that is usually published more for the author's sake than for the publisher's. In the fall The Stand, an 823-page hardcover, appeared and sold 50,000 copies in its first year, returning King to the New York Times bestseller list but also bringing him attention as a serious commentator on contemporary American life. A review in the New Yorker, for instance, observed: "Stephen King takes liberties permitted in science fiction and thrillers (the good guys share clairvoyant powers, and the plot often turns on lucky coincidences), but he grounds his apocalyptic fantasy in a detailed vision of the blighted American vista, and he avoids the formulas of less talented popular novelists. Some readers will no doubt feel a bit nervous this winter when the first symptoms of the flu set in."[4] Doubleday's treatment of that book, however, significantly contributed to King's growing frustration with the company.

King had been unhappy with Doubleday for a number of reasons. For one he was not commanding the advances that his sales suggested he was worth. Another point of contention was the company's refusal to negotiate over its policy of taking a 50 percent cut on the money a title earned through the sales of the paperback rights. King was also displeased with the company's apparent indifference to him. "Every time he came to the office, I'd have to introduce him all over again to the executives,"[5] Thompson recalled. Furthermore, the production values of the books that were released were often bad. "I like books that are nicely made, and, with the exception of 'Salem's Lot and Night Shift, none of the Doubleday books were especially well made. They have a ragged, machine-produced look to them, as though they were built to fall apart. The Stand is worse that way: it looks like a brick. It's this little, tiny squatty thing that looks much bigger than it is,"[6] King later complained. *Carrie* had actually been released without any printed material on the cover, no author name or title.

King's unhappiness with Doubleday had been exacerbated by its treatment of *The Stand* well before it had appeared on bookshelves. "The finished manuscript was over twelve hundred pages long and weighed twelve pounds,"[7] and executives at Doubleday, derisively called "the accounting department"[8] in the preface to the complete edition of the novel that was released in 1990, feared the production costs of such a big book would make it too expensive for the average book buyer. King was told that the manuscript had to be 20 percent shorter, and he was given the choice of making the cuts himself or allowing an in-house editor to do it for him. King reluctantly agreed to perform the task but asked permission to publish a complete version as a collector's edition with another company. The proposal was rejected because of contracts Doubleday had with book clubs.

McCauley was continuing to have success with King's short stories, placing "Children of the Corn" in the March 1977 issue of *Penthouse*, and King accepted McCauley's offer to become his agent. Signing with McCauley may suggest that King was beginning to think more about the money, which was true, but he would also demonstrate his continued commitment to the joy of writing. He placed "One for the Road" in the March–April 1977 issue of the small-circulation *Maine Magazine*, and, in March, entered a *Cavalier* writing competition, submitting the first 500 words of "The Cat from Hell"; it won and appeared in complete form in the magazine's June issue. Perhaps more revealing was King's giving a story that he had written simply to amuse his children to *Flint Magazine*. Originally called "The King Family and the Farting Cookie," the story was populated by King's family, much as some of his childhood stories were populated by his classmates and teachers, and is about a witch who gives him and the rest of the Kings cookies that disable them. King loses the ability to write anything except the word banana; Tabitha's hands are turned into milk bottles, and the children, Naomi and Joe, are unable to stop crying. (Owen had not yet been born, though Tabitha was likely pregnant, since Naomi is said to be six.) In the end the Kings revenge themselves by getting the witch to eat a cookie made of baked beans, which causes her to fart continuously. The story appeared, with illustrations provided by Naomi and Joe, as "The King Family and the Wicked Witch" in August 1977, and in the same month, "The Man Who Loved Flowers" appeared in *Gallery*.

By the time these latter stories had appeared, King, with the help of McCauly, had taken control of his career. He signed a deal worth $2.5 million with NAL for three books, *The Dead Zone*, *Firestarter*, and another book that had yet to be started when the contract was signed in the spring of 1977 but turned out to be *Cujo*, the idea for which came to King later in the year. The deal would reverse the customary publishing arrangement in that King's books were to be bought by the paperback house, who then sold the hardcover rights to another publisher, which would turn out to be Viking. Money wasn't the only reason to sign with NAL, however. Equally, perhaps more, important was that the publisher had supported King in another way, helping him to resolve an issue that he had been grappling with for sometime. He had written more novels than would be released by a publisher—all of whom worked under the assumption that a writer should publish no more than a book a year so that the sales of one would not affect the sales of another. Of the novels he had written before *Carrie*, King believed two, "Getting It On" and *The Long Walk*, were good enough for publication, and he approached NAL about putting them out under a pseudonym. King would later recall, "I originally went to New American Library full-time *because* they published the Bachman books.... [I]t was through the Bachman books that I actually got to know *people* over there, real people."[9]

King denies that his motivation for creating a pseudonym was simply to avoid releasing too many King books, for while the creation of Bachman was done to assuage the fears publishers had about over-publishing him, "this does nothing," King wrote, "to explain why I felt this restless need to *publish* what I write when I don't need the dough." He concluded, "I only publish them...because they are still my friends."[10] The first Bachman book to appear was "Getting It On," a manuscript that had been originally sent to NAL, after King had spoken with his editor, Elaine Geiger (whose last name had become Koster by the mid-1980s), under his grandfather's name, Guy Pillsbury. That King had authored the book soon became common knowledge among NAL employees, and King withdrew the manuscript, resubmitting it as *Rage* without an author name. When NAL were getting ready to print it, King received a call, perhaps from Geiger or from Carolyn Stromberg, the book's editor, and was asked what pseudonym he would like to use. "There was a Richard Stark book on my desk, and the Bachman-Turner Overdrive on the stereo. So I told them to call him Richard Bachman."[11]

Rage was not successful, but it was not expected to be. Indeed, Bachman was not created for success, and no publicity campaign accompanied the appearance of his work. The books were, as King described them, "paperbacks to fill the drugstore and bus-station racks of America." Keeping a low profile would allow Bachman to stay alive. "So, in a sense, the poor guy had the dice loaded against him from the start."[12] The dice were loaded against him in other respects as well. His survival depended on keeping King's secret, but the texts could not hide their author. From the start fans wrote King asking if he were Bachman, and over the years NAL received a fair amount of questions. Koster recalled, "I wanted to jump up and down and say, 'This is Stephen King!' But I couldn't. . . . We just stonewalled it, even though it would be to our advantage not to."[13] Koster and Stromberg did not even tell NAL's CEO, Bob Diforio, who Bachman was. Once Bachman's identity came to be known, the fate of *Rage* changed, and King came to regret publishing the book. The story of a high-school student who brings a gun to school, kills a teacher, and takes students hostage turned inspirational. "Never crossed my mind at the time, but it's a story about—I mean—I'm even hesitant to speak of it. Since [its publication], several kids have killed teachers or held classes hostage who apparently had read that book. One kid in Lexington, Kentucky, had read the book several times."[14]

In the fall of 1977, King decided to move from Bridgton, and putting his house up for sale, he went to England, intending to stay a year and hoping, as he had done when he went to Colorado, to find a different setting for his fiction. "With its history of eerie writers and its penchant for mystery, England should help Stephen King produce a novel even more bloodcurdling than his previous ones—a novel that will only go to prove his title of 'Master of the Modern Horror Novel,'" NAL revealed in a press release cited by George Beahm.[15] The English novel never materialized. Other ideas did, however. Taking inspiration from a story in a Portland, Maine newspaper about a child who was "savaged by a Saint Bernard and killed"[16] and an experience with that breed of dog that he had had while out on his motorcycle in Maine, King drafted a version of *Cujo*. He also met the horror-writer Peter Straub, who had first discovered King after publishing his own first horror novel. "It was sent out for people to do blurbs, and this one guy wrote about it so well, I saw he was on my wavelength, and I read his book 'Salem's Lot and was bowled over. So I wrote to Steve and said, 'You write wonderful books,'" Straub would recall.[17] While having dinner at Straub's home in Crouch End, outside London, King and Straub discussed the idea of writing a book together. Neither had time to work on any projects in the immediate future, but the two would return to the idea. (King did get one short story out of his experience in England, the Lovecraftian tale "Crouch End," the idea for which came to him when he had gotten lost looking for Straub's house and which was first published in *New Tales of the Cthulhu Mythos*, a collection of stories inspired by H. P. Lovecraft that was edited by Ramsey Campbell.)

King, with no English novel in sight, cut his stay in England short, returning to Maine in mid-December, a few weeks following his meeting with Straub. The King's then purchased a home in Center Lovell, in western Maine, where they would live until the following fall, when King once again would find himself living near Bangor, temporarily, he thought.

NOTES

1. Kim Foltz and Penelope Wang, "An Unstoppable Thriller King," *Newsweek* (June 10, 1985), p. 62, http://www.lexis-nexis.com/.

2. Stephen King, *Skeleton Crew* (New York: Viking, 1985), p. 567.

3. Ibid., p. 568.

4. "*The Stand* (Book Review)," *New Yorker* (January 15, 1979), p. 109, http://vnweb.hwwilsonweb.com/hww/login.jhtml.

5. Quoted in George Beahm, *The Stephen King Story* (Kansas City, MO: Andrews and McMeel, 1992), p. 78.

6. Bhob Stewart, "Flix," in *Bare Bones: Conversations on Terror with Stephen King* (New York: McGraw-Hill, 1988), p. 131.

7. Stephen King, *Danse Macabre* (New York: Berkley Books, 1983 [1981]), p. 399.

8. Stephen King, *The Stand: The Complete and Uncut Edition* (New York: Signet, 1991 [1990]), p. xiii.

9. Quoted in Stephen P. Brown, "The Life and Death of Richard Bachman," in *Kingdom of Fear: The World of Stephen King,* ed. Tim Underwood and Chuck Miller (New York: Signet, 1987), p. 129.

10. Stephen King, "Why I was Bachman," in *The Bachman Books: Four Early Novels* (New York: New American Library, 1985), pp. vii, x.

11. Brown, p. 127.

12. King, "Why I was Bachman," p. ix.

13. Brown, p. 129.

14. Quoted in "Stephen King's Biggest Fear is a Dread of Copycats," *Baltimore Sun* (February 14, 1997), p. E2, http://vnweb.hwwilsonweb.com/hww/login.jhtml.

15. George Beahm, *The Stephen King Story,* p. 81.

16. Mat Schaffer, "Interview with Stephen King," in *Bare Bones,* p. 114.

17. Michael Kernan, "Kindred Spirits," *Washington Post* (November 27, 1984), p. C1, http://www.lexis-nexis.com/.

Chapter 6

RESPONDING TO FAME AND FORTUNE

By 1978 King had achieved a level of fame and wealth that few writers ever attain. He, however, altered little about himself, refusing, for example, to carry a credit card, which was a bigger status symbol in the seventies than it is today. In the years that followed, he would be mistaken for a person of ordinary means. Thus, at a World Fantasy Convention, while checking into a hotel, "the lady at Reception . . . suspected Steve of not being able to pay for his hotel booking."[1] King continued to ignore his status, "working hard to retain his country-boy manner," Kim Foltz and Penelope Wang reported for *Newsweek* in 1985. "He lives modestly, for a millionaire, dressing in blue jeans and living on the $200 a week in pocket money his manager doles out. . . . While he's grown accustomed to the fame, his wealth still doesn't seem real to him. 'Basically, I'd like to be like Scrooge McDuck and put all of my money in Shop 'N Save bags and keep it in a vault to play around with. Then it might seem real.'"[2] He had distrusted the monetary value of what he was doing from the start, recalling that after *Carrie* was published, "my wife Tabby got very exasperated with me, saying, 'You've made all this money, you are a success, let's spend some of it.' But I was insecure inside."[3]

King was also, in a way, insecure about his place in the literary establishment, where popular literature, particularly the genre fiction with which King is associated, is looked upon with distrust. Despite being "young enough in those days to worry about that casual cocktail-party question, 'Yes, but when are you going to do something *serious?*,'"[4] he continued doing what he had always done, publishing horror stories, including in such places as *Fantasy and Science Fiction*. There he placed, in February

1978, "The Night of the Tiger"—a story influenced by the episode of the television series *The Fugitive* (1963–1967) in which Dr. Richard Kimble, the fugitive for whom the show was named, took a job cleaning cages at a zoo or a circus. King's story is set at the traveling Farnum & William's All American 3-Ring Circus and Sideshow and told by Eddie Johnston, who puts up tents and cleans cages. Although the circus has only one lion, Green Terror, Johnson hears that two lions had had a fight to the death during a storm, and one has a scar on its neck, in the same place that Jason Indrasil, the lion's trainer, had one. Indrasil is never heard from again. King found the story in an old box and, upon rereading it, decided it was respectable, though it needed to be fixed. He thus rewrote it, and recalling the response to it that he had gotten from *Fantasy and Science Fiction* years earlier, he resubmitted it on a whim. "This time they bought it. One thing I've noticed is that when you've had a little success, magazines are a lot less apt to use that phrase, 'Not for us.'"[5]

King did do some things to call attention to his seriousness, accepting, for example, a position as a visiting writer at UMO. That move simultaneously called attention to his ordinary-Joe attitude and his aspirations to be regarded as a man of letters. On the one hand, he was making himself available at his *alma mater,* in a very personal way, to students who would likely be his fans, suggesting, in a way few famous authors would, that he was much like those who read his books. On the other hand, he was demonstrating that he deserved a place in academia, just like any respectable writer. King would further that impression two years later, when he deposited six boxes of his papers—manuscripts of both published and unpublished material—in UMO's Fogler Library Special Collections division so that those wishing to do research on him could have access to more than just published material. King, as is his wont, downplayed the significance of his donation, commenting, according to James MacCampbell, the library's director, that the papers "were piled up around home and they might as well be here as somewhere else."[6]

Taking the teaching job meant that King had to leave Lovell to be close to the university, and in the fall he took up residence in Orrington, a town near Bangor. Over the next two semesters, he taught creative writing and literature courses. Having to teach, as well as a phone call, would lead him to take up a different mode of writing, a more academic one. Thompson had left Doubleday after *The Stand* had been completed and was now the senior editor at Everest House. In the middle of King's first teaching semester, he called King and asked, "Why don't you do a book about the entire horror phenomenon as you see it? Books, movies, radio, TV, the whole thing."[7] The idea was intimidating to King. After all, he was a fiction writer and had never been obliged to confine himself to facts. The idea grew on him, especially since he was preparing a syllabus for a course on supernatural fiction, which he would teach in the Spring 1979 semester, and "musing aloud to my wife that I was shortly going to be spending a lot of time in front of a lot of people talking about a subject in which I had previously only felt my way instinctively, like a blind man."[8] King decided to take on the project, supposing that he could draw upon the material that he would use in class to develop his argument for the book, which would be published as *Danse Macabre* (1981), while his research for the book would help him prepare for the class.

Of course, King did not abandon his fiction just because he had accepted the challenge of writing a study of horror. In December 1978 *Cavalier* published "Man with a Belly," a revenge tale about a mob boss who humiliates his wife by having her raped. She, in turn, hires the man who raped her, John Bracken, to have sex with her until she becomes pregnant. (The story would reappear the following year in the November–December issue of *Gent*.) Around the time that that story was first published, King had an idea for a new novel. His daughter's cat, Smucky, was killed on the highway near where the Kings were living. (The grave of a cat named Smucky, which reads, "He Was Obedient"[9] and gives his dates as 1971–1974, appears in the novel, calling attention to the origins of the story's idea.) The cat was buried at a cemetery for pets that local children had developed and named, using their own spelling, the "Pet Sematary." The cat's death, and his daughter's demands that God give her cat back to her, led King to wonder about its coming back to life. "And then you say to yourself, 'You have to go a little further. If you're going to take on this grieving process—what happens when you lose a kid—you ought to go all the way through it.'"[10] These musings were the impetus for beginning *Pet Sematary* (1983), which he set to work on in December 1978, finishing the first draft in May 1979.

Louis Creed, a doctor who has taken the position of health director at the University of Maine's medical facility, and his wife Rachel move from Chicago to Ludlow, Maine, with their five-year-old daughter Ellie and year-old-son Gage. Jud Crandal, their neighbor, soon shows them the pet "sematary," which has been built near an ancient Native American burial ground. According to local legend, that which is buried in it will come back to life. Thus, when Ellie's cat, Church, a name derived from Winston Churchill, is run over by a truck, Louis decides to bury it in the Native American part of the cemetery, and Church returns, though he is more wild than he was before. Shortly thereafter, Gage is killed in the same manner as Church had been, and grief stricken, the Creed's decide to take Gage's body from the local cemetery and place him in the pet sematary. He, too, returns but as a soulless monster who kills both Crandal and his mother. Creed, hoping against hope that a quick burial will return his wife to him in a normal condition, quickly buries her. She too returns in the final episode of the book, which then fades into darkness.

King put the book aside, intending not to polish it for publication. "You never know when an idea will turn mean. My wife read it and cried and said, 'You can't publish this.'"[11] He did bring it to the attention of the public, telling *Rolling Stone*, "It's put away. I have no plans to publish it in the near future. It's too horrible. It's worse than *The Shining* or any of the other things. It's too horrible."[12] King then went to work on *Christine* (1983). After his year of teaching ended, he returned to Lovell with the material for *Danse Macabre*, the manuscript for *Pet Sematary*, and the beginning of *Christine*. Soon after his return home, Bachman's second book, *The Long Walk* (1979), was released; like its predecessor, it was given little attention by NAL, but it would develop a small audience, and unlike King's other pseudonymous books, it remained in print as a Bachman book until Bachman's true identity was uncovered.

Later in the summer of 1979, *The Dead Zone*, with a hardcover first printing of 80,000 copies, was released by Viking, who had produced the book with care, referencing the Wheel of Fortune, a device used throughout the story, on the cover. King would later remark that it "is the best-produced of all [his] works…*The Dead Zone* is really nicely put together. It's got a nice cloth binding, and it's just a nice product."[13] The book, which sold 175,000 copies in its first year and placed King in the number one spot on the *New York Times* bestseller list, is the first novel to be set in Castle Rock and tells the story of Johnny Smith, a high school teacher who goes into a coma for four-and-a-half years after being in an automobile accident. When he awakes he finds that he has the ability to see the future of the people that he touches, a power that will allow him to see that Greg Stillson, a third-party candidate for president, will get elected and cause a nuclear Armageddon. Smith thus sacrifices his own life to save the world from the destruction that Stillson will unleash.

In November a television adaptation of *'Salem's Lot*, which had been directed by Tobe Hooper and filmed in Northern California, premiered on CBS. The miniseries starred David Soul, who was known at the time for playing the detective Hutch in the television series *Starsky and Hutch* (1975–1979), as Ben Mears. The four-hour miniseries aired in two two-hour parts on the 17th and 24th of the month. Television critics praised the production at the time. Suggesting it was more for the young than for adults, Tom Shales wrote, "Children, send your parents to bed early tonight. We wouldn't want them coming unglued over *Salem's Lot*. . . . This four-hour version of a Stephen King novel . . . is a more assured exercise in the art of the heebie-jeebies than a number of recent theatrical horror movies have been."[14] King, too, found the work acceptable but was disappointed that the television format had obliged the producers to cut out some of the more gruesome aspects of the book, noting, "Considering the medium, they did a real good job. TV is death to horror. When it went to TV, a lot of people moaned and I was one of the moaners."[15]

Others were harsher. As Tony Magistrale observes, the "critic Michael Collings argues that Hooper's *'Salem's Lot* essentially fails as a result of 'the constraints of television. From the beginning, the project ran afoul of network standards, including prohibitions against overt violence (an element endemic to vampire films), against showing children threatened (a theme consistent throughout practically everything King has written), against the kind of innovative approach that would have made the film noteworthy against the backdrop of the hundreds of vampire films produced over nearly eight decades.'"[16] The idea of producing a version for the theaters, however, proved unfeasible, as a number of screenwriters determined that the story could not be adequately adapted to the time constraints of a movie.

Having agreed to write *Danse Macabre*, King would start looking for other ways to expand his range and would try literary forms other than short stories and novels. Besides the poems he had written in college, he had penned a play called "Accident" and written a screenplay for the movie version of *The Shining*, which the director Stanley Kubrick rejected. King now decided to write a movie project for himself, beginning the screenplay *Creepshow*, which would be released both as a movie and as a collection of graphic stories in 1982. The work incorporated into itself two of King's already published short stories, "The Crate," which had first been published in *Gallery* in July 1979, and "The Lonesome Death of Jordy Verrill," which had been adapted from "Weeds." The work also contained three original pieces, "Father's Day," "Something to Tide You Over," and "They're Creeping up on You."

King would find himself agreeing to tackle yet another mode of writing near the end of the year. Christopher Zavisa, who ran the small publishing house Land of Enchantment, approached him at the World Fantasy Convention, which took place during the 1979 Halloween weekend in Providence, Rhode Island, and discussed the idea of him writing short vignettes, no longer than 500 words each, for a calendar that was to be illustrated by Berni Wrightson. King agreed for three reasons. The first was frivolous: he had had too much to drink and was particularly susceptible to any proposals that were made to him. The other two reasons were more substantial. One, the idea of a story calendar seemed truly originally, and two, King was feeling a little guilty over his financial success, especially when he was in the company of his idols, some of whom were living in poverty. "So, in comes Chris Zavisa at a moment when I am (a) drunk and (b) as ready as I will ever be to do something *small*, something which will show I am a regular guy and...NOT JUST IN IT FOR THE MONEY."[17] King went to his room and began considering what story would fit into "the cyclic nature of the calendar, and by noon the next day something had suggested itself...That something, of course, was the werewolf myth."[18]

Zavisa liked the idea, and King returned to Maine ready to write the 12-part story that would be called *Cycle of the Werewolf*. King thought he would be able to finish it in less than two weeks, doing a vignette a day. After finishing three, a set of galleys arrived that needed to be attended to immediately, and four months went by before he even thought about the project. Nothing suggested itself for the remaining nine vignettes, and King put the project aside, leaving it unfinished for years. "Every now and then," King later recalled, "I would look guiltily at the thin sheaf of pages gathering dust beside the typewriter, but look was all I did. It was a cold meal. Nobody likes to eat a cold meal unless he has to."[19] King would never finish the 12 500-word vignettes, yet that failure has not put him off the idea that he should experiment with different modes of writing. "I like to goof widdit," he would later explain, "do a little media cross-pollination and envelope-pushing....It's not about making more money or even precisely about creating new markets; it's about trying to see the act, art, and craft of writing in different ways, thereby refreshing the process and keeping the resulting artifacts—the stories, in other words—as bright as possible."[20]

NOTES

1. Ramsey Campbell, "Welcome to Room 217," in *Kingdom of Fear: The World of Stephen King*, ed. Tim Underwood and Chuck Miller (New York: Signet, 1987), p. 35.

2. Kim Foltz and Penelope Wang, "An Unstoppable Thriller King," *Newsweek* (June 10, 1985), p. 62, http://www.lexis-nexis.com/.

3. Quoted in George Beahm, *The Stephen King Companion* (Kansas City, MO: Andrews and McMeel, 1995), p. 37.

4. Stephen King, *The Bachman Books: Four Early Novels* (New York: New American Library, 1985), p. ix.

5. Stephen King, *On Writing: A Memoir of the Craft* (New York: Scribner, 2000), p. 41.

6. Quoted in "Names in the News," Associated Press (July 25, 1980), http://www.lexis-nexis.com/.

7. Stephen King, *Danse Macabre* (New York: Berkley Books, 1983 [1981]), p. xiv.

8. Ibid., p. xv.

9. Stephen King, *Pet Sematary* (New York: Signet, 1984 [1983]), p. 43.

10. *The Paris Review Interviews II*, ed. Philip Gourevitch (New York: Paris Review, 2007), p. 475.

11. Aljean Harmetz, "*Pet* Film Rights Sold," *New York Times* (June 8, 1984, Friday), p. C10, http://www.lexis-nexis.com/.

12. Stephen Jones, *Creepshows: The Illustrated Stephen King Movie Guide* (New York: Billboard Books, 2002), p. 57.

13. Bhob Stewart, "Flix," in *Bare Bones: Conversations on Terror with Stephen King* (New York: McGraw-Hill, 1988), p. 131.

14. Tom Shales, "Small Town Vampire: Gruesome Fun in *Salem's Lot,*" *Washington Post* (November 17, 1979), p. B1, http://www.lexis-nexis.com/.

15. Quoted in George Beahm, *Stephen King: America's Best-Loved Boogeyman* (Kansas City: Andrews and McMeel, 1998), p. 59.

16. Tony Magistrale, *Hollywood's Stephen King* (New York: Palgrave Macmillan, 2003), p. 182.

17. Stephen King, *Silver Bullet* (New York: Signet, 1985), p. 9.

18. Ibid.

19. Ibid., p. 10.

20. Stephen King, "Introduction: Practicing the Almost Lost Art," *Everything's Eventual: 14 Dark Tales* (New York: Scribner, 2002), p. xi.

Chapter 7

SETTLING INTO HIS POSITION

In 1980 the Kings moved to Bangor's historic district, buying the William Arnold House, an historic structure that had been built in 1856: the Center Lovell house, which was in an isolated location, became a summer residence. The year before they had "decided the kids would be needing more contact with other kids rather than just the woods.... [W]e had two choices: There was Portland and there was Bangor. Tabby wanted to go to Portland, and I wanted to go to Bangor because I thought that Bangor was a hard-ass, working-class town."[1] King, in fact, wanted to set a novel in that kind of environment. An idea for a story had been percolating in his mind for some years, first coming to him when he was living in Colorado. His transmission had fallen out of his new car, an AMC Matador, and when he was going to pick it up from the dealer a few days later, he decided to walk. As he was crossing a wooden bridge, the sound of his boots on the wood reminded him of the fairytale, "The Three Billy Goats Gruff," and the line, uttered by a troll, "Who is trip-trapping upon my bridge?" King began considering writing a novel about a troll in a real city, which made him think of "Bangor...with its strange canal bisecting the city, and decided the bridge could be the city, if there was something under it. What's under a city? Tunnels. Sewers. Ah! What a good place for a troll! Trolls *should* live in sewers!"[2] Caught up in the business of picking up the car, he pushed the notion out of his mind, but it kept returning to him.

Living in Bangor again King began seriously thinking about his troll novel, but before starting, he walked around town, asking "everybody for stories about places that caught my attention. I knew that a lot of the stories weren't true, but I didn't care. The ones that really sparked my imagination were the myths."[3] As King was thinking about that book, Stanley Kubrick's eagerly awaited film *The Shining*, a big-budget affair starring Jack Nicholson as Jack Torrance, was released. Kubrick, who co-wrote the screenplay with Diane Johnson, was disinterested in King's vision, abandoning it for his own. "The movie is littered with remnants of episodes that were integral to the novel but appear vague or inexplicable on the screen. (Nicholson's first encounter with a ghostly bartender is perhaps the worst example.) And readers of King's novel are likely to feel justifiably contemptuous of two switches at the denouement: an ill-advised change of victims and the abandonment of an apocalyptic disaster in favor of a 'kicker' weakly patterned after the Rosebud gimmick in *Citizen Kane*," Gary Arnold wrote for the *Washington Post*.[4] King was kinder, though equally dismissive, telling David Sterritt, "Kubrick's direction is good, but it's heartless. Technically the movie is flawless, and the acting is great, but it's not very scary."[5] Elsewhere, he would call it "a beautiful film. It's like this great big gorgeous car with no engine in it—that's all."[6]

That summer McCauley's collection of stories, *Dark Forces*, was released, and the piece King had written for it back in 1976 finally saw the light of day. Peter Nicholls, reviewing the story when it was re-released in *Skeleton Crew*, would observe, "'The Mist' (almost a short novel) is by far the best supermarket-menaced-by-horrible-monsters story ever likely to be written, and some of the nastiest monsters are human."[7] Other critics were less impressed. Christopher Lehmann-Haupt would praise the story's opening, writing "'The Mist' begins as a powerful evocation of a small Maine community dealing with the terrifying aftermath of a storm," but he would go on to write, echoing one of the most common criticisms of King's work—that he overwrites his stories—"it quickly deteriorates into a hokey sci-fi thriller full of gigantic spiders and insects created presumably by human tampering with nuclear energy."[8]

King was now seriously working on the troll book under the working title "Derry," the fictional city that corresponds to Bangor in which the novel is set. The name would later be changed to *It* (1986). At the same time *Firestarter*, King's second Viking hardcover, was in the final stages of preparation. The story revolves around the daughter of Andy McGee and Vicky Tomlinson. Andy and Vicky met while serving as paid guinea pigs for an agency of the U.S. government, which tested a mild hallucinogenic substance called Lot Six on them in a research lab known as The Shop. While tripping they fell in love and were genetically altered, something that caused them to develop psychic powers. Vicky is gifted with telekinesis, while Andy is able to hypnotize people with a psychic "push." The problem is that the mixture of their genes in their offspring, a girl whom they name Charlene, or Charlie, gives her the ability to start fires with her thought, a talent the government hopes to use as a weapon. King would write in an afterword, "Most of the novel's components are based on actual happenings, either unpleasant or inexplicable or simply fascinating. Among the unpleasant ones is the undeniable fact that the U.S. government, or agencies thereof, has indeed administered potentially dangerous drugs to unwitting subjects on more than one occasion."[9]

Viking expected the book to do well and printed 110,000 copies for the September 1980 release. It would not disappoint, selling a quarter of a million copies in its first year in print, while getting a mixture of reviews. "Another smasheroo from a writer whose books haunt bestseller lists as well as impressionable imaginations. This is your advanced post-Watergate cynical American thriller with some eerie parapsychological twists, and it's been done so distinctively well that we'd better talk about genius rather than genre," Paul Stuewe proclaimed.[10] Even the *New York Times* critic Lehmann-Haupt, who found King's prose less than compelling, argued that the story is "potent enough to overcome the novel's several faults—the bathos of Charlie's guilt over her talent for toasting her enemies; the author's constant nudging to remind us just how bad the bad guys really are; the occasional heavy talk concerning Charlie's knack ('The power was still growing; it was turning into something that was lithe yet ponderous, an invisible something that now seemed to be feeding itself in a spiraling chain reaction of exponential force.'); and—the only serious flaw in the plot—the spuriousness of Injun John Rainbird's motivation for snuffing out Charlie."[11]

The following January Zavisa contacted King to find out about the progress that he was making on the *Cycle of the Werewolf*. King had done nothing with it since the fall of 1979, but feeling guilty, he lied, telling Zavisa that "it was coming along real well."[12] Deciding that he could pull the project together quickly, King took the work with him to Puerto Rico, where he went on vacation with his family in February. He managed to finish three more vignettes, doing April and May on the way to Puerto Rico and June in the Avis office while waiting for his rental car. Over the next week the manuscript sat on a table in the cottage that he had rented, and when he picked it up during his second week, he was unable to continue. "The vignette form was killing me,"[13] he recalled. King then decided to see what would happen if he told the tale in a narrative form. Not only did he finish July quickly but he could also see what he would write in the later parts as well as how to fix the earlier ones. He completed July, August, and September before returning home and the rest of the manuscript during his first two weeks back in Maine. The 6,000-word idea was now a much longer 12-part novella—which resembled a calendar only in that the chapter titles took their names from the months of the year—about a small town, Tarker's Mills, that is being attacked by a werewolf and is, in the end, saved by a wheelchair-bound boy named Marty. Meanwhile, Zavisa, whom King had told would not be getting text for a calendar, was enthusiastic about publishing the novella.

King's nonfiction project, *Danse Macabre*, appeared in April 1981. The previous December, a bidding war for the paperback rights to the book was fought between five publishers, and Berkeley Books, with a bid of $585,000, won. Everest House produced a first printing of 60,000 copies and organized a $50,000 ad campaign. Surveying the previous 30 years of horror fiction, King attempts to illustrate the value of horror, arguing "that the horror story, beneath its fangs and fright wig, is really as conservative as an Illinois Republican in a three-piece pinstriped suit; that its main purpose is to reaffirm the virtues of the norm by showing us what awful things happen to people who venture into taboo lands."[14] Critics found the work less than enlightening. "There is not a single new idea in *Danse Macabre*, with the exception of: an amusing *précis* of *The Amityville Horror*, which King says 'might as well have been subtitled *The Horror of the Shrinking Bank Account.*'...[H]e is a genial enough guide through the halls of horror trivia, but he is neither a revolutionary nor an intellectual," the influential Canadian film critic Jay Scott complained.[15] Calling the book "a one-man flea market of opinions and ideas," Michele Slung observed that it "will certainly be a treat for those avid readers of horror, fantasy and science fiction....However, for those who have little interest in accompanying Mr. King on a highly discursive ramble through byways lined with other people's monsters and mad scientists, this book may prove both boring and baffling."[16] Such reviews did not repulse the reading public.

In May 1981 George Romero, who won acclaim directing *The Night of the Living Dead* (1968), began filming *Creepshow*—which had an $8 million budget—in Pittsburgh. King, having written the screenplay, joined the crew on the set, where he took a part, that of Jordy Verrill, the farmer in the "The Lonesome Death of Jordy Verrill" segment. While on the set King began writing "Cannibals," a novel that he has not published and probably never finished, though he did get quite far into it, revealing, "I've got about 450 pages done and it is all about these people who are trapped in an apartment building. Worst thing I could think of. And I thought wouldn't it be funny it they all ended up eating each other. It's very, very bizarre because it's all on one note."[17]

Cujo—the novel that King had begun in England—appeared in August. The second King book to be set in Castle Rock, it tells the story of a gentle St. Bernard that is bitten by a rabid bat and traps Donna Trenton and her four-year-old son, Tad Trenton, inside a Ford Pinto, the battery of which has gone dead. "And a moment later Cujo's foam-covered, twisted face popped up outside her window, only inches away, like a horror movie monster that has decided to give the audience the ultimate thrill by coming right out of the screen. She could see his huge, heavy teeth," King writes. "Those red, bleary eyes stared into hers. The dog's muzzle looked as if it had been badly lathered with shaving cream that had been left to dry. Cujo was grinning at her."[18]

Lehmann-Haupt, who had been one of King's harshest critics, was for once impressed, calling the novel "the cruelest, most disturbing tale of horror [King]'s written yet." He concluded: "In the end, I don't really know what Mr. King is trying to say. It may be that there are simply dark places in the world from which blind evil emanates....Or maybe there's nothing more to the problem of evil in *Cujo* than what Mr. King says about his writing: 'I like to scare people, and people like to be scared. That's what I'm there to do. I like to go for the jugular.' He certainly hits the jugular with *Cujo*. But it's a nasty book that leaves you feeling uneasy as well as afraid. It also leaves you with the feeling that none of its evil has been purged."[19] Not everyone, however, found the story so compelling. Bart Testa wrote, "in *Cujo*, King's closeted impulse toward psychological realism capsizes a novel already listing badly with sideline subplots in a narrative channel so constricting that King winds up locking his heroine in a Ford Pinto for 159 pages, more than half of the book's length. King's style is so broad one cannot escape the impression that he has stretched a fair short story idea into a long, suffocated novel. *Cujo* is neither frightening as good horror fiction nor revelatory as psychological fiction." Testa concluded, "King's imagination is growing thinner in each book without compensating refinements in style."[20]

Roadwork, the third Bachman novel, was released around the same time as *Cujo*. Without a promotional apparatus behind it, the book quickly went out of print, but King was getting another novel ready for the press, the one that he and Straub had discussed collaborating on when the two met in England. As Albin Krebs and Robert McG. Thomas Jr. explained, "King had a dream some time ago, and told it to his friend, Mr. Straub, and 'what followed was a phantasmagorical conversation which turned into an outline for a book,' said Mr. King. He said their book would be a 'quest novel envisioned as an epic fantasy-horror tale full of adventure, the supernatural, and the contemporary American landscape.'"[21]

The two would have time to begin working on the novel the following year, after King put the final touches on his next book, *Different Seasons*, a collection of four novellas that was due out in 1982. Straub, who was now living in Connecticut, and King would exchange text over modems, each picking up the story where the other had left off. To do the project King bought a Wang System 5, a word processor with modem-technology, while Straub bought an IBM Displaywriter. "The collaboration was 'like a long-distance tennis game,' [Straub would later say]. For King, 'It was like those marvelous serials in the old *Saturday Evening Post*. I'd look forward to reading what Peter had sent every two weeks.'"[22] King, over the next few years, would continue using an electric typewriter for most of his writing, having his secretary transfer it to the Wang, on which he would do his editing. The procedure proved helpful, and King would declare, "Since I got the computer, my output has doubled."[23]

While finishing *Different Seasons* King also released a number of stories, publishing, in October, what would become the thirteenth chapter of *It*, under the title "The Bird and The Album" in *A Fantasy Reader: The Seventh World Fantasy Convention Program Book*; in November, "Do the Dead Sing?," which would be renamed "The Reach" when it appeared in *Skeleton Crew*, in *Yankee* magazine; and, also in November, "The Monkey" in *Gallery*. That same year King received the Career Alumni award from UMO; at age 34 he was the youngest person ever to have received such an honor from that university.

NOTES

1. Tony Magistrale, *Hollywood's Stephen King* (New York: Palgrave Macmillan, 2003), p. 3.

2. Stephen King, "How *It* Happened," in *Secret Windows: Essays and Fiction on the Craft of Writing* (New York: Book of the Month Club, 2000), pp. 322–323.

3. Magistrale, *Hollywood's Stephen King*, p. 3.

4. Gary Arnold, "Kubrick's $12 Million Shiner," *Washington Post* (June 13, 1980), p. E1, http://www.lexis-nexis.com/.

5. David Sterritt, "When Shivers Came from What You Didn't See," *Christian Science Monitor* (August 28, 1980), p. 18, http://www.lexis-nexis.com/.

6. Craig Modderno, "Topic: Horrors!" in *Bare Bones: Conversations on Terror with Stephen King*, ed. Tim Underwood and Chuck Miller (New York: McGraw-Hill, 1988), p. 143.

7. Peter Nicholls, "*Skeleton Crew*," *Washington Post* (June 16, 1985), Book World, p. 1, http://www.lexis-nexis.com/.

8. Christopher Lehmann-Haupt, "Books of the Times," *New York Times* (July 11, 1985), p. C21, http://www.lexis-nexis.com/.

9. Stephen King, "Afterword," *Firestarter* (New York: Signet, 2003 [1981]), p. 402.

10. Paul Stuewe, "*Firestarter* (Book Review)," *Quill & Quire* 46 (October 1980), p. 40, http://vnweb.hwwilsonweb.com/hww.

11. Christopher Lehmann-Haupt, "Books of the Times," *New York Times* (September 8, 1980), p. C15.

12. Stephen King, *Silver Bullet* (New York: Signet, 1985), p. 10.

13. Ibid., p. 11.

14. Stephen King, *Danse Macabre* (New York: Berkley Books, 1983 [1981]), p. 395.

15. Jay Scott, "Stephen King's *Danse Macabre*," *Globe and Mail* (May 2, 1981), http://www.lexis-nexis.com/.

16. Michele Slung, "Scare Tactics," *New York Times* (May 10, 1981), sec. 7, p. 15.

17. Quoted in Douglas E. Winter, *Faces of Fear: Encounters with the Creators of Modern Horror* (New York: Berkley Books, 1985), p. 248.

18. Stephen King, *Cujo* (New York: Signet, 2004 [1981]), pp. 149–150.

19. Christopher Lehmann-Haupt, "Books of the Times," *New York Times* (August 14, 1981), p. C21, http://www.lexis-nexis.com/.

20. Bart Testa, "The Techniques of Children's Fiction and the Shaggy Dog Story," *Globe and Mail* (September 12, 1981), http://www.lexis-nexis.com/.

21. Albin Krebs and Robert McG. Thomas Jr., "Dreaming up a Book," *New York Times* (September 21, 1981), p. A18, http://www.lexis-nexis.com/.

22. Quoted in John Stickney, "The Latest Word on Word Processing," *Money* (September 1984), p. 129, http://www.lexis-nexis.com/.

23. Ibid.

Chapter 8

NEGOTIATING HIS PRIVATE AND PUBLIC LIVES

The year 1982 proved to be significant for King, prefiguring the direction his career would take in the second half of the 1980s, when he would publish books at an extraordinary pace and belie the legitimacy of the publishing model that dictated that authors should publish no more than one book a year. For the moment, however, King would pay lip service to that model, for although he published more than one book in 1982, only one of them, *Different Seasons*, was a major publication. The other books were *Creepshow*, the collection of graphic stories that served as a tie-in to the movie of the same name; a novel, *The Dark Tower: The Gunslinger*; the fourth Bachman novel, *Running Man*; and the first part of a novel in progress that was called *The Plant*. Most of these publications remained unknown to the general public. *The Dark Tower: The Gunslinger* was given a limited release through a small publisher without a publicity campaign, while *The Plant* was issued through the Philtrum Press—a publishing house that King established for pet projects—and Bachman's connection to King remained a well-kept secret.

The first of the books, which came out in May, was Bachman's *Running Man*, a futuristic story about a television game show on which the losing contestants die. It was originally written in the early 1970s "during a period of seventy-two hours"[1] and rejected by Thompson. King thought it "may be the best of [Bachman's books] because it's nothing but story—it moves with the goofy speed of a silent movie, and anything which is *not* story is cheerfully thrown over the side."[2] He was considering making it his last pseudonymous publication, perhaps because he had gotten concerned that his secret would be discovered if he kept the pseudonym alive.

To throw off the speculators, Bachman was provided with a biography. He reportedly lived in New Hampshire, where he owned a chicken farm; he refused to talk with reporters, who did occasionally ask NAL for quotes or interviews, or make appearances, because his face had been ravaged by cancer. While the book would not be Bachman's last, it would be the last that would be released as a bottom-tier paperback. King changed his mind about retiring Bachman after completing *Thinner* (1984), a manuscript that was shorter than his usual books and that he thought might be used to turn Bachman into a success. He, therefore, offered it to NAL as a hardcover and agreed to allow the company to provide it with a publicity campaign.

King's next book to see print was *Creepshow*, which appeared in the summer of 1982, ahead of the film that would have its general release at Halloween. The print element was a graphic album that was illustrated by Berni Wrightson—whose illustrations for the *Cycle of the Werewolf* would appear in the short novel that would be released in 1983—and featured a cover by Jack Kamen, the preliminary sketches for which "showed a sinister little boy resembling King's son Joe, who ended up playing the part in the film."[3] The movie would not prove successful, failing to find the support of the public after critics pronounced it a failure. Vincent Canby, for example, wrote for the *New York Times*, "*Creepshow* takes its format as well as its style from a horror comic book, a prop that has a significant role in the film's prologue and epilogue. In between are five stories that have nothing in common except that Mr. King wrote them in what appears to have been a hurry.... The best things about *Creepshow* are its carefully simulated comic-book tackiness and the gusto with which some good actors assume silly positions. Horror film purists may object to the levity even though failed, as a lot of it is."[4] King would comment, "I think the critical drubbing it got might have driven some adults away, though a lot of teenagers have flocked to see the film. I expected bad reviews, of course, because *Creepshow* is based on the horror–comic book traditions of the fifties, not a send-up at all but a recreation. And if the mainstream critics had understood and appreciated that, I'd have known right off that we'd failed miserably in what we were trying to do. Of course, a few big-name critics, such as Rex Reed, did love the film, but that's because they were brought up on those comics and remember them with affection."[5]

The novella collection *Different Seasons* appeared at the end of July; the book was not exactly what the publisher had been looking for, and when King pitched it to Alan Williams, his editor at the time, Williams became a little crestfallen, telling King that it had a great ring but then sighing, "the sigh of a good sport who has just taken his seat in third class on Revolución Airways' newest plane—a Lockheed Tristar—and has seen the first cockroach trundling busily over the top of the seat ahead of him."[6] One concern was that King wanted to release a collection of novellas, what he describes in his afterword to the book as "a really terrible place, an anarchy-ridden literary banana republic," the kind of works that "traditionally only sell to the 'genre markets.'"[7] What was perhaps worse, as far as King's editor was concerned, was that the first three stories, "Rita Hayworth and the Shawshank Redemption," "Apt Pupil," and "The Body," weren't horror stories.

The first of the stories, "Rita Hayworth and the Shawshank Redemption," is a prison narrative that begins in the late 1940s in the fictional Maine prison Shawshank, when Rita Hayworth was a popular pinup girl. Told from the perspective of Red, a prisoner who has things smuggled into the prison for the other inmates, the story is about Andy Dufresne, a banker who has been wrongly convicted of the murders of his wife and her lover. Over the next 10 years, Dufresne digs a tunnel, the opening of which is hidden behind a poster of Rita Haworth, and successfully escapes. The second, "Apt Pupil," the longest of the stories, is an exploration of the fascination of a high school student, Todd Bowden, with Kurt Dussander, the Nazi war criminal whom Heinrich Himmler, the leader of the SS, called "an efficiency expert"[8] and whom Todd discovers lives nearby him under the alias Arthur Denker. "The Body," which is set in Castle Rock, is semi-autobiographical in that its narrator, the adult Gordie Lachance, is a successful horror writer whose first three books were made into successful movies but whose work is dismissed as garbage by literary critics. Two of Lachance's early stories, "Stud City" and "The Revenge of Lard Ass Hogan," are actually ones that King had published under his own name. The central story, however, is fiction. A coming-of-age tale that takes place around 1960, when Lachance and his three friends—Chris Chambers, Vern Tessio, and Teddy Duchamp—go off on a two day search for the corpse of Ray Brower, a kid around their age who went missing after going off to pick blueberries. The last of the stories, "The Breathing Method," is the only work in the collection that attempts to cater to the expectations of King's reading public. A ghost story told one Christmas at a club on East 35th Street in New York, where gentleman gather to tell stories, by Dr. Emlyn McCarron, the tale concerns a young woman, Sandra Stansfield, whose baby McCarron had delivered. She is beheaded on her way to the hospital, but her headless body lives on, continuing to employ the breathing method that Sandra had learned to help her cope with pain of childbirth. Dedicated to Straub and his wife, Susan, the story was apparently inspired by Straub's *Ghost*

Story (1979), which also features a men's club, the Chowder Society. King would explain to *Playboy:* "That men's club really is a metaphor for the entire storytelling process. There are as many stories in me as there are rooms in that house, and I can easily lose myself in them. And at the club, whenever a tale is about to be told, a toast is raised first, echoing the words engraved on the keystone of the massive fireplace in the library: IT IS THE TALE, NOT HE WHO TELLS IT. That's been a good guide to me in life, and I think it would make a good epitaph for my tombstone. Just that and no name."[9]

The book was, as Paul Gray wrote for *Time*, King's "bid to be recognized as something other than a writer in a fright wig: 'I've worked on it harder than anything I've ever done,'" King told Gray, who went on to observe, "The book may not win him critical respect, but it does suggest that horror, after all, has been incidental to his stunning success."[10] Gray's seeming dismissal of the literary value of the work was ambivalent, for he argued that the stories are "examples of what can be called postliterate prose. The genre is new, its methods still in the formative stage, but King is its popular master." He went on:

> *Different Seasons* offers a dazzling display of how writing can appeal to people who do not ordinarily like to read. King uses language the same way the baseball fan seated behind the home-team dugout uses placards: to remind those present of what they have already seen. In "Apt Pupil," for example, . . . [w]hen [Todd] confronts the fugitive, the youth is disappointed by the old man's accent: "It didn't sound . . . well, authentic. Colonel Klink on *Hogan's Heroes* sounded more like a Nazi than Dussander did." . . . [M]embers of his immediate family are judged in the same way: "Dick Bowden, Todd's father, looked remarkably like a movie and TV actor named Lloyd Bochner." When Todd finds himself in a dilemma, he mentally goes to the movies: "He thought of a cartoon character with an anvil suspended over its head." Such perceptions spare readers the task of puzzling them out. They short-circuit thought, plugging directly into prefabricated images. . . . In postliterate prose, reality is at its most intense when it can be expressed as an animated drawing.

Other critics had similar responses to that of Gray, as many noted that the stories illustrated King's ability to step outside the horror field and represented a failed attempt to be taken seriously by the literati. The public, however, responded positively, buying 140,000 copies in its first year in print and proving that King's editor's concerns over its commercial possibilities were unfounded. Hollywood was interested as well: three of the stories would by made into movies: "The Body" would be released as *Stand by Me* (1986), "Rita Hayworth and the Shawshank Redemption" would become *The Shawshank Redemption* (1994), and *Apt Pupil* would be released under the same name in 1998, 11 years after Richard Kobritz had begun shooting a version starring Rick Schroder—who was best known as the star of the television series *Silver Spoons* (1982–1987)—that ran into financial difficulties and was never completed. King was later shown the incomplete version and remarked, "That sucker was *real* good!"[11]

King followed *Different Seasons* with a book that marked another major departure from his usual work. Three of *Different Seasons'* novellas may not have been horror stories, but they all clearly fit into the world in which King's other stories, even the post-apocalyptic *The Stand,* took place, that is, a recognizable America. *The Dark Tower: The Gunslinger,* which was inspired by the Robert Browning poem "Childe Roland to the Dark Tower Came" that King had read as a sophomore in college, was radically different. King had begun writing it in 1970—when he had published part of it in the UMO student newspaper during the summer after he had graduated—and had released it in parts through the pages of *Science Fiction and Fantasy* between 1978 and 1981, publishing "The Gunslinger" in October 1978, "The Way Station" in April 1980, "The Oracle and the Mountains" in February 1981, "The Slow Mutants" in July 1981, and "The Gunslinger and the Dark Man" in November 1981. King, however, had not intended to release the piece in novel form, fearing that it departed too much from the real world: "It was more like a Tolkien fantasy of some other world," he told Janet C. Beaulieu.[12] He was also not sure he wanted to put out an incomplete story, what he regarded as "the first stanza in a much longer work"[13]: "[I]t was like 'peg-legged,' it was there, inside its covers, I guess you'd say, it made a certain amount of sense, but there was all this stuff that I wasn't talking about that went on before the book opens, and when the book ends, there's all this stuff to be resolved, including: what the hell is this all about? What is this tower? Why does this guy need to get there? And the rest of it."[14]

Donald M. Grant, a specialty publisher, convinced King to issue a limited edition through his press, Donald M. Grant Publisher, Inc. The book, which King and Grant agreed to have illustrated by Michael Whelan, would be available by mail order, would be advertised in fantasy magazines, and would be limited to a 10,000-copy print run for the trade edition and a 500-copy deluxe edition that was signed by King and came in a slipcase.

No one, except the readers of the fantasy magazines in which Grant advertised, knew the book had been published until the print run sold out.

In his personal life, as in his authorial life, King found himself having difficulties negotiating the demands his success placed upon him. As an author he had created the Bachman persona to satisfy a personal need to get his work into print without undermining the publishing rule not to publish more than a book a year, while he had begun releasing books that were not to be publicized with small presses to reward the fantasy industry that had given so much to him both as a reader and as a young writer in search of places to submit his work. That same industry would begin rewarding him for what he had given to it, honoring him in 1982, after years of nominating him, with the most prestigious fantasy award, the Hugo, which he won for *Danse Macabre,* as well as a Locus Award for *Danse Macabre*, a World Fantasy Award for the short story "Do the Dead Sing?," and a British Fantasy Award for *Cujo.*

Privately, King was besieged by fans. His home had become a tourist attraction, and he was obliged to surround it with a wrought iron fence, which featured two gates that were adorned with bats, spiders and webs, to keep the intrepid from ringing his doorbell and asking for autographs. The finials adorning the fence were also shaped like bats, but fans would cut these bats off to keep as souvenirs. For a while King had them replaced but eventually realized doing so was pointless.[15] Fame also prevented him from enjoying fantasy conventions, which he loved to attend, for he had to hide to escape the mobs of people swarming about him. He eventually stopped attending conventions altogether. Still, King was flattered by the attention that his success brought him and thus agreed to star in a television ad for American Express, something that probably brought him to the attention of the public more than anything else had, since his face was brought into everyone's home, not just those interested in his fiction. The ad, in fact, suggested that the anonymity he sought was the problem: he, walking alone through what seemed like a haunted house, asked "Do you know me?" and went on to observe, "It's frightening how many novels of suspense I've written, but still, when I'm not recognized, it just kills me. So instead of saying I wrote *Carrie,* I carry the American Express card. Without it, life's a little scary."[16] King, belying the lines he uttered each time his commercial appeared, ended the year on a very private note, releasing the first part of a novel in progress, *The Plant,* through the Philtrum Press, sending 200 copies to personal friends in lieu of Christmas cards.

NOTES

1. Stephen King, "Why I Was Bachman," in *The Bachman Books: Four Early Novels* (New York: New American Library, 1985), p. ix.

2. Ibid., p. x.

3. Rita Kempley, "*Creepshow* is the Word," *Washington Post* (November 12, 1982), p. 17, http://www.lexis-nexis.com/.

4. Vincent Canby, "*Creepshow*, In Five Parts," *New York Times* (November 10, 1982), p. C.23, http://www.lexis-nexis.com/.

5. Eric Norden, "*Playboy* Interview," in *Bare Bones: Conversations on Terror with Stephen King,* ed. Tim Underwood and Chuck Miller (New York: McGraw-Hill, 1988), p. 42.

6. Stephen King, *Different Seasons* (New York: Viking, 1982), p. 506.

7. Ibid., pp. 502–503.

8. Ibid., p. 127.

9. Norden, "*Playboy* Interview," pp. 55–56.

10. Paul Gray, "Master of Postliterate Prose," *Time* (August 30, 1982), p. 87, http://www.lexis-nexis.com/.

11. Quoted in Stephen Jones, *Creepshows: The Illustrated Stephen King Movie Guide* (New York: Billboard Books, 2002), p. 52.

12. Janet C. Beaulieu, "An Interview with Stephen King," http://carolina navy.com/navy/creativewriting/sking/view.html.

13. Stephen King, *The Dark Tower: The Gunslinger* (New York: Signet, 1989 [1982]), p. 307.

14. Beaulieu, "An Interview with Stephen King."

15. Donald E. Westlake related the story about the stolen bats in 1994, during a promotional tour for one of his novels. See Patricia Ward Biederman, "On the Road for a Novel Tour: Prolific Author Donald E. Westlake is Now Signing Copies of His Latest Work, *Baby Would I Lie?*, for Fans at a Bookstore Near You," *Los Angeles Times: Valley Life* (September 23, 1994), p. 9, http://www.lexis-nexis. com/.

16. The ad can be seen at: http://teamsugar.com/brand/American_Express?v= ABwy2nFh1Vo&t=Stephen%20King%20&%20American%20Express%20 (commercial)&ra=4.37&rc=38.

Chapter 9

SOMETHING DIFFERENT

Having ended 1982 by privately printing *The Plant* for friends, King started the next year on an even more personal note, beginning a book specifically for his daughter. In January 1983 King stopped off at his house in Center Lovell on his way to an event at which he was speaking and began a new novel, the working title of which was "The Napkins" but became *The Eyes of the Dragon* when King released it through the Philtrum Press in 1984. He had been considering doing such a book for some months, hoping to develop a story that would please his daughter, who had yet to read one of his novels. She had, King wrote for the jacket copy of the 1987 Viking edition, "made it clear that she loves me, but has very little interest in my vampires, ghoulies, and slushy crawling things." He was determined to write something she would want to read. "Eventually the tale was told," King continued on the jacket copy, "and Naomi took hold of the finished manuscript with a marked lack of enthusiasm. That look gradually changed to one of rapt interest as the story kidnapped her. It was good to have her come to me later and give me a hug and tell me the only thing wrong with it was that she didn't want it to end. That, my friends, is a writer's favorite song."[1]

The tale would not be finished that night; King didn't have the time to keep going, but he had thirteen pages written in longhand.[2] Nor would he finish it soon after. He had professional interests to attend to, such as the publication of *Christine*, which was to arrive in bookstores in March. The year had started with the appearance, in the January issue of *Playboy*, of the short story "Word Processor of the Gods," which would be adapted for a *Tales from the Darkside* episode in 1985. The piece drew its inspiration from King's use of his word processor. The main character, Richard Hag-strom, uses his Wang much like King used his, primarily for editing, taking advantage of its ability to change text easily. The twist is that Hagstrom edits his life, recreating his reality with the help of the delete key, with which he erases those people who are making him miserable, and the execute key, with which he reorganizes his existence.

Submitting stories to such high-profile magazines as *Playboy* and having them accepted was an ordinary event by this period in King's career, but the history behind the forthcoming novel was far from ordinary. King had only taken a dollar advance for *Christine*. He had insisted upon taking such a small sum, at a time when he could command at least a million dollars for a novel, for two reasons. First, he did not need the income and felt it was unnecessary to tie "up money other writers could get for advances."[3] Second, the contract that he had signed for the first three novels that NAL had published called for staggered payments on his advance so that he only got paid a portion of what was owed to him each year. He had not finished receiving his advances on those books, even though they should have already earned much more for him than the advance. Consequently, he had yet to get the royalties that were owed to him. Taking a dollar for *Christine* would ensure that he started receiving his royalties immediately.

Set in Libertyville, a town near Pittsburgh, Pennsylvania, in the late 1970s, *Christine* tells the story of the relationship between Arnie Cunningham, a teenager who is hoping to prove he is more than just the loser that everyone thinks he is, and his car, a 1958 Plymouth Fury, the Christine of the title, which is haunted by its original owner, Roland D. LeBay. Arnie is seduced by the car when he first sees it, even though it is little more than a piece of junk, and after he restores it to its original condition, trouble begins. The car, or LeBay's ghost, turns out to be a killer who, prowling the streets, sets out to kill those people who have wronged Arnie.

The book received mixed to positive reviews. Jonathan Yardley called King's prose "competent but melodramatic, and heavily weighted with foreshadowing. Considering he is the author of what is said to be an authoritative *pronunciamento* on horror fiction, King himself can be surprisingly maladroit at it, especially when it comes to tipping his hand. Worse than that, in *Christine* he commits the horror novelist's cardinal sin: he is boring."[4] Others found the book more compelling. "In this novel," Phillipe Van Rjndt, observed, "Mr. King proves once again that there is no substitute for the art of storytelling. His narrative carries such momentum that the reader must force himself to slow down in spite of the desire to turn to the next page and the next one. Much of the story's appeal derives from Mr. King's use of the American teenager's love affair with the automobile. (The lyrics that preface each chapter—by performers like Chuck Berry, Bruce Springsteen, Janis Joplin and the Beach Boys—reflect this popular obsession.)"[5]

Fans were indifferent to any negative criticism: *Christine* sold 330,000 copies in its first year. Discussing its success years latter, King told Marshall Blonsky, "I guess you'd say it's a monster story. But it's also a story about cars and girls and guys and how cars become girls in America. It's an American phenomenon in that sense. *Christine* is a freeway horror story. It couldn't exist without a teenage culture that views the car as an integral part of that step from adolescence to adulthood. The car is the way that journey is made."[6] Within the horror industry readers saw what the fans would see, and Richard Kobritz, who had produced the *Salem's Lot* miniseries and had seen the manuscript the year before *Christine* was published, bought the movie rights for $500,000. He recalls, "You *knew* it was going to be a bestseller. That was axiomatic."[7] Filming on the movie, which was based on a screenplay by Bill Phillips and was directed by John Carpenter, began in April.

King soon took his first steps into a business outside the publishing industry. In May it was announced that he was buying the financially troubled AM Bangor radio station, WZON. "I've been interested in radio since I was about 3 years old, but this is the first involvement of this kind," King said when the sale was announced.[8] The deal would be finalized at midnight on Halloween, although Christopher Spruce, the station manager and King's brother-in-law, noted, "It was more of an accountant's dream (to take possession on the first day of the month) than a Halloween dream." Spruce went on to observe that King was planning to be involved in the station's programming. "He likes rock-and-roll, and will have some very definite things to say about the music we play."[9] Indeed, King bought the station, in part, because he feared that it would change its format, getting rid of rock-n-roll, to which he listens while he writes, for something more profitable. Over the years King tried to incorporate the station into other aspects of his life, if only in an attempt to make the venture profitable. In 1985, for instance, the station held a drawing, the winner of which would become an extra in the movie *Maximum Overdrive,* the film on which King would make his directorial debut. Such promotions did little to help the station, which continued to lose money, and in 1988 King transformed it into a nonprofit. Two years later, he sold it, but he would get involved in Bangor radio again a few years later.

Also in May 1983, David Cronenberg began shooting the film *The Dead Zone* for an October release. The movie, Cronenberg explained, "is certainly not a horror film. It's tense and disturbing. But if people go to it expecting nightmarish terror, they'll either be disappointed or surprised."[10] Janet Maslin, writing for the *New York Times*, agreed: "The combined talents of the novelist Stephen King, the director David Cronenberg (*Scanners*) and the producer Debra Hill (who has the second and third *Halloween* films to her credit) would seem to suggest something much scarier than *The Dead Zone*, a well-acted drama more eerie than terrifying, more rooted in the occult than in sheer horror. It's a sad, sympathetic and unsettling movie, quietly forceful but in no way geared to the cheap scream."[11]

King would not need to wait until October to see a movie based on one of his books reach the big screen. *Cujo*—a film that was made on a $5 million budget, directed by Lewis Teague, and based on a script written by King, though heavily revised by Barbara Turner, under the pseudonym Lauren Currier, and Don Carlos Dunaway—was released in June with a happy ending. (In the book the four-year-old Tad dies; in the movie, he survives.) Reviews were generally negative, partially because the main characters, Donna and Tad Trenton, were trapped in a car for too long, though that was not the only criticism. Gary Arnold snidely remarked, "Although the material is conventionally manipulated to provoke terror by exploiting Cujo as a mad dog—a four-footed Jaws as a shameless matter of fact—moviegoers are likely to feel too appalled at the way a sick animal is systematically neglected."[12]

King's second novel of the year, *Pet Sematary*, was going to be released by Doubleday in November. It would be the first time that two King books were released by major publishers in a single year. King was not exactly happy about the situation. He wasn't concerned about over-publishing himself; he was annoyed about being forced to publish with Doubleday to settle his financial arrangements with the company. *Pet Sematary* was the only manuscript that he had available to conclude the deal.

The original agreement that King had with Doubleday called for staggered payments on his royalties. His books had sold so well that King would be dead long before the company would be obligated to finish paying him. King thus wanted to change the agreement so that he could get all the royalties that were owed him in a lump sum. Doubleday's executives at first refused to renegotiate the original deal but then said they would change it if King would publish two more books with them, although they settled for one. King showed his irritation with the arrangement by refusing to participate in any promotional activities. Doubleday, nonetheless, had high expectations, printing 335,000 copies for the novel's first run, and the book proved a financial success, selling 657,000 copies.

Pet Sematary was also critically successful. Christopher Lehmann-Haupt praised the book for "the authenticity of the story's Down East characters, particularly nice old Jud Crandall, who lives across the road from the Creeds and shows them the 'sematary.'... What has always made Mr. King so effective as a storyteller is his instinct for subtly exploiting the unconscious hostility and consequent guilt that men and women feel in the routine of living with each other and raising their children. And what works particularly well for him in this latest of his fictional nightmares is the way old Jud Crandall seems to be offering relief to Louis Creed."[13] "This is vintage King," Mary K. Chelton observed, "with the suspense slow, savored, and inexorable, with all the little familiar and ironic touches King is master of. Creed, for example, pays for his son's funeral with a MasterCard. Possibly the best thing about the book is that the ending is inevitable and known almost instinctively early in the book, but the reader simply cannot help finding out how Creed gets there."[14]

The appearance of *Pet Sematary* also created interest in one of King's low-key projects. *The Dark Tower* had been placed on a list of King's previous books on *Pet Sematary*'s front matter, sparking interest in the title. King's fans, for the most part, had been unaware of its existence, and, annoyed that they were unable to get it, they began pressuring King to make it available, writing to his publisher to find out where they could find a copy and complaining that they had not been offered the opportunity to buy one. These letters were forwarded to King, who initially resisted the idea of allowing another printing but then gave in, authorizing, in 1984, a second printing of 10,000 copies, which quickly sold out. In the latter part of the 1980s, a trade paperback edition was published. The book would not only become a standard King title but would take on central importance in King's *oeuvre*.

Just as King's fans were finding out about the *Dark Tower*, they were being denied a chance to read the novella *Cycle of the Werewolf*, which was released in the fall of 1983. The print run was limited to 7,500 copies, as well as a signed collector's edition of 250 copies. As with *The Dark Tower*, publicity for the *Cycle* was limited to ads in fantasy magazines. The book soon went out of print, but King would end up making the story available to general readers anyway. Dino DeLaurentiis, the movie producer who had bought the movie rights to the *Dead Zone*, as well as *Firestarter*, would call King on occasion to ask him if he had anything that might make a good movie. In 1984 King sent him the *Cycle*, though he didn't expect the story to be of any interest to DeLaurentiis, as three recent werewolf movies—*The Howling* (1981), *An American Werewolf in London* (1981), and *Wolfen* (1981)—had not proved successful at the box office. King was wrong. DeLaurentiis not only bought the movie rights but also convinced King to write the screenplay, and in 1985 *Silver Bullet,* a title derived from the name Marty has given to his wheelchair, was released, along with an accompanying book, also titled *Silver Bullet,* that contained the original novella as well as King's screenplay and stills from the movie. (NAL released a paperback under the original title, without the screenplay.)

The movie version of *Christine* was released in December 1983, the concept of the car having been altered slightly. For the purposes of the movie, it is not haunted by its first owner; it is itself the demon, displaying murderous behavior even before getting off the assembly line, where it slams its hood on the arm of a factory worker. "*Christine* is only a moderately engrossing film.... Mr. King's device of turning mundane objects into terrible threats—demonic car, demonic dog (*Cujo*)—may simply work better on the page than on the screen. Even a car that playfully locks out one person while trying to kill another, as its radio plays 'Keep a-Knockin' But You Can't Come In,' still seems more like something to drive than something at the heart of a bad dream."[15] Such reviews could not stop the King inspired movies coming out of Hollywood. Indeed, as *Christine* was playing in the theaters, the filming of *Firestarter* had just been completed and was scheduled to appear in May, while *Children of the Corn,* which had been filmed in Iowa during the last month of the summer, was to be released around the same time.

The movies, perhaps more than the books—since a large number of Americans do not read—further raised King's profile among the general public, even when they were less than successful, and King would come to understand that, later remarking, "You would freak—or maybe you wouldn't—if you knew how many people walk up to me on the street and say, 'Steve, I love your movies.' These people have no idea I do anything *but* movies."[16] King continued to try to illustrate, at least to those whom he knew well, that he was an ordinary guy, writing more for the love of doing it than for the money that he could earn, and he ended the year sending out the second installment of *The Plant*—which was again issued through the Philtrum Press—to 226 select friends for Christmas.

NOTES

1. Stephen King, *The Eyes of the Dragon* (New York: Viking, 1987).

2. See George Beahm, *Stephen King: America's Best-Loved Boogeyman* (Kansas City, MO: Andrews and McMeel, 1998), p. 82.

3. Ibid.

4. Jonathan Yardley, "Stephen King's New Thriller: It's a Long, Deadly Road," *Washington Post* (March 23, 1983), p. B1, http://www.lexis-nexis.com/.

5. Phillipe Van Rjndt, "The Other Woman was a Car," *New York Times* (April 3, 1983), sec. 7, p. 12, http://www.lexis-nexis.com/.

6. Marshall Blonsky, "Hooked on Horror," *Washington Post* (August 13, 1989), p. B1, http://www.lexis-nexis.com/.

7. Richard Zoglin, "Giving Hollywood the Chills," *Time* (January 9, 1984), p. 56, http://www.lexis-nexis.com/.

8. Quoted in "Names in the News," Associated Press (May 27, 1983), http://www.lexis-nexis.com/.

9. Quoted in United Press International (November 4, 1983), http://www.lexis-nexis.com/.

10. Quoted in "Here Comes the Fall!" *People* (August 29, 1983), p. 75, http://www.lexis-nexis.com/.

11. Janet Maslin, "*Dead Zone*, From King Novel," *New York Times* (October 21, 1983), p. C8, http://www.lexis-nexis.com/.

12. Gary Arnold, "*Cujo:* A Really Bad Dog," *Washington Post* (August 16, 1983), p. B11, http://www.lexis-nexis.com/.

13. Christopher Lehmann-Haupt, "Books of the Times," *New York Times* (October 21, 1983), p. C31, http://www.lexis-nexis.com/.

14. Mary K. Chelton, "*Pet Sematary* (Book Review)," *Voice of Youth Advocates* 7 (April 1984): 32, http://vnweb.hwwilsonweb.com/hww.

15. Janet Maslin, "*Christine*, A Car," *New York Times* (December 9, 1983), p. C10.

16. Quoted in George Beahm, *Stephen King From A To Z: An Encyclopedia of His Life and Work* (Kansas City, MO: Andrews McMeel, 1988), p. 204.

Chapter 10

KING'S STATUS RISES

While a number of King films were to be released in 1984, King had only one book that was officially scheduled to appear, the one on which he was collaborating with Straub. As in previous years King would publish projects that were more discreet, a Bachman book and the novel that he had written for his daughter. The Bachman book, the working title of which was "Gypsy Pie," had been completed in 1982. Although it was unlike his other pseudonymous efforts in that it was a horror novel, it was also different from King's own books in that it was quite short and, King thought, had a Bachman feel to it. Determining not to publish the book under his own name, King decided to see if it could change the direction of Bachman's career, transforming him from a third-tier paperback novelist into a hardcover author competing for a spot on bestseller lists. "There is a book that I had thought would become the next Bachman novel," King said. "It's a novel called *Misery*, and it's got a Bachman feel to it. So I thought: let's say that Bachman sells thirty thousand copies of *Thinner* in hardcover. Let's say that it doesn't become a bestseller, but it does pretty well. If I could have come back with another hardcover, I think I could have made the guy a bestseller in two or three years, completely on his own."[1] Setting out to change Bachman's profile, King would change the nature of his own.

NAL, attempting to show King what it could do with a hardcover book and convince him to let it become more than his paperback publisher, went all out to publicize *Thinner*, handing out advance copies at the Annual Booksellers Convention on Memorial Day weekend and revealing that there would be a first printing of 50,000 in November. There was, of course, greater interest in *The Talisman*, the King–Straub collaboration about Jack Sawyer, a 12-year-old boy who sets off in search of a talisman to save his mother's life that Viking was publicizing for an October release. King would thus have to wait to find out about Bachman's future. In the meantime he had two new short stories on the magazine racks, "Gramma," which had been published in the Spring 1984 issue of *Weird Book*, and "Mrs. Todd's Shortcut," which was in the May 1984 issue of *Redbook*. Two other stories would become available in the summer, "The Ballad of the Flexible Bullet," which appeared in the June 1984 issue of *Fantasy and Science Fiction*, and "The Revelations of Becka Paulson," an excerpt from *The Tommyknockers* (1987) that *Rolling Stone* printed in August.

Fans were also given the opportunity to see two King movies. The first was *Children of the Corn*, which was adapted for the screen by George Goldsmith, who was hired to write the script after King's own was rejected, and directed by Fritz Kiersch. The second was *Firestarter*. These films were not successful, either financially or artistically. *Children of the Corn*, which King later called a dog, earned $7 million at the box office, only $4 million more than it cost to make. It nonetheless did receive some vaguely positive reviews. Vincent Canby, writing for the *New York Times*, for example, noted, it was "fairly entertaining, if you can stomach the gore and the sound of child actors trying to talk in something that might be called farmbelt biblical."[2] *Firestarter*, which was directed by Mark L. Lester and based on a script written by Stanley Mann, was a little different, having a budget of $15 million and some big name stars, most notably the nine-year-old Drew Barrymore, who played the firestarter Charlie McGee. The film failed to impress critics, Liam Lacey, for example, remarked, "*Firestarter* may be the one film version of King's work that most accurately captures the experience of reading his rambling, modern gothic novels: the movie is overly long, structurally unwieldy and chock-a-block with characters so two-dimensional they'd have trouble winning an audition for *The Bugs Bunny-Roadrunner Hour*. And although the rewards barely justify the time spent waiting for the puffed-up plot to deflate to its conclusion, it's a reasonably entertaining way to kill a couple of hours."[3] Moviegoers were even harsher, mostly ignoring it, and it took in a measly $7.5 million.

Such failures did very little to stop the momentum of King's career or his reputation from improving. Indeed, King's status as a legitimate literary figure began to establish itself, as a body of secondary material concerning his work started to appear, clearly distinguishing it from that of other popular novelists. The first to publish a book about King was

Edward J. Zagorski, who brought out, in 1981, *Teacher's Manual: Novels of Stephen King*. Douglas E. Winter followed, releasing *Stephen King* through a small press, in 1982. Winter then approached King's publisher about doing something more extensive. NAL accepted the proposal, and with the approval of King, who made himself available to Winter, *Stephen King: The Art of Darkness* was issued in the fall of 1984. A number of popular and academic studies on King have followed, including *The Unseen King* (1988) by Tyson Blue; *Stephen King: Man and Artist* (1991) by Terrell; and *The Dark Descent: Essays Defining Stephen King's Horrorscape* (1992), a collection of essays edited by Tony Magistrale. Over the years, college course devoted to King, as well as academic conferences, would be added to the books. Magistrale would explain the phenomenon in these terms: Stephen King is "telling us something about ourselves and our culture that we would seek to repress."[4] King, at least at times, has embraced the phenomenon, providing, for example, Tim Underwood and Chuck Miller with a foreword to their 1986 anthology of essays, *Kingdom of Fear: The World of Stephen King,* and participating in Stephen Jones's *Creepshows* (2002), a book that covers films based on King's books, as well as those developed around his characters, for example, the five straight-to-video sequels to *Children of the Corn,* which were made despite the lack of interest in the original movie.

After the summer of disappointment at the movie theaters, King's fiction began appearing in the medium with which King always found success—at least as far as the reading public, if not the critics, were concerned. The short story "Beachworld" appeared in the fall issue of *Weird Tales*, and *The Talisman*, to which Steven Spielberg had bought the movie rights, appeared in October. Some critics weren't sure what to make of the King–Straub collaboration. John Skow complained about "the mechanical series of adventures King and Straub have invented for Jack to battle through on his way to the talisman. The hoodoos encountered in a rancid roadhouse in New York, a corrupt orphanage in Ohio, and a nuclear-wasted parallel-Nevada in the Territories are maggoty and colorful, but also wearisomely repetitive. The horrors there on the page are visually ingenious, but they never echo in the mind. Jack Sawyer has two unvarying reactions, fearfulness and pluck. The co-written sentences are so gaudy and muscular they seem phony, like the deltoids of a bodybuilder."[5] Others found that the collaboration worked brilliantly. "*The Talisman* is exactly what it sets out to be—a fine variation on suspense and horror filled with many surprises, a ground King and Straub have plowed before with great success, together and individually. Together, they demonstrate once more that they are the Minnesota Fats of the novel-into-film. When they say six ball in the side pocket, that's where the six ball goes."[6] Readers agreed, buying almost 900,000 copies in the first months after the book's appearance.

Bachman's *Thinner* then appeared. The novel is about Billy Halleck, an obese lawyer who runs over a gypsy woman while driving, killing her. He is exonerated of responsibility when the case goes to trial, but the women's father curses him, touching Halleck's cheek as he leaves the court and saying "thinner." Thereafter, Halleck loses weight at a danger-ous rate, despite eating more and more. Those who had no idea about its possible connection to King's body of work paid little attention to its appearance. Lois Horowitz called it "an interesting fantasy thriller" in her Books/Writers column in the *San Diego Union-Tribune*,[7] simply noting that Bachman had published four paperbacks and was now trying to break in to the hardcover market. Those more connected to the horror industry seemed to assume that the book was King's. "There have long been rumors that Stephen King's earlier and weaker work was being published under pseudonyms, and Bachman is widely believed, at least among horror afi-cionados, to be one such identity," Everett F. Bleiler observed and went on to argue that *Thinner* belonged among King's weaker novels, pointing out that "The basic idea is reminiscent of the historical incident in which the Gypsy conwoman Volga Adams cursed a New York police detective into thinness, making me wonder whether the novel might not have been written many years ago and touched up for the modern market. In any case, it is not good King, although here and there the power of the major King flashes out."[8]

King remained tightlipped, as did those who were in the know at NAL, even though revealing the truth would have led to more book sales. The chain bookstore Walden, for example, promised to order 30,000 copies if NAL would confirm that King was the author, even if Walden were for-bidden to advertise that fact. King seemed to have foreseen such questions arising and had gone further to disassociate himself from Bachman than ever before, publishing Bachman's picture, which had been supplied by a friend of his agent, on the flap. King also seemed to slyly hint at his con-nection to the book, having a character tell Billy Halleck at one point, "You were starting to sound a little like a Stephen King novel for a while there, but it's not like that."[9] For the moment King had another project about to be released that neither the press nor the general reader would learn about for sometime. In December the Philtrum Press issued *The Eyes of the Dragon*, a signed and numbered limited edition that was designed by Michael Alpert and illustrated by Kenny Ray Linkous under the pseud-onym Kenneth R. Linkhauser. Only 1,250 copies were printed, and 1,000 copies, which were autographed and numbered, were sold by lottery. The other 250 copies, autographed and numbered in red ink rather than black ink, were sent to King's friends as Christmas gifts in lieu of an installment of *The Plant*.

The novel, a fantasy epic that was dedicated to King's daughter and Peter Straub's son, Ben, was for young readers but also, as Barbara Tritel observed when the trade edition was published in 1987, "addresses the child within the adult. To the author's credit, it is written so simply and so honestly that the prose is only rarely sloppy or jarring."[10] It tells the story of the final years of King Roland the Good's reign over the land of Delain and the first years after his murder, and the difficulties faced by his two sons, the heroic Peter, who is imprisoned by the evil court wizard Randall Flagg, and his younger brother, the cowardly and jealous Thomas, who, as his father had been, is manipulated by Flagg. With Peter imprisoned and Thomas under control, Flagg takes control of the kingdom.

Gary Webb-Proctor found the story to be a failure and snidely remarked, "If…his 14-year-old daughter doesn't relate to his other stories, he should forget about it and try to impress her by raising her allowance. He can console himself with the knowledge that while she may not like his genre, many of the paperback sales of his horror books are undoubtedly to her age group."[11] Similarly, Vern Perry observed, "The major problem with King's latest effort is the story itself. Not only does it crawl across the pages at a pace that makes a snail seem like Secretariat in full gallop, but it also contains precious little action and characters that are both predictable and dull. What can you expect of a story where the fierce dragon of the title is dispatched by Page 6, and the rest of the plot hinges on napkins?"[12] Others saw something more valuable in the book. "Like the best fairy tales, *The Eyes of the Dragon* is really a veiled commentary on the precarious relationship between parents and children, and among the siblings themselves. Envy, resentment, fear of isolation and homicidal tendencies all appear at various points in the novel and all are dealt with in their turn," Henry Mietkiewicz asserted. He went on to note, "Stylistically, this is a refreshingly different Stephen King who charts a brand new course midway between the childish simplicity of the standard fairy tale and the Wagnerian heavyhandedness of so many sword-and-sorcery epics. Most important, there is never a sense that King is talking down even to the youngest of his readers."[13]

Meanwhile, the rumors concerning King's relationship to Bachman continued to grow, and by early January 1985 one King aficionado, Stephen Brown, had confirmed his suspicions that King was Bachman. Brown, who lived in Washington, looked up the copyright registration at the Library of Congress and found that the copyright to *Rage* had been registered to King, thanks to a mistake made by someone from NAL at the beginning of Bachman's career, and Brown wrote to King about the discovery. A notice in *Castle Rock*, the King newsletter that was launched by his sister-in-law and personal assistant, Stephanie Leonard, in January 1985, that a long-held King secret would soon be revealed was then published. Later in the month King was contacted by someone from the *Bangor Daily News*, to whom King reluctantly said that his output had created "a chronic problem not wanting to over-publish,"[14] and in early February *Entertainment Tonight* hinted that King was Bachman. Other traces of King's secret began to emerge, such as the fact that the only known address for Bachman was care of Kirby McCauley and that the UMO library had once had a file card that read "Stephen King also writes under the name of Richard Bachman"[15] but had removed it from circulation at King's request.

NAL tried to keep the secret a little longer, asserting until the middle of February that Richard Bachman wasn't King, but such denials were by that time pointless: the secret had escaped and even King was no longer trying to contain it. Bachman, King thus proclaimed, was dead, but that death resolved his publisher's concerns about King's overpublishing. *Thinner* had sold about 28,000 copies as a Bachman book, quite a success for a practically unknown author, but once the book was reissued as a King novel, the following fall, it sold 300,000 copies. By the end of 1985, the first four Bachman books were issued together as *The Bachman Books: Four Early Novels* and also reached bestseller lists. King's publisher was now convinced that its conservative approach to publishing books, at least King's books, was wrongheaded. There seemed little need to limit his publishing schedule to a novel a year.

Little changed about King's writing life. Those who had subscribed to *Castle Rock* were treated to a serial story, "Dolan's Cadillac," the first segment of which came out in February with a new segment appearing every month until June. The same month that *Castle Rock* readers were getting the last segment of the early version of "Dolan's Cadillac," *Skeleton Crew* appeared in book stores, a collection that contained twenty stories, including the novella "The Mist," and two poems "Paranoid: A Chant" and "For Owen." The book found a positive reception: "There's only one perfectly sane and rational explanation for Stephen King's continuing and deserved success: He has made a pact with the devil," Curt Schleier raved. "But if that's not the case, one thing is clear. There are forces at work here that shouldn't be tampered with. Consider *Skeleton Crew*, King's latest collection of short and gripping fiction, and a book that can only enhance his already considerable reputation."[16] While less enthusiastic in his assessment, Peter Nicholls was similarly impressed, noting "Four stories are classics ['The Mist,' 'Mrs. Todd's Shortcut,' 'The Monkey,' and 'Big Wheels: A Tale of the Laundry Game (Milkman #2)']. The other 16 are, without exception, highly readable; eight definitely above average and none of them contemptible. Other critics might call the score a little differently, but overall there can be no argument: the big guy from Bangor, Maine, has made another touchdown. No question, King is the most successful good ol' boy in the book business, though he continues to give the impression (can it be true?) of being unspoiled by success."[17]

Despite all the box-office failures, King's stories continued to find their way onto the big screen. Earlier in the year, *Cat's Eye* appeared in theaters. The idea for the movie dated back to 1983, when, during the shooting of *Firestarter*, DeLaurentiis became so enamored of Drew Barrymore that he asked King to develop a project for her. King went home, where he dashed off a fifteen-page script about a girl threatened by dark forces but who is protected by a cat. DeLaurentiis loved the script, but since it was too small for a full-length movie, it needed to be blended with at least two other stories, which turned out to be "Quitters Inc" and "The Ledge" from *Night Shift*. The movie was shot the following summer under the direction of Lewis Teague, who had made *Cujo*. Critics responded favorably. Vincent Canby noted, "*Cat's Eye*...mixes elements of Roald Dahl's urbane, unsentimental humor with Mr. King's somewhat more commonplace affection for things magical and occult. Even though the mix contains lumps, *Cat's Eye* is the best screen adaptation of any King work since Brian De Palma's *Carrie*."[18] Others were not quite as impressed, though most found the movie successful. Calling it the best of three recently released anthology movies—*The Twilight Zone: The Movie* (1983) and *Nightmare* (1983) were the other two—the *Arkansas Democrat-Gazette* observed, "*Cat's Eye* is 9 million times better than *Children of the Corn*. It is not as good as *Cujo* or *Christine*. It is better than *The Shining* but not quite as good as *The Dead Zone*. It is about 1 percent as good as *Salem's Lot*, one of the most frightening movies ever filmed, even if it was a made-for-TV effort."[19] Still, moviegoers were uninterested, and *Cat's Eye*'s box office numbers were the worst of any King movie up to that point.

The following July King was making his directorial debut on "Overdrive"—the movie that was released the following year as *Maximum Overdrive*—working from a script that he had adapted from the short story "Trucks." Having been unhappy with a number of the movies based on his work, King had been telling people since the early eighties that he wanted to take over the director's chair, assuming that he could do just as well as the directors that he had felt mangled his work. "There's been this sort of progression from *The Shining*," King explained. "Each one makes less money than the one before. Because people are sort of wised up, I guess, to saying, well, it isn't there. And there's always been this sort of unanswered question: Would it be different if I went in and did it myself, would the translation happen? So that's what brings me out here, to see whether or not it will, not because I want a career in directing. And after this, who knows? I might not have a career in anything."[20]

King, who was paid $70,000 for the work, found that his lack of understanding of the director's job was a problem; working with actors, as well as the trucks, wasn't very easy. He also found that directors had terrible hours. "I'd jump on my motorcycle while the sun was coming up and stop at McDonald's for breakfast and then shoot all day on locations in 95-degree heat....On Sundays I'd become a vegetable."[21] Matters were made worse by the language barrier between him and the crew, who mostly spoke Italian, but after shooting was complete, King felt he hadn't done a bad job. The week the movie was to be released, he observed, "I don't think I'd like to direct another movie. It's not as much fun or as challenging as writing novels. But I must say that I like *Maximum Overdrive* better than any film made from my books."[22]

In the fall *Silver Bullet*, the movie based on *Cycle of the Werewolf*, was released, along with the tie-in publication, but critics found it wanting, not simply because of its production values—though those elements were criticized, especially the quality of the werewolf costume—but also because of the story. King, Ron Base remarked, "is slow to understand that the movie's sole claim to originality lies in the appearance of Marty Coslow (Corey Haim), a 13-year-old, crippled since birth and confined to a motorized wheelchair....It is only when Marty and his sister Jane (Megan Follows) begin to believe there is a werewolf, and discover its identity, that the movie comes to fitful life."[23] Others simply pronounced it boring, and the movie quickly disappeared from the theaters, having made only $5.4 million, $1.6 million less than it had cost to make.

King ended the year on a private note, printing the third installment of *The Plant* and sending it to friends for Christmas. The story would be left untouched—as King abandoned it after the appearance of *Little Shop of Horrors* (1986), which he felt was too similar—until 2000, when he revived the idea, reworking the parts for a serialized e-novel that was made available through his official Web site. At the time King's voracious need to see his work in print would soon be almost completely satisfied by a mainstream publisher, who agreed, in 1986, to release four books over fourteen months: *It* in 1986 and *The Eyes of the Dragon*, *Misery*, and *The Tommyknockers* in 1987. King had also continued working on the Dark

Tower series and would release, again in a small run of 10,000 copies, *The Dark Tower II: The Drawing of the Three* in May 1987. "[T]hose books are there, and I'm tired of just seeing them sit in a drawer. They're not doing me any good, they're not doing anybody else any good. One of them has been there since 1981, *The Tommyknockers*," King explained to Weingarten. "So it was Tabby's idea. She said publish them all at once, and get done with them, and then don't publish any more for a couple of years. And it struck me as a real good idea. Do the four in one year, and people will say 'Well, he really overloaded the market this time,' and maybe I will, and maybe that's not such a bad thing. You know, feed people enough pumpkin pie and they won't want any more."[24]

NOTES

1. Stephen P. Brown, "The Life and Death of Richard Bachman," in *Kingdom of Fear: The World of Stephen King,* ed. Tim Underwood and Chuck Miller (New York: Signet, 1987), pp. 131–132.

2. Vincent Canby, "*Children of the Corn:* Based on King Story," *New York Times* (March 16, 1984), p. C7, http://www.lexis-nexis.com/.

3. Liam Lacey, "Young Star Saves *Firestarter:* Barrymore a Hot Property," *Globe and Mail* (May 14, 1984), http://www.lexis-nexis.com/.

4. Michael Ollove, "Typhoid Stevie," *Baltimore Sun* (October 27, 1996), p. J1, http://www.lexis-nexis.com/.

5. John Skow, "Monstrous: *The Talisman,*" *Time* (November 5, 1984), p. 88, http://www.lexis-nexis.com/.

6. Frank Herbert, "When Parallel Worlds Collide," *Washington Post* (October 14, 1984), Book World, p.1, http://www.lexis-nexis.com/.

7. Lois Horowitz, Books/Writers, *The San Diego Union-Tribune* (November 6, 1984), p. 5, http://www.lexis-nexis.com/.

8. Everett F. Bleiler, "The Ghosts of Christmas Present," *Washington Post* (December 23, 1984): Book World, p. 11, http://www.lexis-nexis.com/.

9. Stephen King, *Thriller* (New York: Signet, 1985), p. 109.

10. Barbara Tritel, "What the Wicked Magician Did," *New York Times* (February 22, 1987), sec. 7, p. 12, http://www.lexis-nexis.com/.

11. Gary Webb-Proctor, "The Little Fable *Eyes of the Dragon,*" *Globe and Mail* (April 4, 1987), http://www.lexis-nexis.com/.

12. Vern Perry, "Fantasy Failures: Snail Could Outrun Pace of King's *Eyes of the Dragon,*" *Orange County Register* (February 1, 1987), p. L8, http://www.lexis-nexis.com/.

13. Henry Mietkiewicz, "King of the Horror Novels Has Light Touch in Fairytale, *The Eyes of the Dragon,*" *Toronto Star* (February 22, 1987), p. A18, http://www.lexis-nexis.com/.

14. Quoted in "Stephen King Penned Five Novels Under Pseudonym," United Press International (February 10, 1985), http://www.lexis-nexis.com/.

15. Ibid.

16. Curt Schleier, "Stephen King's Stories Offer Evidence of Pact with the Devil," *Chicago Tribune* (June 9, 1985), p. C35, http://www.lexis-nexis.com/.

17. Peter Nicholls, *"Skeleton Crew,"* *Washington Post* (June 16, 1985), Book World, p. 1, http://www.lexis-nexis.com/.

18. Vincent Canby, "The Screen, *Cat's Eye,"* *New York Times* (April 12, 1985), p. C8, http://www.lexis-nexis.com/.

19. *Arkansas Democrat-Gazette* (April 26, 1985), http://www.lexis-nexis.com/.

20. Paul Weingarten, "Meeting the Tiger: Stephen King's Books Keep America on Edge, But Oh, Those Frightful Films," *Chicago Tribune* (October 27, 1985), p. C10, http://www.lexis-nexis.com/.

21. Vernon Scott, "King Takes Wheel on His Vehicle," *Chicago Tribune* (July 24, 1986), p. B15, http://www.lexis-nexis.com/.

22. Ibid.

23. Ron Base, "Toronto Kids Carry King's Werewolf Movie," *Toronto Star* (October 15, 1985), p. B1, http://www.lexis-nexis.com/.

24. Weingarten, "Meeting the Tiger," p. C10.

Chapter 11

THE SENSE OF AN ENDING

King's focus at the beginning of 1986 was on *Maximum Overdrive*, which was scheduled for release in March but which ran into difficulties after a special screening in February. The Motion Picture Association of America (MPAA) regarded it as excessively violent and gave it an X-rating, something that would guarantee that the film would never reach mainstream audiences. The release was thus delayed until the summer, as cuts, most significantly of two particularly gory scenes, were made. King wasn't very happy about being forced to make changes but was nonchalant when he discussed the matter, saying, "I don't think we lost anything at all."[1]

King's public life expanded beyond that of a writer in other ways, as he started getting more directly involved in politics. He had revealed something of his distrust for the government in *Firestarter*, where he had called attention to the U.S. government's experimenting with drugs on citizens in the afterword. He had also publicly supported Colorado Senator Gary Hart in his failed attempt to become the Democratic nominee for president in 1984. In 1986 a referendum, which was sponsored by the Christian Civic League, to establish a law limiting the availability of pornography in Maine was held. Vehemently opposed to censorship of any kind, King joined those fighting the proposed law, appearing in television ads and debating the leader of the Christian Civic League, Jasper (Jack) Wyman, the night before Maine was to vote on the measure. King was worried that the law would lead to the banning of important books, as similar laws had done in the past, despite Wyman's assertions to the contrary, and told Wyman, "Jack, you can sit there and say you know what it [the law] will do, but you don't. No one does. And that's why I'm against it. I'm against what I don't know about."[2] The anti-censorship campaign was successful: 72 percent of Maine's electorate voted against the proposed lan on June 10, 1986.

Ironically, the version of *Maximum Overdrive* that arrived in theaters in July had been censored, but that fact had nothing to do with the movie's failure. Critics found even what the censors allowed to stand offensive. "Stephen King, the author dissatisfied with what the movies did to his books, has made the worst Stephen King movie ever. It is not about rampaging machines. It is about crap. And whatever else is wrong with *Maximum Overdrive*, there is one thing you have to say for it: The crap is right up there on the screen," Ron Base wrote in a typical response.[3] King initially put a positive spin on such dismissals, saying "a measure of my success in achieving what I set out to do was that one New York newspaper gave it zero stars and said, furthermore, there was a bathroom scene that was vulgar beyond description. And I thought, 'Hot damn, I've succeeded!'"[4] He later admitted that he hadn't done a good job, accepting that the film was an artistic, as well as financial, failure.

At the beginning of August, a couple of weeks after the premier of *Maximum Overdrive,* the second summer movie based on one of King's stories appeared, *Stand By Me,* which was adapted from the novella "The Body" and directed by Rob Reiner. Initially set to be released with the title King gave the story, those involved began to worry that moviegoers would believe that it was another King horror flick and stay away. Reiner's suggestion, *Stand by Me,* the title of a 1961 Ben E. King song, was found to be the least objectionable of all the suggestions for the new title. The King connection was also deemphasized in the promotions. The movie turned out to be the most successful King movie since *The Shining,* earning $50 million at the box office and the respect of the critics. "How odd that the best little movie of the summer of '86 should arrive as the summer winds to an end and with almost no advance notice," an anonymous reviewer wrote for the *Arkansas Democrat-Gazette.* "*Stand by Me...*is the sleeper of the summer. It's a marvelous little surprise, full of the sort of nostalgic humor that is certain to strike chords of recognition in almost every viewer."[5] King had been moved as well. "I remember we had a private screening of *Stand By Me,* and Stephen got very emotional, because the book was so close a part of his own life," Reiner said. "He told me it was the best film that had been done from his books. Before I could get too excited he quickly added, 'But that isn't saying very much.'"[6] Reiner subsequently formed a production company called Castle Rock Entertainment with four partners: Martin Shafer, Andy Scheinman, Glenn Padnick, and Alan Horn.

The run of successive movie failures was not the only constant in King's life to come to an end in the latter part of 1986. King began the process of putting his abuse of drugs and alcohol behind him. He, on some level, had understood that he was an alcoholic as early as 1975. Like most addicts he ignored his problem and was eventually drinking a case of 16-ounce beer cans a night. In the 1980s he had added a cocaine addiction to his problems. Shortly after the summer of 1986, his wife "organized an intervention group formed of family and friends, and I was treated to a kind of *This Is Your Life* in hell. Tabby began by dumping a trash bag full of stuff from my office out on the rug: beer cans, cigarette butts, cocaine in gram bottles and cocaine in plastic Baggies, coke spoons caked with snot and blood, Valium, Xanax...."[7] His wife finally said that he had a choice: he could keep his addiction or his family. She gave him two weeks to come to a decision. King chose his family, even though he had been telling himself for years that he might not be able to write without the alcohol and drugs.

King, now working on maintaining his sobriety, was back promoting his prose fiction in the fall. *It,* the first novel to feature the fictional town of Derry and one of four novels to be published by mainstream publishers in roughly four-month intervals over the following year, appeared. Five years in the making, *It,* a 1,138-page monster, was the longest book King had published and was his most complicated experiment. The story is narrated by seven main characters, all members of the Losers Club—Bill Denbrough, Beverly Marsh, Rich Tozier, Stan Uris, Ben Hanscom, Mike Hanlon, and Eddie Kaspbrak—in a nonlinear fashion, as the narrative jumps back and forth between the summer of 1958, when the Club first encounters the monster, and the summer of 1985, when the grown-up club members return to Derry to finish it off. Negotiating the jumps between the two time periods was only a part of the difficulty. The novel serves, as Michael Collings has written, "as a virtual encyclopedia of horror.... Almost every variation on the monster [as *It,* capable of metamorphosis, takes on a number of guises, including that of a clown] is present at one level or another, if not physically as one of It's many manifestations, then imagistically in the form of metaphor or simile, or verbally as King embeds the language of horror into his text."[8] King was also trying to put an end to a stage of his career, regarding the writing of the story as "an act of closure, as the summation of all his preceding children-under-threat novels,"[9] Collings reports. King would call the book "my final exam as far as supernatural horror went, like my master's thesis on everything. I'd done vampires and werewolves, now let's do it all at once, and call it by that quintessential movie-poster word *IT*."[10]

Terrell later pronounced the novel, "King's Masterpiece to date," arguing that "critics may have difficulty placing the book [just as critics had difficulty placing such literary experiments as T.S. Eliot's *The Wasteland* and Ezra Pound's *The Cantos*] because with *It* [King] has created a new form."[11] Terrell's assessment seems to have been substantiated by those reviewing the book when it appeared. David Gates saw in it "King's apparent desire to be a literary heavy," observing "The exciting and absorbing parts of *It* are not the mechanical showdowns and shockeroos—and certainly not the 'ideas'—but the simple scenes in which King evokes childhood in the 1950s. If—fat chance—he ever takes a vow of poverty and tries for true literary sainthood, this intensely imagined world would be a good place to begin his pilgrimage."[12] Other reviewers were overwhelmed by the sheer size of the book, finding that King's ambition to include everything undermined its power. "Where did Stephen King, the most experienced crown prince of darkness, go wrong with *It?*" Walter Wager asked. "Almost everywhere. Casting aside discipline, which is as important to a writer as imagination and style, he has piled just about everything he could think of into this book and too much of each thing as well."[13]

It would put an end to King's focus on childhood and adolescence, though his next novel to appear seemed to belie the direction in which King was taking his career, as he decided to allow his publishers to release an edition of *The Eyes of the Dragon*, which sold 525,000 copies in its first year in print. (He would again illustrate his interest in the psychology of children in the 1990s, when he would publish, at the beginning of the decade, "The Library Policeman," a novella in *Four Past Midnight* [1990] that was inspired by his son's fears about not returning books to the library on time, and, at the end of the decade, *The Girl Who Loved Tom Gordon* [1999], a short novel about a young girl lost in the woods.) In May King released the second volume of The Dark Tower Series, *The Dark Tower II: The Drawing of the Three*, another book that was published by Donald M. Grant with little promotion and a print run limited to 30,000 copies, plus 850 that were signed by King and its illustrator, Phil Hale. In this installment of the series, Roland is thrust into the complications of the twentieth century, as he finds a gateway into our world.

More continuity in King's career was suggested in the theaters. *Creepshow 2* opened the same month that the second Dark Tower book became available. Romero had written the scripts, adapting King's "The Float" and providing the dialogue for two scenarios that King had developed, "Old Chief Wood'nhead," which is about a cigar-store Indian who takes revenge on hoodlums who kill his owner and wife, while robbing their store, and "The Hitchhiker," which is about a woman who runs down a hitchhiker who won't die, as well as a wraparound story. Produced on a budget of $3.5 million dollars and directed by Michael Gornick, the movie was like many King movies: it failed to win the support of the critics or the public, taking in a mere $5 million at the box office. "Where the first *Creepshow* effectively recreated the old E.C. style—complete with wacky camera angles and bright primary colors and the traditionally icky 'final frame'—told with the necessary tongue in cheek, *Creepshow 2* is merely an imitation of the imitation," Rob Salem wrote.[14]

Misery, the book King had once hoped would make a bestseller out of Richard Bachman, was released in June. It had been begun in the early 1980s, when King fell asleep on a flight to London and "had a dream about a popular writer (it may or may not have been me, but it sure to God wasn't James Caan [the actor who played the writer's part in the movie adaptation]) who fell into the clutches of a psychotic fan living on a farm somewhere out in the back of the beyond. The fan was a woman isolated by her growing paranoia. She kept some livestock in the barn, including her pet pig, Misery. The pig was named after the continuing main character in the writer's best-selling bodicerippers."[15] King wrote the dream down on a napkin, and during his first night in London, unable to sleep, he found the concierge at Brown's Hotel, where he was staying, and asked if there was anywhere that he could write. The concierge directed him to a desk, which was once owned by Rudyard Kipling, and King completed 16 handwritten pages that contained the germ of the story: Paul Sheldon, a romance novelist who is famous for his Misery Chastain novels but who has decided to write more serious fiction, has awoken and discovered that he is a prisoner of Annie Wilkes, a fan who demands that Sheldon write another Misery Chastain novel, which comes to be called *Misery Returns*, just for her.

The novel, the first in which King would explore the relationship between the writer and his fans, was more inwardly psychological than anything he had written before. His new approach to his genre was well received. Kim Newman, writing for the *New Statesman*, observed, "in *Misery* [King] opens up a whole new area of potent neuroses and complexes that make the novel the most shatteringly horrid he has ever done. Also, in Annie Wilkes, he has created his most monstrous of monsters: Ultimate Evil as Ultimate Banality."[16] John Katzenbach, in the *New York Times*, responded equally positively, writing: "This book is built on a single cliff and hangs there throughout its length. But the novel functions as well on a more sophisticated level. Mr. King...muses on the literature of possession and the idea that art is an act in which the artist willingly becomes captive. He delves deeply into the psychology of creation, and it is to his credit that much of the tension in the book stems from the devilish dilemma the author-hero discovers: his book based on psychotic demand is actually quite good, by far the best he has written."[17]

King had begun, by this time, to earn a reputation for kindness, and he would end the summer furthering that reputation, demonstrating "once again what a nice guy [he] really is"[18] when, in August, he issued through the Philtrum Press *The Ideal, Genuine Man* by Don Robertson, a writer whom King had long admired but who had been having difficulty finding a publisher. "I had become," Robertson explained to David Streitfeld, "redundant in publishing circles."[19] King thought the novel deserved to be read and thus offered to release it and bring attention to Robertson, who subsequently sold *Companion to Owls* (1989), his next novel, to a major publisher, Crown.

As King's fourth major novel to be released in 12 months, *The Tommyknockers*, was being prepared for the press, rumors were circulating that he was preparing to retire, something that was untrue, though King was preparing to take a break from publishing. After all, he had been releasing stories at an extraordinary pace, five novels over the previous 12 months as well as four short stories, "For the Birds," in the collection *Bred Any Good Rooks Lately?* (1986), which was edited by James Charlton; "The End of the Whole Mess," in the October 1986 issue of *Omni;* "The Doctor's Case," in the collection *The New Adventures of Sherlock Holmes* (1987); and "Popsy," in the collection *Masques II: All-New Stories of Horror and the Supernatural* (1987). Still, the rumor persisted, and *The Tommyknockers*—a book King had reworked the previous "spring and summer...often working until midnight with my heart running at a hundred and thirty beats a minute and cotton swabs stuck up my nose to stem the coke-induced bleeding"[20]—was "greeted as a summation of some kind,"[21] Collings later reported, when it appeared in November, especially since the story is extremely self-referential, making allusions to a number of other King books, including *The Talisman, It, The Dead Zone, Firestarter, Cycle of the Werewolf, Thinner, Pet Sematary, Cujo, Roadwork,* and *'Salem's Lot,* as well as himself, as if he were constructing what Collings called "an encyclopedia of Things-King."[22]

Inspired by the nursery rhyme—"Late last night and the night before, / Tommyknockers, Tommyknockers, / Knocking at the door. / I want to go out, don't know if I can, / 'cause I'm so afraid / of the Tommyknocker man"[23]—*The Tommyknockers* transforms the original fairy-tale like creatures into aliens, who, after remaining in stasis underground for millions of years, wake up and begin giving the residents of Haven, Maine great abilities, while turning them into Tommyknockers. Reviewers found the novel failed to deliver what readers had come to expect from King, and even his fans regard the book as among the worst in the King cannon. "King pulls out all the stops—besides the alcoholic everyman doing his best in an extreme situation, there are the kindly grandfather, the lost little boy, and the tough, but honest, cop. None ever really comes alive on the page," David Nicholson complained. "And despite his use of the honorable tricks of the trade—weaving together three or more stories and interrupting a section of the narrative just before the climactic moment—the book lacks intensity."[24]

As *The Tommyknockers* arrived in bookstores, the next King movie, *The Running Man*, which was marketed as a Richard Bachman movie, appeared in the theaters, much to the disappointment of its distributors, who were unable to release it in the summer, because its star, Arnold Schwarzenegger, prevented them from playing it against his other film, the summer blockbuster *Predator*. That was only the last of a number of disappointments. The movie, which transformed Ben Richards, the novel's main character, from a desperate out-of-work character into a former police officer wrongly convicted of manslaughter, seemed doomed from the start, as more than one director was replaced and the picture ran $17 million over budget, more than it took in while it was in the theaters. Despite that letdown, King had had an extraordinary year, as he became the first author to have four hardcover books on the *New York Times* bestseller list in a single year, an achievement that led David Streitfeld to remark, even before the publication of *The Tommyknockers*, "King has passed beyond bestsellerdom into a special sort of nirvana reserved for him alone."[25]

NOTES

1. Quoted in Stephen Jones, *Creepshows: The Illustrated Stephen King Movie Guide* (New York: Billboard Books, 2002), p. 46.

2. Quoted in Christopher Spruce, "Stephen King Helps Spearhead Censorship Referendum Defeat," in *The Stephen King Companion*, ed. George Beahm (Kansas City: Andrews and McMeel, 1995), p. 156.

3. Ron Base, "Stephen King Makes the Worst Stephen King Movie Ever Made," *Toronto Star* (July 25, 1986), p. D12, http://www.lexis-nexis.com/.

4. Jones, *Creepshows*, p. 46.

5. *Arkansas Democrat-Gazette* (August 22, 1986), http://www.lexis-nexis.com/.

6. Quoted in Patrick Goldstein, "Rob Reiner Takes on *Misery*," *Los Angeles Times* (April 29, 1990), p. 8, http://www.lexis-nexis.com/.

7. Stephen King, *On Writing: A Memoir of the Craft* (New York: Scribner, 2000), p. 97.

8. Michael Collings, "*It*," in *The Stephen King Companion*, p. 263.

9. Ibid., p. 262.

10. Quoted in Matt Roush, "It Calms King's Fear of TV," *USA Today* (November 16, 1990), p. D3, http://www.lexis-nexis.com/.

11. Carroll F. Terrell, *Stephen King: Man and Artist* (Orono, ME: Northern Lights, 1991), p. 140.

12. David Gates, "The Creature that Refused to Die," *Newsweek* (September 1, 1986), p. 82, http://vnweb.hwwilsonweb.com/hww.

13. Walter Wager, "More Evil Than a 15-Foot Spider," *New York Times Book Review* (August 24, 1986), p. 9, http://www.nytimes.com/books/97/03/09/life times/kin-r-it.html.

14. Rob Salem, *"Creepshow 2:* Really a Monster Bore!" *Toronto Star* (June 3, 1987), p. C3, http://www.lexis-nexis.com/.

15. King, *On Writing*, p. 165.

16. Kim Newman, "*Misery* (Book Review)," *New Statesman* (September 11, 1987), p. 30, http://vnweb.hwwilsonweb.com/hww.

17. John Katzenbach, "Summer Reading," *New York Times* (May 31, 1987), p. 20, http://www.lexis-nexis.com/.

18. David Streitfeld, "Ideal Genuine Man," *Washington Post* (February 7, 1988). p. X15, http://www.lexis-nexis.com/. King has proved himself a nice guy throughout his career, perhaps most notably, sending Billy Johnson, a man whose King collection was stolen with the rest of his belongings, signed copies of *Misery, It, The Dark Half, Gerald's Game, Four Past Midnight,* and *Needful Things,* as well as the audio version of *Nightmares & Dreamscapes,* after hearing about the incident in the news. See Judith Lynn Howard, "Stephen King Eases the Misery," *Dallas Morning News* (February 27, 1994), p. A33, http://www.lexis-nexis.com/.

19. Streitfeld, "Ideal Genuine Man," p. X15.

20. King, *On Writing*, p. 96.

21. Michael Collings, *"The Tommyknockers,"* in *The Stephen King Companion,* p. 273.

22. Ibid., p. 274.

23. Stephen King, *The Tommyknockers* (New York, Signet, 1988 [1987]), p. 124.

24. David Nicholson, "Stephen King and Strange Happenings in Haven, Maine," *Washington Post* (November 29, 1987), p. X9, http://www.lexis-nexis.com/.

25. Streitfeld, "Stephen King's No. 1 Fans: The Author Gives His Readers a Lively Dose of *Misery," Washington Post* (May 8, 1987, Friday), p. D5, http://www.lexis-nexis.com/.

Chapter 12

LETTING PEOPLE RECOVER

King published no original novels in 1988, although he did publish three "bland and obscure"[1] stories—"Dedication," "Sneakers," and "The Reploids"—in Douglas E. Winter's *Night Visions V,* which was reissued as *Dark Visions* at the end of 1989; "My Pretty Pony,"[2] a short story put out as a collectors edition by the Whitney Museum of Art; and at the end of the year, an introductory essay to *Nightmares in the Sky,* a collection of photographs of gargoyles taken by the photographer f-stop Fitzgerald that Viking incorrectly thought might gain an audience by attaching King's name to it. The lack of a full-length novel seemed to confirm the rumor of the previous year that King had gone into retirement, despite an article in *Castle Rock* that assured readers that he would continue to write, though it did say that he was going to take some time off from releasing new books. "I did the four novels in one year because it was a good time for me to clear the decks," King explained, remaining silent about The Dark Tower novel that had also appeared. "Books get old, get stale, like bread. They don't keep well in a desk drawer. But it's time to let people recover."[3]

King wasn't the only one withholding new fiction: Hollywood brought no new King movies to the screen in 1988. King's work, however, was introduced to another medium. *Carrie* was recast as a musical, which, in the mid 1980s, had been adapted for the stage by Lawrence D. Cohen, who had written the screenplay for the 1976 movie, and contained a rock-and-roll score by Dean Pitchford and Michael Gore. It had been announced, in 1985, that *Carrie* would open on Broadway in 1986, but the financing was pulled and the production cancelled. Terry Hands, whose reputation had been built staging classical drama and who was the artistic director at the Royal Shakespeare Company, had been picked to direct. He revived the project, staging it on the Royal Shakespeare Company's main Stratford-upon-Avon stage for three weeks at the end of February and the beginning of March of 1988. The production was then brought to Broadway for a May opening. "*Carrie* is an experiment, an exploration of a form that we would like to get better at," Hands explained. "What fascinates me is trying to do a story through song and dance and popular culture.... We definitely want to do more. I haven't had so much fun in years!"[4] The Broadway run didn't last long, closing after only five performances.

Around the time that the musical was given its brief run, the Whitney released its $2,200 collectors edition featuring King's "My Pretty Pony"—a story taken out of an incomplete Bachman novel of the same name that King began and abandoned in the early 1980s—and lithographs by Barbara Kruger. Bound in "stainless-steel and a leather jacket with an inset digital clock, a bow to the story's interest in the passage of time,"[5] only 280 copies were printed, 150 of which were made available to the public. Recalling his decision to send the story to the Whitney, King wrote in *Nightmares & Dreamscapes*, the short-story collection in which he placed a more polished version, "*My Pretty Pony* I junked...except for a brief flashback in which [Clive] Banning [the novel's main character]... remembers how his grandfather instructed him on the plastic nature of time. Finding that flashback—marvellously complete, almost a short story as it stood—was like finding a rose growing in a junkheap."[6] The following year Knopf reissued a more affordable edition, printing 15,000 copies, which sold for $50, a price that still seemed expensive for a 9,000-word short story. "While the merits of the design are certainly open to doubt, the story itself is a charming fable of an old man's passing of a timepiece, and a lesson, to his favorite grandchild. This is the writer at his most avuncular, a bittersweet fiction in which he takes our hands and walks with us toward that long, dark night ahead,"[7] Winter wrote.

King had nothing to do with the *Carrie* musical and little to do with the edition of "My Pretty Pony," which he described as "overpriced (and overdesigned, in my humble opinion),"[8] after he had sent the story to the Whitney. In fact, he was suffering writers' block for the first time in his career between January and May. Still, he remained busy, releasing, through NAL, an audio-version of *The Dark Tower: The Gunslinger*—on which he read—in July. King had also agreed to allow that novel, as well as later books in The Dark Tower series, to be released as trade paperbacks. His agent, McCauley, negotiated a deal worth $8 million with NAL for the rights to the books, and the first volume of the series appeared in August, though King apparently did not proof the pages or reread the limited edition. One critic complained that "he might at least have taken the trouble...to emend or delete the more egregious errors and saucheries before letting an unwary (or undiscriminating) publisher put them into print. Witness: A donkey on one page becomes a mule on the next. Centrifugal force is described as 'gravity.' The hero, traveling through a tunnel, feels touched by 'a claustrophobic hand,' whatever that might be."[9] King, perhaps struck by such criticism, as well as complaints that the book had no real story that could be followed, released a heavily revised edition in 2003.

After *The Gunslinger* made its paperback appearance, a number of changes took place in King's professional life. Stephanie Leonard, King's assistant and the editor of the newsletter *Castle Rock*, announced that she was leaving her job. Christopher Spruce, who was the general manager of King's radio station, WZON, took over her editorial responsibilities. The other major change that King made at the time was to split from McCauley and hire Arthur B. Greene, a lawyer, as his business manager. As the year was ending, Greene was negotiating with NAL for four books—*The Dark Half* (1989); the novella collection *Four Past Midnight* (1990); an as yet unnamed book, presumably *Needful Things* (1991); and *Dolores Claiborne* (1992), although *Gerald's Game* (1992) would appear before the Claiborne novel. An agreement, worth between $30 and $40 million dollars, was announced in February 1989, and in March the Book-of-the-Month Club bought the rights to print the four novels "for what it describes as a 'mid-seven figure' sum"[10] and announced plans to offer its members a collection of twenty King titles the following year.

The month after the book-club deal was announced, the film *Pet Sematary*, for which King had provided the screenplay and in which he made a cameo as the minister, was released in 1,500 theaters. Directed by Mary Lambert, who was primarily known for videos, it was the first King movie to be filmed in Maine, something King had gotten written into the contract when he sold the movie rights for a $1,000 in the mid-1980s, after turning down a $1 million offer that would have completely left him out of the decision-making process. Shooting in Maine, King said, "adds a lot," and he predicted that audiences would appreciate such authenticity. "They're going to know that it's Maine. And just as important, they're going to know that it's not California."[11] King was, in fact, enthusiastic about the film, but critics were less than impressed. Some dismissed it as a complete failure: Richard Harrington called it "DOA—Dog on Arrival,"[12] while Jerry Bokamper called it a "Puerile potboiler...barely deserving even of ridicule."[13] At least one critic found it adequate, writing: "*Pet Sematary* falls somewhere in the middle of the films made from Stephen King's novels. It's better than *Cujo* and *Firestarter*, but nowhere near *Carrie* and *The Shining,* which it dimly echoes."[14] Moviegoers responded more positively. *Pet Sematary* grossed more than $33 million at the box office in its first three weeks on the screen and $60 million before its run ended.

King released another limited edition of a short story in 1989, publishing "Dolan's Cadillac" with John Lord Press, a specialty publisher. Unhappy with the story as it had appeared in *Castle Rock* back in 1985, which was partly because he had been overwhelmed by the technical details that the story required him to know, King rewrote the story. As he explains in *Nightmares & Dreamscapes,* "I am an extremely lazy sod when it comes to research and technical details. I have been twigged again and again by readers and critics...for my lapses in these areas."[15] He decided he could not fudge on details when it came to "Dolan's Cadillac," but with 15,000 words, he didn't want to give up on it and called his brother, Dave, for help. About a week later King received a video on which Dave explained the technical information, using matchbox cars to illustrate his points. King then finished the story but, still unhappy with it, placed it in a box, where he thought it would remain, never to be published in its final form. Then Herb Yellin, the publisher who ran the John Lord Press, called and asked if King had a story that could be printed in a limited edition. "Because I love his books, which are small, beautifully made, and often extremely eccentric, I went out into what I think of as the Hallway of Doom and hunted through my boxes to see if there was anything salvageable. I came across 'Dolan's Cadillac,' and once again time had done its work—it reread a lot better than I remembered it."[16]

In April King's focus turned to baseball, an annual ritual when it came to watching the Red Sox, something King shaves his beard for every year. In 1989 he was also following his son Owen's little league team, which made a successful run for the state championships under the direction of the coach Dave Mansfield, whom King, a little league coach during his college years, helped. King would continue coaching for some years after, something that led him to donate, in 1991, $1.2 million to build a semi-pro field behind his home for the local Senior Little League team. The field, completed in 1992, affectionately came to be known as "The Field of Screams," though its official name is the Shawn Trevor Mansfield Complex, after coach Mansfield's son, who died at the age of fourteen. King apparently was good at discerning a player's talent. Matt Kinney, who was among the players that King coached over the years and who later became a Major League pitcher, recalled that King had told him, "You probably won't be a good hitter, but I think you'll be a pretty good pitcher."[17]

King had become, by the time he provided the money for the baseball field, known as quite a philanthropist in Maine, donating in the late

1980s, through the Stephen and Tabitha King Foundation, $1.5 million for the expansion of the library in Old Town, Maine, where Tabitha had grown up. The foundation had also given millions to the Eastern Maine Medical Center and has continued to donate money to important charities, including Bangor homeless shelters; the University of Maine, to which the foundation gave $4 million in 1997; and Family Crisis Services, to which Tabitha gave $50,000 to open a shelter for women and children who are victims of abuse.

Late in 1989 King moved his office from his house to a building in downtown Bangor. He had altered his workspace in his home after becoming sober, getting rid of the large oak desk that he had worked on since 1981—the type of desk that he had dreamt about owning since the days when he wrote in the laundry room of his rented trailer. He "put in a living-room suite where it had been, picking out the pieces and a nice Turkish rug with my wife's help...[and] got another desk—it's handmade, beautiful, and half the size of the *T. rex* desk. I put it at the far west end of the office, in a corner under the eave."[18] Redecorated, the space proved more family friendly, someplace where his kids could hang out, watch TV, and spend time with their father, though he would continue, at least part of the time, to write at home.

November saw the appearance of *The Dark Half*, which had a record-breaking first printing of 1.5 million copies and became the second best-selling novel of the 1980s—Tom Clancy's *Clear and Present Danger* (1989) took first place, but King's book remained on bestseller lists during the first weeks of 1990. The novel was built using material from a book King had almost completed in the early 1980s and had considered releasing as a Bachman novel. It was to be called "Machine's Way," the title of the book written by the main character, Thad Beaumont, under the pseudonym George Stark, a name that is itself an *homage* to Bachman, whose first name was borrowed from Richard Stark, the pseudonym used by Donald E. Westlake, whom King phoned when he was working on *The Dark Half*. "'I want the other half of your pen name,' he said," Westlake recalled. "'Okay,' I said. And so the pseudonym come to murderous life...was named George Stark."[19] Stark, who writes horror fiction that supports Beaumont's serious and respected literary endeavors, however, is more than simply a pen name: he is the remains of an unborn twin brother, who had been absorbed into Beaumont's fetus and who now survives in Beaumont's brain. Stark thus fights back when his status as Beaumont's pseudonym is discovered and Beaumont decides to kill him off. King acknowledged Bachman in another way, writing in an introductory note: "I'm indebted to the late Richard Bachman for his help and inspiration. This novel could not have been written without him."[20]

Critics wrote largely positive, if qualified, reviews. George Stade was representative: calling the story "a parable in chiller form of the popular writer's relation to his audience," he observed:

> King is tactful in teasing out the implications of his parable.... No character in the novel comes right out and says, for example, that writers exist (at least to readers) only in their writing, that each person (at least to himself) is his own fiction, that the writer's imagination can feel alien to him, a possessing and possessive demon, a Dracula arisen to prey on the whole man and his family. Nor does anyone in the novel say outright that reality inevitably leaks fiction, which then floods reality, that reality and fiction feed on and feed each other, that they are at war yet they are twins—so identical that attempts to say which is which only lead to more fictions. Such things are better left unsaid, anyhow. Stephen King is not a post-modernist.

Stade concluded that King "mostly succeeds...in spite of occasional clichés of thought and expression and bits of sophomoric humor (the F.B.I. is 'the Effa Bee Eye,' marijuana is 'wacky tobaccy')."[21] Similarly, Tasha Diamant proclaimed, "the author has, for the most part, succeeded with *The Dark Half*. As he writes of a character in the novel, King himself has ideas 'as dark as bats in a deserted church steeple.' At times, the premises of his stories are too farfetched to be credible. But even then, Stephen King still has the capacity to terrify."[22]

As 1989 came to an end, the last issue of *Castle Rock* was published. Spruce, who was about to begin graduate school, would no longer be able to prepare the newsletter, and King decided to put the publication to rest, as its circulation was declining. "Rushing to haul the next issue together begins just about the time the previous issue rolled off the presses," Spruce noted in his last column, explaining his inability to continue putting the newsletter together. "It was always done in between this, that and the other thing. Sometimes it looked that way, too. For the most part, however, it seemed to come out all right. Your letters and cards over the years confirmed that impression."[23]

NOTES

1. John North, "This King Can't Win Them All," *Toronto Star* (December 30, 1989), p. M11, http://www.lexis-nexis.com/.

2. Many sources give the publication date of the Whitney's *My Pretty Pony* as 1989, the year Knopf came out with a $50 substitute. Riva Castleman's *A Century*

of Artists Books (New York: Museum of Modern Art, 1994), however, gives the date as 1988, and discussing the Knopf edition, David Streitfeld wrote for his "Book Report" in the *Washington Post* (August 20, 1989, p. X15, http://www.lexis-nexis.com/), "*My Pretty Pony* was first published last year by the Whitney Museum as a $2,200 limited edition. The price has come down quite a bit—to $50—but the edition will again be restricted, to 15,000 copies."

3. Quoted in David Streitfeld, "Ideal Genuine Man," *Washington Post* (February 7, 1988), p. X15, http://www.lexis-nexis.com/.

4. Linda Joffee, "Terry Hands Explains Interest in *Carrie*," *Christian Science Monitor* (May 6, 1988), p. 21, http://www.lexis-nexis.com/.

5. Michael Collings, "My Pretty Pony," in *The Stephen King Companion*, ed. George Beahm (Kansas City, MO: Andrews and McMeel, 1995), p. 278.

6. Stephen King, *Nightmares & Dreamscapes* (New York: Viking, 1993), p. 683.

7. Douglas E. Winter, "Venturing a Bit into the Magical," *Washington Times* (November 29, 1989), p. E2, http://www.lexis-nexis.com/.

8. King, *Nightmares & Dreamscapes*, p. 683.

9. Gary Jennings, "King, Haunted by His Past," *Washington Post* (August 26, 1988), p. B3, http://www.lexis-nexis.com/.

10. Edwin McDowell, "Book Notes," *New York Times* (March 22, 1989), p. C25, http://www.lexis-nexis.com/.

11. Quoted in Jerry Harkavy, "Horror Film Rooted in Author's Experience," Associated Press (April 21, 1989), http://www.lexis-nexis.com/.

12. Richard Harrington, "*Pet Sematary:* King's Crass Menagerie," *Washington Post* (April 22, 1989), p. C1, http://www.lexis-nexis.com/.

13. Jerry Bokamper, "*Sematary* is a Shody Potboiler," *Arkansas Democrat-Gazette* (April 22, 1989), http://www.lexis-nexis.com/.

14. Jay Carr, "*Pet Sematary:* No Flowers, Please," *Boston Globe* (April 21, 1989), p. 46, http://www.lexis-nexis.com/.

15. King, *Nightmares & Dreamscapes*, p. 677.

16. Ibid., p. 678.

17. Quoted in Chris Haft, "Giants Pitcher Attached to Fame at an Early Age," *Contra Costa Times* (September 23, 2005), p. F4, http://www.lexis-nexis.com/.

18. Stephen King, *On Writing: A Memoir of the Craft* (New York: Scribner, 2000), p. 100.

19. Donald E. Westlake, "Richard Stark Introduced by Donald E. Westlake," in *Payback* by Richard Stark (New York: Mysterious Press, 1999 [1962]), p. vii.

20. Stephen King, *The Dark Half* (New York: Signet, 1990 [1989]), unnumbered page.

21. George Stade, "His Alter Ego is a Killer," *New York Times* (October 29, 1989), sec. 7, p. 12, http://www.lexis-nexis.com/.

22. Tasha Diamant, "Supernatural Meanderings," *Maclean's* (December 18, 1989), p. 57, http://www.lexis-nexis.com/.

23. George Beahm, *Stephen King From A To Z: An Encyclopedia of His Life and Work* (Kansas City, MO: Andrews McMeel, 1988), p. 32.

Chapter 13

TAKING A STAND

In January 1990 Doubleday announced that its lead title that spring would be *The Stand*, with a first printing of 400,000 copies, plus a collector's edition, bound in leather and signed, 1,250 of which would be made available to the public. The reprint was promoted, even in its preface,[1] as the version that King had originally wanted to publish. The 150,000 words that he had been forced to cut, it was asserted, had been restored. The book's complete title was *The Stand: The Complete and Uncut Edition*. King, however, had done more than simply restore the novel to its original condition: he updated the setting from 1980 to 1990 and left some of the material that he had been forced to take out "on the cutting room floor," deciding that it "deserved to be left there."[2] King explained his reasoning in the following terms: "I am republishing *The Stand*...not to serve myself or any individual reader, but to serve a body of readers who have asked to have it. I would not offer it if I myself didn't think those portions which were dropped from the original manuscript made the story a richer one, and I'd be a liar if I didn't admit I am curious as to what its reception will be."[3]

The Stand, which now replaced *It* as King's longest novel, appeared at the end of April, a couple of weeks after King broke into print in the *New Yorker*, a magazine that he once complained was uninterested in his type of writing, with "Head Down," an essay that recounted his son Owen's little league team's championship season, and a couple of weeks before the first of four King movies appeared, *Tales From the Darkside*, an anthology film that included King's "Cat From Hell"—the screenplay for which George Romero had originally written for *Creepshow 2*. Meanwhile, *The Stand* was generating extraordinary interest, becoming the first hardcover reprint to land on the *New York Times* bestseller list and forcing Doubleday to set up "a 1–800 number for people to call and find out what the differences are in the new version," Ellen Archer, a Doubleday spokesperson, said.[4]

Some critics, as King had predicted in his preface, complained, as they had back in 1978, that the novel was too long. "In short (well, not so short), this is the book that has everything—adventure, romance, prophecy, allegory, satire, fantasy, realism, apocalypse, etc., etc. Even Roger Rabbit gets mentioned," Robert Kiely observed. "*The Stand* does have some great moments and some great lines. A desperate character trying to save his mother reaches an answering machine: 'This is a recording made at Mercy General Hospital. Right now all of our circuits are busy.' And there is a wonderful description of 'mankind's final traffic jam.' But the overall effect is more oppressive than imposing."[5] The length didn't bother everyone. Discussing the process by which King builds the narrative, Ray Murphy praised King's ability to pick up characters' stories "again and again throughout the book in a series of self-contained vignettes, each of them of lapidarian brilliance. It is these short telling scripts that make King so much the writer of his time, the 'post-television writer,' like the episodic script writers of *Hill Street Blues*. The jarring bits make a whole and build into a crackling structure with explosive climaxes."[6]

The Stand was followed, in August, by *Four Past Midnight*, a collection of novellas, which were written in 1988 and 1989. The first of them, "The Langoliers," is about a flight that travels through a rift in time and ends up in the past, where monsters, the Langoliers, a nonsense term coined by King, devour what is left. The next, "Secret Windows, Secret Garden," is about a writer, who, while overcoming a divorce and suffering writers block, is accused of plagiarism. "The Library Policeman" is a tale in which Sam Peebles, who is unable to return library books because they have been sent to the recycling center, is tormented by the ghost of a librarian; and "The Sun Dog" is about Kevin Delevan's getting a Polaroid Sun camera for his birthday that takes pictures of a frightening black dog.

Each of the novellas was as long as other authors' novels, and some critics found them to be the best stories King had written in some time. "With the exception of this story ["Sun Dog"], which suffers from the digressions and repetitions that have marred King's last few novels, the tales in *Four Past Midnight* are exceptionally well crafted," Michael A. Morrison observed. He continued, "King shapes his material with the sure hand of a master woodworker, tossing off unexpected similes, deftly using dreams to reveal character, subtly planting clues to coming revelations, and skillfully managing the coincidences on which his stories often hinge. If, like me, you have loved King's work for years but were pretty disappointed in his last several novels, then you'll be delighted with *Four Past Midnight*, his best work since *Pet Sematary*."[7] Robert Chatain was similarly impressed, proclaiming "this may be Stephen King's best book" and arguing: "*Four Past Midnight*, like most of its predecessors, deserves its expected success. Despite being four individual stories instead of a novel, it's a serious, heavyweight effort. The tales are rich; the compression of complex narratives and large effects into 200 rather than 600 pages gives each of them an intensity that never loosens its hold on the darker corners of our minds. They are also fast, tricky, even perverse, like carnival rides that look easy from the ground but turn unexpectedly nasty and vertiginous when we're up in the air."[8]

The year 1990 ended with a succession of three King films. The first of them to appear was *Graveyard Shift*. The movie, which was an adaptation of the early short story of the same name, had been first planned in 1986, when King reportedly sold the rights for under $100 to George Demick, a friend of Romero's who, at 22, was already working for Brimstone Productions and had film-making experience. Demick managed to get the screenplay, which was written by John Esposito, but he could not get the production off the ground before his option expired. King then sold the rights to William J. Dunn, a Maine resident who had been involved in the formation of The Maine Film Commission, for $2,500. Using Esposito's script and hiring Ralph S. Singleton to direct, Dunn arranged to have the film shot in Bangor during the summer of 1990, on a budget of $10.5 million. It premiered in October and reviewed badly. "*Graveyard Shift*," John Hartl observed, "is not the most auspicious start for this festival of Kingly horror, even if this does appear to be the most appropriate season for it. As a Halloween special, it's neither scary nor original. In fact, it's something of a chore to sit through."[9] King suggested that those assessments were correct but pointed out that there were other motives for allowing such films to be made. "I got spanked in *People* magazine for allowing *Graveyard Shift* to be made, which is ridiculous. Ralph Singleton had never directed a film. John Esposito had never written a film. Now they both have a movie credit. They'll do better next time. This is why you do it." He continued: "Look, there was a time I was out there knocking on doors, and there were some people who opened them for me. I'll never forget that.... To me that's where the pleasure and the power is, to say 'Yes, you can' rather than 'No, you can't.'"[10]

The next two King films turned out to be much better. One of them was the ABC miniseries *It*, a version of the story told in a linear fashion—a change to the original text that was felt to be necessary to make the movie more intelligible. Romero had been hired to direct but a scheduling conflict forced him to remove himself from the project. Tommy Lee Wallace was thus in the director's chair when filming began earlier in 1990 in Vancouver, Canada. The script, written by Lawrence Cohen of *Carrie* fame, had also been cut down from seven to four hours so that the movie could be aired over two nights. *It*, of course, didn't have to worry about box office receipts: ratings were the issue.

Airing on November 18 and November 20, the movie garnered mostly positive reviews, though the first night's installment, which focuses on the events of 1958, when the characters are children, was regarded as the more artistically successful. Rick Kogan observed, "In *It*, King finally gets his scary due, studded with familiar TV faces: Harry Anderson, Dennis Christopher, Richard Masur, Annette O'Toole, Tim Reid, John Ritter and [Richard] Thomas,"[11] who played It when the monster appeared as a clown. Television viewers also responded positively. The first installment was the fifth most watched television program the week it aired, helping ABC secure second place during the November sweeps, and the second installment was the second most watch show the following week, beating, among other shows, *Monday Night Football*.

The final King film of 1990 was *Misery*, which starred Kathy Bates—who was appearing in her first major role in a feature film—as Annie Wilkes, the crazed fan who imprisons the writer Paul Sheldon, who was played by James Caan. King had considered not allowing the novel to be adapted for film because of all the previous disasters, but he changed his mind when Reiner, whose *Stand by Me* had so impressed him, showed interested in doing it. William Goldman wrote the screenplay, changing the Sheldon character in that he is more active on screen than in the book. King approved the changes, and once the film was complete, he called it his favorite adaptation to date and gave Reiner, as Reiner told Sean Mitchell, "a big hug" at the private screening.[12] Many critics echoed King's assessment. William Arnold, for example, called it "a surprisingly intelligent character study that also manages to deliver 108 minutes of non-stop, edge-of-your-seat suspense," and although he found the gory ending unfortunate, he concluded, "*Misery* is still a big success, and a most pleasant surprise. It is the most entertaining suspense piece to come along this year. And it is also the best treatment King has yet received."[13] The film found favor with the public, too, grossing $61 million, as well as with the Hollywood establishment, which nominated it for an Oscar for best picture and awarded Bates the Oscar for best actress.

King would have his own Sheldon-like experience in 1991, as two fans tried to impose themselves on his personal life. One, Anne Hiltner—a

New Jersey woman who had been harassing King with letters for a decade and once complained to her local police department that he "flew over her house in an airplane equipped with listening devices to eavesdrop on her"[14]—sued him for plagiarism, claiming that he had stolen eight unpublished manuscripts and that at least 90 percent of *Misery* was copied from one of them. She also complained that the character of Annie Wilkes, whom the press got great pleasure out of comparing to her, was based on her. The other, Eric Keene, a Texas man who at one point said he was Hiltner's nephew and was out to get revenge for King's theft, traveled to Maine, harassed the staff at King's office, and the next day broke into the King residence, while Tabitha was home, threatening to detonate a bomb, which turned out to be fake. He would also claim that he was writing a sequel to *Misery*. These bizarre incidents, in time, would become bad memories, though Hiltner would not completely disappear from King's life, accusing him of stealing a manuscript of her brother's in 2000, and suing him, in 2005, for invading her privacy by developing a caricature of her with Annie Wilkes. King, as usual, was focusing on his work. The television movie *Sometimes They Come Back*, which was adapted from the short story of the same name, was going to be aired on CBS, which had also agreed to do an original series, *Stephen King's Golden Years*, during the summer, and he had two forthcoming novels, *Needful Things*, which King intended to be the last of his stories to be set in Castle Rock, and *The Dark Tower III: The Waste Lands*.

Sometimes They Come Back, a story that was first developed for inclusion in *Cat's Eye* was reportedly completed in January 1991, but its director, Tom Mcloughlin, was unable to deliver the final cut for inclusion in the CBS lineup during the February sweeps, and it premiered during the later sweeps period on May 7, when it received positive reviews. "It's a good, creepy idea and *Sometimes They Come Back* is good and creepy as a result. No one in the cast seems to be coasting—not least [Tim] Matheson [who starred as Jim Norman], who seems authentically and increasingly disturbed. CBS didn't provide the names of the kids who play his tormentors, but they perform with nasty zest,"[15] David Klinghoffer wrote. Despite the critical success the movie failed to draw in a big audience. King would explain, "If all my regular readers were to tune in a TV show on a given week, you'd still have less than one rating point. *Sometimes They Come Back* had my name on it, but we still couldn't beat Roseanne Barr."[16]

The two-hour premier of the *Golden Years*, aired on July 16. King had often been approached to do television but as a host in the tradition of Rod Sterling, who had introduced the *Twilight Zone* each week. King did not want to host. "At some point, though, I started to play with the idea of what would happen if somebody did an original novel for television. What's always bothered me about dramatic series is that they have a be-ginning, then a middle and another middle and another middle, with no end or resolution.... I wondered about doing the equivalent of an original paperback novel for television." That novel was the *Golden Years*. A sequel, in a way, to *Firestarter*, it featured "the same shadowy organization, known as The Shop, in [a] story about an experiment that goes wrong and some ordinary people who get caught up in it. It seemed like a natural for TV, but I originally wanted to do it as a novel that would run the length of a television season, instead of just six or eight hours. I sat down to write it, but at that point, nobody seemed to have any real interest in it."[17]

The success of *It* and *Misery*, however, changed King's position, and when Richard P. Rubenstein approached him about developing some-thing for television, King jumped at the chance, writing the first six of the eight hours of the series, the two-hour opener and the next four one-hour episodes. (Josef Anderson wrote the final two episodes.) The story focused on Harlan Williams, a 70-year-old custodian of a government laboratory who survives exposure to the experiment and begins to get younger. The government, intent on keeping the experiment a secret and finding out more about it, sends an agent from The Shop to take care of him. Despite adequate ratings CBS did not pick up the option on the series and refused to give King four hours of airtime the following spring to bring the story to a conclusion. Anderson thus provided an optimistic ending for the made-for-video version, which only runs for four hours.

Both *Needful Things* and *The Dark Tower III: The Waste Lands* were issued in October. The Dark Tower novel was again published in a lim-ited edition by Donald M. Grant, making it unavailable to the majority of King's readers, but unlike the previous books in the series, *The Waste Lands* would be released three months later in a trade paperback and was reviewed in the mainstream press. Richard E. Nicholls, writing for the *New York Times*, called it "an uncertain hybrid of horror and fantasy" and went on to observe, "at its best it demonstrates a subtlety and an assured sense of pacing new to Mr. King's massive body of work."[18] Others were more laudatory. Charles de Lint noted in the *Ottawa Citizen*, "What sets this series far above King's other work and that of many of his contem-poraries is not just King's trademark immediacy of character definition and gift for storytelling, but the beauty of the prose.... [T]hroughout *The Waste Lands* there is an unexpected lyricism and surprisingly evocative sense of description."[19]

When King wrote *Needful Things*, he planned to put an end to Castle Rock—the setting of *The Dead Zone*, *Cujo*, and *The Dark Half*, as well as the novellas "The Body" and "The Sun Dog" and a number of short stories. He wanted, he said, to "do it with a bang."[20] The novel opens with a prologue in which its characters are introduced and the coming of Leland Gaunt to Castle Rock and his plans to open the store Needful Things is announced. After opening his store Gaunt caters to the fantasies of his customers, selling them, for ridiculously low prices, the things they most covet, but he demands that they perform an act of evil on one of their neighbors as well. Gaunt's interest is souls, not money, and he manages to foster an atmosphere of paranoia among Castle Rock's residents, who, in the end, violently destroy their town.

Critics did find things to enjoy in the book. Even Walter Kendrick—whose review was so offensive to King that he condemned it in a letter to the editor of the *Washington Post* where the review ran—found something to enjoy. He noted, "The design of *Needful Things*... is plain very early, and King wastes little energy on suspense. Such pleasure as the novel affords comes from watching the design inevitably complete itself, and from seeing a townful of ordinary people degenerate into mindless, bloodthirsty brutes," but Kendrick felt such enjoyment was "a childish pleasure, and a spiteful one, since Castle Rock is supposed to be a typical American place. Given the chance, [King] seems to say, we'd all blow our neighbors' brains out for the sake of our needful things. A mean message from America's most popular novelist. But King has spat in his readers' faces before, and they have lapped it up."[21] Others found fault with the writing. Joe Queenan complained that the book was filled with "hundreds of pages of rambling, turgid 'clots and clumps' churned out in Mr. King's trademark dark-and-stormy-night style. Though verbose, Mr. King is a lazy writer who uses his own brand of prefabricated imagery to depict events he himself is otherwise incapable of describing. As a result, the book is loaded with fill-in-the-blank descriptions such as this: 'They made him look smart, like Harrison Ford in *The Mosquito Coast*."[22]

The book, nonetheless, proved wildly successful, selling over a million copies, and found many defenders. Collings has called it "one of [King's] most complex, multifaceted narratives,"[23] and Stephen J. Spignesi asserted, "*Needful Things* is an amazing mélange of vividly drawn characters, exciting scenes of violence and terror, and a powerful narrative pull that takes us to a finale that forces us to bid adieu to one of the most beloved locales in all of Stephen King's writings."[24] Beloved Castle Rock may have been, but King felt he needed to move on, if he were to grow: "It's easy to build yourself a rut and furnish it, and I'd done that a little bit in Castle Rock. Going back to Castle Rock for me has been a little bit like slipping into an old smoking jacket or an old pair of blue jeans and settling down.

After a while I started to feel excessively comfortable there, and I don't think that's a good state for a novelist to be in, particularly if you've sold a lot of books."[25]

NOTES

1. See Stephen King, "A Preface in Two Parts: Part 2: To Be Read after Purchase," *The Stand* (New York: Signet, 1991 [1990]), p. xii.

2. Ibid., p. xiv.

3. Ibid., p. xii.

4. Quoted in "Names in the News," Associated Press (May 5, 1990), http://www.lexis-nexis.com/.

5. Robert Kiely, "Armageddon, Complete and Uncut," *New York Times* (May 13, 1990), sec. 7, p. 3, http://www.lexis-nexis.com/.

6. Ray Murphy, "Stephen King's 'New' *Stand*," *Boston Globe* (May 16, 1990), p. 73, http://www.lexis-nexis.com/.

7. Michael A. Morrison, "Stephen King: Time Out of Joint," *Washington Post* (August 26, 1990), p. X9, http://www.lexis-nexis.com/.

8. Robert Chatain, "King of the Creeps: Four Chilling Tales from Stephen King, Our Modern Master of Suspense," *Chicago Tribune* (August 26, 1990), p. C3, http://www.lexis-nexis.com/.

9. John Hartl, "Thin Script, Uninteresting Characters Help Bury *Graveyard Shift*," *Seattle Times* (October 27, 1990), p. C3, http://www.lexis-nexis.com/.

10. Quoted in Daniel Cerone, "What Does King Think?," *Los Angeles Times* (November 18, 1990), p. 82, http://www.lexis-nexis.com/.

11. Rick Kogan, "Come and Get *It*—Stephen King on TV," *Chicago Tribune* (November 16, 1990), p. C1, http://www.lexis-nexis.com/.

12. Sean Mitchell, "Rob Reiner in Hollywood: The Sweet Misery That Fame Brings," *Los Angeles Times* (November 25, 1990), p. 5, http://www.lexis-nexis.com/.

13. William Arnold, "Stephen King's *Misery* Never Lets up on the Thrills," *Seattle Post-Intelligencer* (November 30, 1990), p. 5, http://www.lexis-nexis.com/.

14. Quoted in "Woman Claims Stephen King's *Misery* as Her Own," United Press International (April 20, 1991), http://www.lexis-nexis.com/.

15. David Klinghoffer, "High-School Bullies are Real Ghouls in King Tale," *Washington Times* (May 7, 1991), p. E1, http://www.lexis-nexis.com/.

16. Quoted in Jay Bobbin, "Stephen King: TV with Twist," *St. Louis Post-Dispatch* (July 14, 1991), TV Magazine, p. 5, http://www.lexis-nexis.com/.

17. Ibid.

18. Richard E. Nicholls, "Avaunt Thee, Recreant Cyborg!," *New York Times* (September 29, 1991), sec. 7, p. 14, http://www.lexis-nexis.com/.

19. Charles de Lint, "King Has Us Gasping for More," *Ottawa Citizen* (October 12, 1991), p. 13, http://www.lexis-nexis.com/.

20. Quoted in Christopher Wiater et al., *The Complete Stephen King Universe* (New York: St Martin's Griffin), p. 165.

21. Walter Kendrick, "Pacts with the Devil," *Washington Post* (September 29, 1991), p. X9, http://www.lexis-nexis.com/.

22. Joe Queenan, "And Us Without Our Spoons," *New York Times* (September 29, 1991), sec. 7, p. 13, http://www.lexis-nexis.com/.

23. Michael Collings, "*Needful Things,*" in *The Stephen King Companion,* ed. George Beahm (Kansas City: Andrews and McMeel, 1995), p. 290.

24. Stephen J. Spignesi, *The Essential Stephen King* (Franklin Lakes, NJ: New Page Books, 2003), p. 95.

25. Quoted in Jocelyn McClurg, "With 3 Books Due, Guess Who's King of Book Convention?" *Hartford Courant* (June 16, 1991), p. G3, http://www.lexis-nexis.com/.

King makes a cameo appearance in his television miniseries The Stand, *filmed in 1993.* ©ABC / Photofest.

In the mid-1980s, King took on the role of director for the first time, for Maximum Overdrive. ©De Laurentis Entertainment Group (DEG)/Photofest.

An avid reader, King is also a great promoter of reading. ©ABC/Photofest.

King in the early 1980s during the promotion of the movie The Dead Zone. ©Paramount Pictures/Photofest.

King, undated photo. ©HBO/Photofest.

King took part in New York ComiCon in 2007, the year parts of The Dark Tower were first released in comic-book form. ©Pinguino Kolb.

King, an avid Red Sox fan, finally got to see the Sox win the World Series in 2004. ©Michael Femia.

King and his wife, Tabitha, take part in a ceremony at the governor's office in Augusta, Maine, in 2004. AP Photo/©Pat Wellenbach.

Chapter 14

KING'S FEMINIST SENSIBILITY

When King's four-book deal was announced at the beginning of 1989, *Dolores Claiborne* was among the titles that were reported to be included in the contract, but in November 1991 King read what M. R. Montgomery described for the *Boston Globe* as a "just-finished novel"[1] at a benefit for homeless resettlement agencies. That novel was *Gerald's Game*, which, it was announced in the spring, would be published in the summer of 1992, before *Dolores Claiborne*, which was now scheduled for publication in 1993. King had considered publishing the two novels together, under the title "In the Path of the Eclipse." Having published them separately, he explained their connection. In the foreword to the paperback edition of *Dolores Claiborne*, he notes that the protagonists are linked by their experience of the total eclipse of 1963, the last one to be "visible in northern New England until the year 2016"[2] and that the novels "are tales of women in the path of the eclipse, and of how they emerge from the darkness."[3]

Before King's new novel appeared, two movies—*The Lawnmower Man* and *Sleepwalkers*—were released. *The Lawnmower Man*, which was filmed the previous summer, appeared first, arriving in theaters in early March. King had had nothing to do with the production, having sold the rights to the story back in 1978 when *Night Shift* appeared, and learned about its release the same way everybody else did, when he saw an ad announcing the appearance of another King movie. The movie had very little to do with the story from which it took its title. The screenwriters, Brett Leonard and Gimel Everett, found it impossible to expand that story into a feature film and developed a script using another screenplay that Everett had written called "Cybergod," which was about the dangers of virtual reality. The content of King's "The Lawnmower Man" was reduced to a two-minute scene. King was disgusted and sued to get his name removed from all merchandise related to the film, including video releases. "The TV ads said 'From the mind of Stephen King.' Well, it is not from the mind of Stephen King. I felt like I was being raped," King recalled.[4] In June Constance Baker Motley, the judge hearing the case, ruled in King's favor, saying in her decision, "the billing that the movie is 'based upon Stephen King's "Lawnmower Man"' is 'false on its face.'" King was awarded $3.4 million in damages. Allied Vision and New Line Cinema appealed, and while they were denied the right to call the movie *Stephen King's Lawnmower Man*," they retained permission to include "'based on' a King short story" in the credits.[5] New Line Cinema, however, ignored the court order, something King had discovered by launching his own investigation into the marketing of the movie after he won his lawsuit, and in 1993 the company was held in contempt of court and ordered to pay King all the profits it had earned on the movie during the period in which it was in contempt of the court's ruling, plus $10,000 for each day, following a 30-day grace period, that it refused to comply with the court order thereafter. On appeal that fine was dropped.

A month after *The Lawnmower Man* appeared, *Sleepwalkers*, a movie for which King had written the script, even before he had been approached by anyone about making the movie, was released. The idea was sparked by seeing Joe, his oldest son, ask a girl who was working at the concession stand at the local movie theater out on a date. King began to wonder how she could really know if his son, a stranger to her, were safe to be alone with. From there King developed the story about the incestuous couple Charles Brady and his mother, Mary, who are half reptilian, half feline creatures—perhaps the last of their species—and resemble vampires in that they consume humans' life force to live. They roam from small town to small town, victimizing young women, whom Charles seduces. The movie opens as the two settle into Tavis, Indiana, where Charles meets Tanya Robertson and sets out to turn her into a victim. He falls in love with her instead. As with *Maximum Overdrive's*, *Sleepwalker's* original cut was deemed too violent by the MPAA and scenes had to be removed for it to get an R rating. The result was a film with which King "wasn't ENTIRELY satisfied. This was a controversial story about incest and love and what people do to survive, and a lot of that is gone from the movie. I like it, I think it's funny, and it's got some neat things in it. There's an ambivalence about the bad guy; you hate him, but you like him a little, too."[6]

Reviewers were impressed by the story but not the movie. "*Sleepwalkers* is no masterpiece, but it's hard not to admire the slickness of its storytelling. With just a few deft hints, King sets up the viewer to believe that *Sleepwalkers* will be the story of a young sleepwalking fellow's coming to fall in love with his victim. Then King pulls the rug out."[7] The problem was the director, Mick Garris. Critics complained that he handled the material inefficiently: he let, Gene Seymour wrote, "scenes go on too long and has a faulty sense of rhythm, with shots bumping haphazardly into each other,"[8] while Jeffrey Staggs observed, "Garris abandons Mr. King's attempt to critically examine the [horror] genre [specifically, its misogynistic nature] in *Sleepwalkers* and simply makes another horror movie. Yes, it's all there: lots of blood, bones popping through skin, the obligatory turning-around-and-being-startled shots, ridiculous makeup, the whole schmear."[9] The film took in $29 million at the box office.

At the annual American Booksellers Association's gathering in May, King tried something new, joining a number of other writers, including Amy Tan, Dave Barry, Robert Fulghum, Barbara Kingsolver, Michael Dorris, Ridley Pearson, and Tad Bartimus, to play rock-'n'-roll on the stage at the Cowboy Boogie, a club in Anaheim, California. Taking its name from book remainders—those books that can't be sold and are returned to the publisher—the band was called The Rock Bottom Remainders. The press was amused: "You haven't lived until you've heard Stephen King croak 'Teen Angel,' the seminal Top-40 ballad about young lovers whose romance goes up in smoke in a car crash,"[10] Max McQueen observed, but those not in attendance would be denied the chance to do so. The owners of the song's rights thought King was so bad that they forced a video of the night's performance to be pulled from the shelves. Interest in the band, especially because of King's place in it, continued, and The Rock Bottom Remainders did a short tour in 1993 and has occasionally gotten together for live performances since. Barry, discussing the phenomenon with Sarah Lyall and Marjorie Williams, suggested that King's participation was particularly important, noting, as paraphrased by Lyall and Williams, "whenever the band went to play anywhere, dozens of King zealots would come out of nowhere, their arms in front of them like zombies, intoning, Stephen, Stephen."[11]

King had joined the band for the fun of it, explaining, "It's liberating! Real powerful. And what I normally do, I do in a room all by myself. I very rarely do it in front of a thousand screaming beered-up patrons."[12] The real reason for his presence at the bookseller's gathering was to promote his forthcoming novel, which was appearing in June. It was, in a way, an apt follow up to his recent movie. If *Sleepwalkers* subtly undermined the misogyny of horror movies—particularly during the scene in which Charles takes Tanya, who is cast as a date-rape victim, to a cemetery with the intention of dining on her—*Gerald's Game* more radically addressed misogyny, opening with a more realistic rape scene. Gerald Burlingame handcuffs his wife, Jessie, to their bed for a sex game. She becomes uncomfortable and asks Gerald to stop, something he interprets as goading. He thus gets more aggressive. She kicks him below the belt, and he dies of a heart attack, leaving her handcuffed to the bed and unable to reach the keys. What follows is a more than 300-page monologue in which Jessie not only considers her present situation but her life, including her being molested by her father.

Reviewers found King's handling of the material beautiful. Calling it "a solo version of *Misery*," Albert Mobilio wrote, "King deftly captures the jagged rhythms of a mind under pressure and seamlessly weaves telling details from Jessie's life into the particulars of her dilemma." He went on to note that the story "never flags or spins its wheels. It is propelled by meticulously plotted escape attempts, each of which draws not only on Jessie's strength and ability to stand pain, but on her reaching back into an episode of childhood sexual abuse to discover how she might free herself, from that memory and from her handcuffs."[13] The *New York Times* critic Lehmann-Haupt, drawing more attention to the feminist tendencies of the story, found it equally compelling, observing, "The story of *Gerald's Game* is finally the brutal metaphor of a woman trying to fight free of male oppression, the various guises Mr. King evokes effectively with his almost too great facility at building his prose out of the odds and ends of popular culture....But whatever this yarn adds up to, its details build so powerfully that near the climax you become afraid to turn the next page."[14]

The public responded as it typically does to a King book, putting *Gerald's Game* on the number one spot in the *New York Times* bestseller list a week after it appeared in bookstores and keeping it there throughout the summer. Such sales prompted Viking to move up the publication of *Dolores Claiborne*—another book that explored the darker side of men—from January 1993 to November 1992. Dolores, like Jessie, has suffered in her relationships with men. She was married to Joe St. George, a philanderer, a drunk, a thief, and a spousal abuser, whom she tolerated until he threatened to rape their daughter. She then murdered him. Now, 30 years later, she is accused of killing her senile employer, Vera Donovan. During the course of proclaiming her innocence in the latter crime, she confesses to the former one, weaving the story of her life with her husband into that of her life with Vera. "All is told first-person in an ill-educated backwoods-Maine dialect by Dolores, confessing to local authorities. It's an unlikely and awkward device; one can't imagine cops patiently listening for hours to Dolores' slow, deliberate soul-baring. Yet its directness and vernacular serve the yarn well. And telling good yarns is what King is all about," Bruce Westbrook wrote.[15]

Many critics remarked that King seemed to be abandoning his monsters for more real horrors, but there was an evident continuity between the earlier supernatural stories and his new novels. Indeed, in some respects, *Dolores Claiborne* was, as Sean Piccoli observed, "vintage bone-yard King: the tiny town, the secret lives. Murder and mayhem lurk reliably behind the tranquil veneer."[16] Fans again made the novel a bestseller, keeping it on the *New York Times* bestseller list for months, and Castle Rock Entertainment bought the movie rights for an estimated $1.5 million.

As a consequence of the early release of *Dolores Claiborne*, King would publish no new novel in 1993. In fact, he had not written one in 1992. He was working on the screenplay for *The Stand's* eight-hour miniseries. "Screenplays never end...," he explained. "When I started doing screenplays I described it as work for idiots, but it's really work for strong, passionate idiots. The difference between writing a novel and a screenplay is like [the difference between] playing singles tennis and baseball. With screenplays, it's a team sport. This screenplay is 400 pages long but I rewrote it six times. That's 2,400 pages and the reason a novel didn't get written last year."[17]

In lieu of a novel, King published another collection of short stories, *Nightmares & Dreamscapes*. Before that collection became available, three movies based on King's work were released. The first was *The Dark Half*, which was adapted for film and directed by Romero. It had been scheduled for release in the fall of 1992, but its distributor, Orion Pictures, had declared bankruptcy. For a while King—who, despite never appearing on the set, was consulted by Romero during the shooting of the film—feared no one would get to see it. Having concluded bankruptcy proceedings Orion was able to start distributing its backlog, and even though it had several films older than *The Dark Half* on its shelves, it decided to release the King movie first, something Timothy Hutton, who played Thad Beaumont/George Stark, regarded "as a vote of confidence,"[18] John Hartl reported. The response did not substantiate such confidence, as the public stayed away and critics condemned it. Richard Harrington, for example, complained, "Romero's film starts out well and clearly benefits from some higher-on-the-line elements, ranging from the cast to the cinematography of Tony Pierce-Roberts (*A Room with a View, Mr. & Mrs. Bridge*). But like too many King transfers to the screen, it falls apart in the last reel."[19] However, the following year, it was, for a time, among the top rented movies in the country.

During sweeps week, on May 9 and 10, ABC aired the second King movie of the year, *The Tommyknockers*, starring Jimmy Smits as James Gardner, but the station did not have the kind of success that it had with *It*, as the four-hour series proved a critical failure and had much fewer viewers. Matt Roush, in a representative review, observed, "While not nearly as odious as some of his big-screen flops, *Tommyknockers* is just a sprawling, uninspired *Invasion of the Body Snatchers* knockoff, with one of King's quaint Maine burgs (Haven Falls) succumbing to a mysterious underground object that emits an emerald aura of power....What might have been an effective *Outer Limits* episode, with the trademark King theme of magic as a dangerous elixir for human frailty, instead bloats to fill two nights with incidents more silly than sinister."[20] King himself would remark, "I thought they did a pretty decent job with a book that wasn't top drawer to begin with."[21]

The third movie adaptation, *Needful Things*, followed in August. Directed by Fraser Heston, the son of the celebrated actor Charlton Heston, it was expected to give a boost to the young Heston's directing career. Things didn't work out that way, as the critics were unimpressed with the work. Mick LaSalle, for example, observed, "like most Stephen King movies, this one falls into that range between awful and mediocre. People who think all Stephen King movies are a raging delight might very well find reasons to like *Needful Things*, but for everyone else, the strain won't be worth the effort."[22] The public took such reviews to heart, and the movie had a disappointing box-office draw, taking in about $13 million.

King might have failed at the box office, but the release of *Nightmares & Dreamscapes* in October put him back on top, placing his name on the top of bestseller lists with over 1.3 million copies sold before the year ended. The collection contained stories written over the previous 20 years; the *New Yorker* piece about his son's little league team; a screenplay called *Sorry, Right Number*; and a poem, "Brooklyn August," about memories of Ebbets Field. The horror stories proved the main draw, as Gary Graff explained when he called the baseball piece "a nice diversion" and noted "the real strength of *Nightmares & Dreamscapes* is what we ultimately expect of King—the scary stuff. He delivers with little blasts of his warped and limitless imagination, chilling and thrilling his way through a compendium that's as rewarding as any of his more celebrated, full-length novels."[23]

King, during the year, had taken advantage of his more family-friendly home office to foster his connection to his family, particularly his youngest son, Owen, with whom he had taken to watching the MTV cartoon *Beavis and Butt-head*, a show he at first didn't understand. "When I started to get what was going on, I couldn't understand why anybody would let it on," King revealed. "Then, the next thing I knew, I was laughing hysterically."[24] King, now that he was sober, was using a lot of his time for his family, for although he writes everyday, except on his birthday, the Fourth of July, and Christmas, he often was able to fulfill his quota in four hours, leaving him the rest of the day free.

NOTES

1. M. R. Montgomery, "King of Fear—and Philanthropy," *Boston Globe* (November 22, 1991), Metro, p. 1, http://www.lexis-nexis.com/.

2. Stephen King, *Dolores Claiborne* (New York: Signet, 1993 [1992]), p. xvi.

3. Ibid., p. xvii.

4. Quoted in Rene Rodriguez, "King of Horror," *Hamilton Spectator* (October 29, 1992), p. 5, http://www.lexis-nexis.com/.

5. "2nd Circuit Allows 'Based on' Credit for 'Lawnmower Man': Lanham Act: King v. Allied Vision Ltd.," *Entertainment Litigation Reporter* (November 23, 1992), http://www.lexis-nexis.com/.

6. Quoted in Rodriguez, "King of Horror," p. 5.

7. Mick LaSalle, "The Naughty *Sleepwalkers*," *San Francisco Chronicle* (April 11, 1992), p. C3, http://www.lexis-nexis.com/.

8. Gene Seymour, "Reigning Cats in King Country," *New York Newsday* (April 11, 1992), Part II, p. 23, http://www.lexis-nexis.com/.

9. Jeffrey Staggs, "*Sleepwalker* Trips over Its Horror," *Washington Times* (April 13, 1992), p. D4, http://www.lexis-nexis.com/.

10. Max McQueen, "Horror Hits Music World: King's Rocking with Novel Band," *Gazette* (November 10, 1992), p. G7, http://www.lexis-nexis.com/.

11. Sarah Lyall and Marjorie Williams, "*Dreamcatcher*," *Slate Magazine* (April 4, 2001), http://www.lexis-nexis.com/.

12. Jim Washburn, "Writers Rock Around the Clock," *Los Angeles Times* (May 28, 1992), p. E7, http://www.lexis-nexis.com/.

13. Albert Mobilio, "Dark Nights of the Soul," *New York Newsday* (June 28, 1992), p. 36, http://www.lexis-nexis.com/.

14. Christopher Lehmann-Haupt, "Books of the Times: To Be Read in Daylight, Away from Hungry Dogs," *New York Times* (June 29, 1992), p. C13, http://www.lexis-nexis.com/.

15. Bruce Westbrook, "Man as Monster: Horror Still the Engine that Drives King's Novel," *Houston Chronicle* (November 15, 1992), *Zest*, p. 30, http://www.lexis-nexis.com/.

16. Sean Piccoli, "King's Newest Horror Tale Is Decidedly This-Worldly: *Dolores* Doesn't Need Supernatural," *Washington Times* (January 11, 1993), p. D2, http://www.lexis-nexis.com/.

17. Quoted in Peter Johnson and Brian Donlon, "Screenwriting *The Stand* a Horror for Stephen," *USA Today* (February 18, 1993), p. 3D, http://www.lexis-nexis.com/.

18. John Hartl, "*Dark Half*: Hutton's Double Duty," *Seattle Times* (April 22, 1993), p. D4, http://www.lexis-nexis.com/.

19. Richard Harrington, "*The Dark Half*: The Gory Penalties of Using a Pen Name," *Washington Post* (April 23, 1993), p. D7, http://www.lexis-nexis.com/.

20. Matt Roush, "King Clunker," *USA Today* (May 7, 1993), p. D3, http://www.lexis-nexis.com/.

21. Quoted in Stephen Jones, *Creepshows: The Illustrated Stephen King Movie Guide* (New York: Billboard Books, 2002), p. 85.

22. Mick LaSalle, "*Needful Things*: High Budget but Still Low Grade," *San Francisco Chronicle* (August 27, 1993), p. C4, http://www.lexis-nexis.com/.

23. Gary Graff, "Stephen King's Short Stories Long on Chills and Thrills," *Ottawa Citizen* (October 30, 1993), p. B7, http://www.lexis-nexis.com/.

24. Quoted in "People in the News," Associated Press (November 22, 1993), http://www.lexis-nexis.com/.

Chapter 15

THE KING MACHINE ROLLS ON

At the beginning of 1994, the promotional blitz began for the ABC mini-series *The Stand*, which was scheduled to air in the spring, about a half a year later than ABC had planned. Filming had taken place the previous year over a period of six months at 120 locations—although the majority of the work had been done in Utah, Nevada, and Pennsylvania. Laurel King Productions, a company that was formed when King joined Laurel Productions specifically to adapt *The Stand*, was in control of the set, something that was important to King. He had refused to endorse a film-adaptation for more than twelve years, because its length made television the only viable medium for playing a movie based on the book, as the time constraints associated with the big screen would have prevented the story from being told properly. King, however, had worried about the appropriateness of television, observing, "You can't do the end of the world, then break in and say, 'And now a word from Charmin toilet tissue.'"[1] Another problem when doing television was dealing with network censors and the standards-and-practices people's sometimes crazy demands. King thus got assurances from the network. "My question to ABC was, can we do the book or are you going to make this deal and then say there's stuff you can't do? And they said, yes, we will stand away and let you do the book that you wrote."[2]

Other problems arose after the agreement had been made with ABC. A workers' dispute disrupted the production, forcing ABC to abandon its plans for a November 1993 premier. Laurel King Productions was concerned that the size of the project would cause it to go over budget, and to save money, the company—in addition to getting such stars as Molly

Ringwald and Rob Lowe to take less than their usual fees—had hired non-union workers for its crew. Those workers were under the impression that the company would sign a deal with the International Alliance of Theatrical Stage Employees (IATSE) and provide union benefits. When such benefits failed to materialize, they went on strike until they were granted union status, which happened in July after Laurel King Productions agreed not only to provide benefits but also to give those who had refused to cross the picket line their jobs back.[3]

The Stand would be the first major King project to appear in 1994, but a different one that few would hear about came out first. Troupe America, a theatrical touring group based in Minneapolis, performed Ghost Stories—a compilation of King stories that were adapted for the stage by Robert Pridham—in South Bend, Indian in the middle of January and then traveled to Pittsburgh, Pennsylvania later that month. Three months afterward, The Stand aired on May 8, 9, 11, and 12. Some critics found the production dull. "[V]iewers may be tempted to doze...," Tony Atherton wrote. "The fault lies mainly with the screenplay."[4] Mark Dawidziak, by contrast, recalling that many critics had regarded the miniseries a dead form, remarked, "hey, lifeless bodies are nothing new to horror master Stephen King. So, look out, friends and fiends, guys and ghouls. Here comes the King of Horror with a four-night miniseries that's electrifying enough to reanimate the corpse."[5] Most important, television audiences were intrigued, making The Stand the highest rated show in its time slot for May 8, with about 32 million viewers watching, and they remained interested, giving the series fairly steady ratings over the following three nights. With numbers better than it had expected, ABC was likely pleased that it had wrapped up a deal with King to do a miniseries based on "The Langoliers" in the days before The Stand premiered and was now anticipating another winner.

At the beginning of October 1994, two more King projects were brought to fruition. The Shawshank Redemption, the adaptation of the novella "Rita Hayworth and the Shawshank Redemption" that was filmed during the summer of 1993, arrived in theaters, and Insomnia, which King had hinted at the beginning of the year would have some connection to The Dark Tower series, appeared in bookstores. The book had originally been written in 1990 but, unhappy with it, King put the manuscript down, picking it up a few years later when he "saw what had gone wrong. It all had to do with a pivotal character named Ed, a research chemist. 'In the first draft of the book, Ed drove off to take a vacation on the coast of Maine on page 40,' said King, who is not the kind of writer who sticks to a rigid outline. 'The characters do pretty much what they want to do....I let them scurry where they want to scurry and Ed just sort of scurried away.'"[6] Once he figured out how to correct the problem, King wrote quickly "'I got down to three hours of sleep a night' while writing the book, he said. 'I became very conscious of when I was going to sleep and as I was sliding off to sleep, I'd think, "Oh, I'm going to sleep. It's happening." And I'd get all excited and wake up.'"[7]

The Shawshank Redemption was among the more successful King films. Frank Darabont, who debuted as a feature film director with the production, had written to King in 1987, asking permission to do the film. Darabont was only 24 at the time, but he had, in 1983, successful adapted King's "The Woman in the Room" for PBS. On the strength of that film, King granted Darabont the rights to make Shawshank, though he later recalled, "I never in a million years thought he'd get the film made."[8] Over the next few years, Darabont wrote the screenplay, sending it to King in the early 1990s. King liked it, and Darabont approached Castle Rock Entertainment about producing it. Castle Rock offered him $2.4 million for the script, an offer he turned down for the chance to direct for a much smaller paycheck. His decision paid off, as The Shawshank Redemption's success brought him greater recognition.

Although a few reviewers claimed the movie was no more than a typical prison movie, Janet Maslin wrote for the New York Times, "There are times when The Shawshank Redemption comes dangerously close to sounding one of those 'triumph of the human spirit' notes. But most of it is eloquently restrained. Despite an excess of voice-over narration and inspirational music, Mr. Darabont's film has a genuine dignity that holds the interest. It is helped greatly by fine, circumspect performances from Morgan Freeman as a rueful lifer named Red and Tim Robbins as Andy, the new kid on the cellblock."[9] More positive notices followed, some seeing the movie's success as an illustration of King's superiority as a teller of realistic tales. "King's novella, titled 'Rita Hayworth and Shawshank Redemption,' happens to be the second from his book Different Seasons to be translated into a movie," Frank Bruni wrote. "The first was 'The Body,' which became the noteworthy Stand by Me. Together, they make a case for filmmakers looking to King's lesser-known works for inspiration. They also make a case that King's a better writer when the genre isn't horror. Some of the gorgeous dialogue and voice-over narration in The Shawshank Redemption are lifted precisely from his prose."[10] Darabont seemed to agree with such an assessment, at least as far as the quality of the writing went, saying, as Robert W. Butler reported, "Many of the things people have been praising in the movie can be credited to King. He wrote a prison story in a way I'd never seen before. It played off of those prison clichés and tap-danced around them at the same time. Very amazing."[11]

As *The Shawshank Redemption* was playing in theaters, King was doing an uncharacteristic book tour, one that stopped only at independent bookstores, which were the first stores to have copies of *Insomnia*. While he was always open to signing books—telling his daughter when she complained about the time he spent doing so that "Those people buy your shoes"[12]—King had not been actively promoting his books with appearances for ten years. He didn't really need to. This tour served to promote the value of independent booksellers, or as King put it, "I'm concerned about the effect that the price cutters are having on American popular culture. And, God knows, American popular culture is debased enough without giving too much economic power to mega-stores that basically want to reduce diversity to 25 fiction titles, 25 nonfiction titles and 100 record albums, most of which are by the Beastie Boys."[13] The tour also gave King a chance to display his status as an ordinary guy, since he did it by riding his Harley Davidson across the nation, making stops in Ithaca, New York; Lexington, Kentucky; Nashville, Tennessee; Colorado Springs, Colorado; Sun Valley, Idaho; and Santa Cruz, California, among other places.

The tour, however, also called attention to King's celebrity status, not just because of the interest generated by his appearances but also because of the unwanted attention of a particular man, Steve Lightfoot. On the last stop in Santa Cruz, Lightfoot showed up with a large sign that read, "Stephen King is a murderer. It's true or he'd sue."[14] Lightfoot, who believed King was responsible for killing John Lennon, had been told to stay out of the bookstore and was arrested for trespassing after he entered shortly before King's arrival. "Steve Lightfoot has been a stone in my shoe for a lot of years," King said when he learned about the incident. "But more importantly, he's been a stone in his own shoe."[15] King, coincidentally, may have had a tangential connection to Mark Chapman, Lennon's killer. Chapman had, King believes, met him outside a television studio in New York. Describing himself as King's number one fan, Chapman urged King to pose for a photograph with him. "The guy was weird, man. He was like a quasar. He just wasn't there," King said. "But someone took the picture [with a Polaroid camera], and when it came out, I wrote, 'To Mark, best wishes, Stephen King.'"[16]

Following the tour *Insomnia* became available everywhere. Set in Derry the story is built around the lives of the elderly, or more specifically what they see. Ralph Roberts, who has recently lost his wife, has insomnia and spends his nights looking out his window onto Harris Avenue. He soon starts to see auras around people, as do others, including his friend Lois Chasse and his younger neighbor Ed Deepneau, who has recently begun to abuse his wife and rail against Susan Day, an abortion-rights activist who is planning to come to Derry for a rally. Ralph and Lois are then called upon to fight the forces of evil, little bald men that have infiltrated this world from a different plane of existence, the element of the novel that connects it to The Dark Tower series, and with whom Ed, who plans to kill everyone at the pro-choice rally, becomes associated.

Some objected to King's addressing the issues of abortion and spousal abuse in the context of a horror–fantasy tale. Chris Bohjalian, for instance, wrote, "There are some truly haunting scenes in the book about wife abuse and fanaticism, as well as touching observations about growing up and growing old, but they're quickly consumed by more predictable sensationalism: the smell of rotting guts, a decapitation, giant deadly catfish, cockroaches streaming from a human skull. It's clear that Mr. King had ambitious (perhaps epic) hopes for his new book. Sadly, what might have been a diamond of a novel is instead a Stephen King bauble."[17] Others welcomed King's return to his usual form. "King's last few novels have been, by his standard, slim and economical," Ray Olson observed. "With this dark fantasy based on the conception of a multilevel ultimate reality, he returns to the massiveness of The Stand and It and The Tommyknockers. . . . This is a yarn so packed with suspense, romance, literary reference, fascinating miscellaneous knowledge, and heart that only Stephen King could have written it. Marvelous—that is, full of marvels."[18]

That fall King also participated in perhaps his most literary publication to date, publishing the short story "Blind Willie" alongside work by Ernest Hemingway, F. Scott Fitzgerald, Joyce Carol Oates in the final issue of Antaeus, a journal described by Oates as "the greatest literary magazine that America has had."[19] The editor, Daniel Halpern, had called King and invited him to send a story and found, "he's a guy who's so happy to be in a literary magazine."[20] The issue sold out and was reprinted at the beginning of 1995, a year in which the King machine rolled on with the appearance, in March, of The Mangler, a film, which was a failure in every sense of the word, based on the early short story of the same name.

The Mangler was followed at the end of March with the film-version of Dolores Claiborne, which saw Kathy Bates return to a starring role in a King-inspired movie. The movie reviewed well. Michael Wilmington, for instance, wrote, "It's rare to see a pop bestseller come out this well in the movies. Thanks to Kathy Bates, Jennifer Jason Leigh, Tony Gilroy, Taylor Hackford—and King—the movie Dolores Claiborne offers much more than the usual techno-fright show. It shows us people in life's worst traps, death, misadventure, evil and murder springing up in the everyday sunshine, under a wind that ceaselessly beats the shore."[21]

The final King movie of the year was the ABC miniseries *The Lango-liers*. Like the previous year's *The Stand*, it aired during the May sweeps period. King had little involvement in the project. He had wanted and got Tom Holland to direct, but thereafter he, for the most part, stayed away, even though it was filmed in Bangor. "I sent the finished script to him, and he returned it with no comments. He was buried in his writing, tied to his word processor," Holland said. "I picked all the cast members from auditions and lists from the network, and Stephen approved every actor. And he showed his support by playing a cameo role. He only does that when he likes how his work has been adapted."[22] Holland may have been discussing King's approval of the script's faithfulness to his novella, but neither the critics nor King considered the film a very good one. In a fairly typical review, John J. O'Connor wrote, "the two-part film is dotted with clever tensions and neat touches, not least a drinks trolley eerily rolling down the aisle of the near-empty plane. But the inflated story goes fairly predictable in a hurry, and the underlining is heavy handed.... This latest King excursion into primal anxieties plucked from the dark closets of childhood is likely to elate only his most die-hard fans."[23] King himself would remark, "I wasn't crazy about it. That was more of a TV thing. But given what it was, it was fine. The best thing about it was that it gave Tom Holland and Richard Rubinstein the bona fides they needed to get Spelling Productions to go ahead with *Thinner*,"[24] the movie of which appeared in 1996. For ABC the miniseries was a success, with an average of 31 million viewers per night.

In June *Rose Madder* appeared. The book, like King's previous three novels, addresses spousal abuse. The plot is set off when the long-abused Rose, or Rosie, leaves her husband, a police detective named Norman Daniels, whom Rene Rodriguez described as "one of King's scariest human monsters."[25] Daniels follows her, for even though she assumes her maiden name, McClendon, Rosie leaves a trail by using his credit card. As Daniel closes in on her, leaving a number of corpses in his wake, Rosie buys a painting, "Rose Madder," which is a portrait of a woman who resembles her. It offers her an entrance into another dimension—one that connects the story to The Dark Tower series and *Insomnia*—where she finds a protector, Rose Madder, whose name comes from a red pigment used by painters.

Reviews were on the positive side. "*Rose Madder* plunges headlong and unapologetically into feminist territory," Rodriguez noted, "from the tightly knit sorority at Daughters and Sisters, the women's shelter where Rosie finds refuge, to the fantastical world of monstrous retribution she discovers inside a bewitching painting. Perhaps it's a sign that King is tiring of the constraints of the horror genre, but the serious undertones don't detract from the scary stuff."[26] Elizabeth Hand went further: finding King's writing better than usual, she observed that his "famously over-the-top prose style is in check for much of *Rose Madder*, which makes for an unusually moving tale of an ugly duckling whose transformation relies as much on her intelligence and perseverance as on special effects.... And the chapters dealing with Norman's bad temper should satisfy those with a taste for oozing eyeballs and other anatomical atrocities. The rest of us can hunker down with a warm blanket and *Rose Madder*."[27]

Despite its critical success, *Rose Madder* failed to reach the top of the *New York Times* bestseller list, and as King would not release another original book that year, he would fail, in 1995, to publish a number one bestseller for the first time in a number of years. His other publications, in 1995, included an essay in *Mid-Life Confidential: The Rock Bottom Remainders Tour America with Three Chords and an Attitude* and "Umney's Last Case," a story that had appeared in *Nightmares & Dreamscapes* that Penguin released as an individual book in September. In December he also released a 90-minute video of a public appearance at the Bangor Auditorium, where he read from his forthcoming novel *Desperation* (1996). Profits from the video went to the campaign to preserve the Bangor Public Library's Capital Campaign, a charity that King had supported earlier in the year through an appearance on ABC's *Celebrity Jeopardy* and to which Tabitha King had donated $2.5 million. Perhaps of bigger import for King was that he bought two more radio stations: Bangor's WNSW-AM and the nearby Brewer's WKIT-FM, adding to WZON, the radio station he had owned in the 1980s and reacquired in 1993, after having sold it in 1990.

NOTES

1. Quoted in "New Stand on *The Stand*," *Sun-Sentinel* (January 15, 1994), p. A2, http://www.lexis-nexis.com/.

2. Quoted in Diane Werts, "Stephen King's Strongest Work," *New York Newsday* (May 8, 1994), p. 20, http://www.lexis-nexis.com/.

3. See "IATSE, Laurel King Near Agreement on *Stand Off*," *Daily Variety* (July 9, 1993), p. 6, http://www.lexis-nexis.com/.

4. Tony Atherton, "King Novel Wilts in TV Adaptation," *Ottawa Citizen* (May 7, 1994), p. F7, http://www.lexis-nexis.com/.

5. Mark Dawidziak, "It Grabs You by the Throat and Refuses to Let Go," *Calgary Herald* (May 8, 1994), p. C4, http://www.lexis-nexis.com/.

6. Quoted in Rebecca James, "Stephen King Says He Sometimes Scares Himself," *Post-Standard* (October 7, 1994), p. D1, http://www.lexis-nexis.com/.

7. Ibid.

8. Stephen Jones, *Creepshows: The Illustrated Stephen King Movie Guide* (New York: Billboard Books, 2002), p. 92.

9. Janet Maslin, "Prison Tale by Stephen King Told Gently, Believe It or Not," *New York Times* (September 23, 1994), p. C3, http://www.lexis-nexis.com/.

10. Frank Bruni, "Human Spirit Triumphs in Prison Drama *Shawshank*," *Detroit Free Press* (September 23, 1994), p. 4D, http://www.lexis-nexis.com/.

11. Quoted in Robert W. Butler, "Hello, This is Oscar Calling: It Could Happen," *Kansas City Star* (October 7, 1994), p. H20, http://www.lexis-nexis.com/.

12. Quoted in Patricia Ward Biederman, "On the Road for a Novel Tour: Prolific Author Donald E. Westlake is Now Signing Copies of His Latest Work, *Baby Would I Lie?*, for Fans at a Bookstore Near You," *Los Angeles Times* (September 23, 1994), *Valley Life*, p. 9, http://www.lexis-nexis.com/.

13. Quoted in David Streitfeld, "Book Report," *Washington Post* (November 13, 1994), p. X15, http://www.lexis-nexis.com/.

14. Lee Quarnstrom, "All This for *Insomnia*: Author Ends Tour in Santa Cruz," *San Jose Mercury News* (October 25, 1994), p. B1, http://www.lexis-nexis.com/.

15. Ibid.

16. Quoted in David Streitfeld, "'Strange' Fans Gave King Idea for Novel," *Toronto Star* (May 17, 1987), p. D7, http://www.lexis-nexis.com/.

17. Chris Bohjalian, "The Ghouls Next Door," *New York Times Book Review* (October 30, 1994), p. 24, http://vnweb.hwwilsonweb.com/hww.

18. Ray Olson, "*Insomnia* (Book Review)," *Booklist* (August 1994) p. 1,988, http://vnweb.hwwilsonweb.com/hww.

19. Quoted in Gwen Florio, "Turning the Page, 25 Years Later: A Literary Kingmaker—*Antaeus*—Hits the End," *Philadelphia Inquirer* (January 16, 1995), p. A1, http://www.lexis-nexis.com/.

20. Ibid.

21. Michael Wilmington, "Deadly Intent: Kathy Bates Brings Humanity to Horrifying *Dolores Claiborne*," *Chicago Tribune* (March 24, 1995), p. C2, http://www.lexis-nexis.com/.

22. Quoted in Cliff Wirth, "Look Out for Flying Furballs!," *Chicago Sun-Times* (May 7, 1995), p. NC1.

23. John J. O'Connor, "An Eerie Plane Trip, Piloted by Stephen King," *New York Times* (May 12, 1995), p. D18, http://www.lexis-nexis.com/.

24. Quoted in Jones, *Creepshows*, p. 101.

25. Rene Rodriguez, "After Rosie Walked Out, Norman Got Madder," *Miami Herald* (June 11, 1995), p. 31.

26. Ibid.

27. Elizabeth Hand, "The Very Picture of Menace," *Washington Post* (June 18, 1995), p. X2, http://www.lexis-nexis.com/.

Chapter 16

BREAKING NEW RECORDS

In November 1995 an announcement about King's next book sparked a flood of interest in the direction that his career was taking. King had signed a deal to release a novel in monthly installments over a period of six months, reportedly for an advance of $1 million per installment. The plan immediately led to comparisons between King and Charles Dickens, who had released his novels in serial form. King, however, noted that "he 'isn't as good' as Dickens and does not expect his book to match the fanatical readership the British author's work enjoyed."[1] Still, it was memories of Dickens that led Ralph Vicinanza, who sells the foreign rights to King's books, to bring the idea of doing a serial book to King in September 1995. He was intrigued by the idea, not because it reminded him of Dickens but because it reminded him of the serial stories that he read as a child in the *Saturday Evening Post*. "I've really been tripping on this," he told Mary B. W. Tabor. "I love it. People can't peek ahead. They can't cheat. They can't know what's going to happen."[2]

King enjoyed serial stories, he recalled in his foreword to the 2000 hardcover edition, "because the end of each episode made the reader an almost equal participant with the writer—you had a whole week to try to figure out the next twist of the snake. Also, one read and experienced these stories more *intensely*, it seemed to me, because they were rationed."[3] King had played with the serial form privately in the mid-eighties, and when Vicinanza suggested King play with it again, he already had an idea that he thought might work as a serial: it was a story of the electric chair—tales of which he had been fascinated with as a child—set in 1932 called *The Green Mile*, a title taken from the color of the linoleum that lines the hallway leading to the Cold Mountain penitentiary's electric chair. By February 1996 three volumes had been completed and the fourth was being worked on. "The rest is somewhere in my brain. If I die it would become like *The Mystery of Edwin Drood* [the novel that Dickens was writing when he died]. Some of the other books I've written, I haven't really known where I was going, either, but it's dangerous. It's like taking off in an airplane and not knowing if the landing gear works," King told Dana Kennedy.[4]

The first part, "The Two Dead Girls," was issued on March 25, 1996, and was accompanied by a large publicity campaign. King even appeared in a 30-second television commercial that advertised the book: "I'm Stephen King," he said, "and it's my job to think about new ways to scare people to death."[5] Such publicity seemed necessary. The venture, after all, was a risky one. King may have asserted in a letter to booksellers, "As a writer, I get to keep an otherwise impossible measure of control and pace over the reader, letting the anticipation build and allowing time for the reader to imagine the possibilities to come next month,"[6] but readers had as much, if not more, control: they could abandon the story, if they didn't like the beginning, without having to pay for the rest. Part one's sales, which quickly placed the book on paperback bestseller lists, boded well for the experiment. Reviews also suggested that readers would want to read future installments: "*The Green Mile*, a Depression-era death-row yarn, is one of King's most immediately engaging page-turners in ages.... The format lets King deliver the punch of a short story (one of his specialties) with tantalizing hints of a broader, richer scope,"[7] Matt Roush raved. Readers kept reading: each installment—"The Mouse on the Mile," "Coffey's Hands," "The Bad Death of Eduard Delacroix," "Night Journey," "Coffey on the Mile"—became a bestseller in its own right.

A month after the last volume of *The Green Mile* appeared, King released another two books, *Desperation* and *The Regulators*, the latter of which was published as a Bachman book. Set in very different parts of the United States, the first in Desperation, Nevada, and the second in Wentworth, Ohio, the books are, in a sense, two versions of the same story. They contain a number of the same characters—including the Carvers, a family who lives in Wentworth; Johnny Marinville, a writer; and others—though each character has a different role in each novel. The characters of *Desperation* find themselves living in an Ohioan suburban street in *The Regulators* but seem very different people; Marinville, who is famous in *Desperation*, is only mildly successful in *The Regulators*; and the Carver family has been inverted, the parents having become the children and the children, the parents. The result is that *The Regulators* serves as "a sort of Bizarro universe of *Desperation*," Ted Anthony wrote.[8] The same evil force, an entity called Tak that possesses humans, however, serves as the adversary in both books.

The King novel begins with the Carvers (Ralph, Ellie, David, and Kirsten) getting arrested in Desperation—where Marinville, who is traveling in search of inspiration, has also found himself—while driving to their Lake Tahoe vacation. In Desperation, Collie Entragian, a monstrously large deputy, has become possessed by Tak and is randomly imprisoning people, Ralph, Ellie, and David Carver and Marinville among them. (Kirsten is killed before she is brought to jail.) Young David Carver proves something of their salvation, managing to escape and release the others. He then begins to believe that God, with whom he has a direct connection, has sent him to defeat Tak, but it is Marinville who takes on the role of Tak's slayer. In *The Regulators* the characters, peacefully ensconced in middle America, are suddenly besieged by the Regulators, Tak's henchmen, a gang that is modeled after one from a 1958 film of the same name and composed of television characters, those loved by Seth, an autistic child who is possessed by and defeats Tak with the aid of his aunt, with whom Seth communicates telepathically.

The two books, though published under different imprints of Penguin, Viking and Dutton, were available as a set, along with a free reading lamp. The relationship between them was further suggested by the covers, which formed a single illustration when placed next to each other. They could stand alone, but seemed to work more powerfully together. "The subtle interconnections King weaves through this diptych of terror resonate in the mind long after both books are finished," Michael A. Morrison wrote. "Separately, each is a compelling tale of supernatural horror; together they constitute a tour-de-force, King's second this year, and I'll wager his 'constant readers' [what King had come to call his readers in his introductions] will relish their visits to Wentworth and Desperation as much as the long trek down *The Green Mile*."[9]

Despite not attempting to assert Bachman's independence, King played with Bachman's fictional biography, getting his personal editor, Charles Verrill, to write an account of how this new Bachman book found its way to the publisher. According to Verrill's account, the former Mrs. Bachman, now Claudia Eschelman, found a box of manuscripts in her basement, when she was moving in 1994, and among a number of incomplete stories and novels, there was *The Regulators*, to which Verrill "made a few small changes, mostly updating certain references (substituting Ethan Hawke for Rob Lowe in the first chapter, for instance), but...otherwise left it pretty much as I found it."[10] The books, each selling over a million copies before the end of the year, held the number one and two spots on the hardcover bestseller lists for a while, even as five installments of the *Green Mile* remained on the paperback list, selling an average of 3.5 million copies each.

At the end of October, *Thinner*, a movie that King was very interested in seeing succeed, finally appeared on movie screens. King had been involved in many stages of the production, polishing the screenplay, checking out on a regular basis what was happening on the set, and making a cameo as a pharmacist. Richard Rubinstein, who had bought the rights to the book in the late 1980s, had spent six years trying to get the project made, and the movie had been filmed the previous year in Camden, Maine, which charged only $6,000 for the use of the town from mid-July to mid-October, to the displeasure of many Camden residents, particularly business owners, who complained that they lost money when film crews shut down streets during the day. Initially scheduled for an April release, the production ran into trouble when test-screening audiences found fault with the ambiguity of the ending, which did not definitively reveal that Billy and his family died. A new ending had to be shot over six days in April. In the end Spellings Films, which was financing the picture, took creative control over the final cut, and King was unhappy with the version that was released. Indeed, he realized early on that things were going wrong. He observed, during a live chat with fans on America Online in April, "I'm not too crazy about *Thinner*, from what I've seen of it. Fingers crossed."[11] Crossing his fingers could not save the movie, and it was out of the theaters three weeks after it arrived, though King claims the $17 million production made a small amount of money.

The failure of *Thinner* did not detract from King's extraordinary year. Selling around 25 million books, his name had dotted bestseller lists from the moment the first installment of *The Green Mile* appeared. Indeed, after *Desperation* and *The Regulators*, he had seven bestsellers, five on the paperback list and two on the hardback list. He also had won an O. Henry Award for the short story "The Man in the Black Suit," which had been published in the *New Yorker* in 1994, further establishing his literary credentials. At the time he was also pursuing another dream, getting a film version made of *The Shining* that was faithful to his vision. King, who had publicly expressed his displeasure with Kubrick's 1980 film, had written a screenplay that Kubrick had dismissed. King, after securing permission to do the project from both Warner Brothers and Kubrick, revamped his script, expanding it for a six-hour miniseries for ABC. He served as the executive producer and made a cameo as the bandleader of a dead orchestra. After reviewing a rough cut of the movie—which had been shot in the first half of 1996 in Colorado, at The Stanley, the hotel where he first had the idea for the book—King was reportedly pleased, and at the beginning of 1997, he promised that the new version would be "the scariest thing ever to air on American television."[12]

To get the rights to remake the movie, King had agreed to say nothing more about what he thought of the original film, but he and the director, Mick Garris, who had also directed *The Stand*, sought to clearly distinguish the new version from the old one. Garris, for instance, noted, "Stanley Kubrick is a genius. He made Stanley Kubrick's *The Shining*. I felt my job was to make Stephen King's *The Shining*. There are a lot of important elements in the book that we thought should have been treated in a cinematic manner, particularly the whole subject of abuse and alcoholism and responsibility, and the whole idea of parental guilt."[13] Comparisons with Kubrick's film were inevitable: Kubrick's was pronounced artistically superior, but the miniseries, according to the critics, did achieve something that Kubrick's did not. "King tells the story more clearly and establishes the characters better than Kubrick did. Yet the first four hours...amount to a slow buildup to the finale, with its harrowing showdown between Wendy and Jack, who wields a croquet mallet,"[14] Hal Boedeker observed. While a lot of hype surrounded the production, King's *Shining* was not as big a ratings draw as were some of the previous King miniseries, averaging only 18.7 million viewers a night.

Three other King inspired movies would appear in 1997; none of them would be great successes. The first, directed by Garris, was *Quicksilver Highway*—a television movie that combined King's story "Chattery Teeth" and Clive Barker's story "The Body Politic"; it aired on Fox in May but got little publicity and few watched. *Trucks*, a made for TV movie that was based on the same story as *Maximum Overdrive*, aired on October 29 on the USA Network, and while considered the better filmic version of the short story, it failed to draw an audience. *The Night Flier*, which was directed by the newcomer Mark Pavia, debuted on HBO in November and had a limited released in theaters the following February. The movie, a gory vampire tale in which a tabloid reporter, Richard Dees, who was played by Miguel Ferrer, gets his comeuppance for publishing trash, reviewed badly and ended its run quickly. "The story has been so poorly adapted that intriguing clues to the killer's motives and *modus operandi* are introduced, then left hanging. Richard's assignment is complicated by the fact that his unscrupulous editor, Merton Morrison (Dan Monahan), a cackling yuppie fiend, pits Richard against a rookie reporter, Katherine

Blair (Julie Entwisle), in a contest to chase down the story."[15] King, none-theless, professed his approval, remarking, "I love it. There's an inner 14-year-old in me that still says rip 'em up and really gross people out."[16]

As far as publishing books was concerned, King remained relatively low key, reviving his private publishing concern, the Philtrum Press, for the first time since the 1980s to release *Six Stories*. Only 1,100 signed and numbered copies, which contained "Autopsy Room Four," "Blind Willie," "L.T.'s Theory of Pets," "Luckey Quarter," "Lunch at the Gotham Café," and "The Man in the Black Suit," were printed. King's one major publi-cation of the year was *The Dark Tower IV: Wizard and Glass*, which like *The Waste Lands* was first released as a limited edition hardcover through Grant and then as a paperback with Penguin, who developed a market-ing campaign around the book on the internet, launching the *Wizard and Glass* Web site at the end of October, a week in advance of the release of the paperback. The Web site served as a portal through which fans could get together and chat about the series; compete for prizes, including a trip for two to The Stanley Hotel in Colorado; and play games, The Dark Tower Trivia Challenges, one for each book.

King had finish a new novel, *Bag of Bones* (1998), but he didn't just send it to his usual publisher, shopping it around to a number of oth-ers instead. He was annoyed, it was rumored, because Viking, which had become a part of Pearson PLC, had given Tom Clancy a much bigger ad-vance than he was being offered, though King's lawyer/business manager, Greene, denied the notion, saying "It isn't a dollars-and-cents issue. It was time for a change."[17] That may have been part of the truth. The following year, describing his "marriage with Viking," he said, "I played the woman's part. I felt like the little housewife who stays home and works all day, while my husband is out taking all the credit and sporting around town in his nice tailored suit. And I felt that I wasn't being respected and I was being taken for granted."[18] Verrill described the problem in these terms: "I think the fact that he loves this book had a great deal to do with the fail-ure of negotiations.... I think that psychologically he was offered a little bit less for a novel that he loved so dearly and, at this point in his career, it came as a kind of wound or blow. Money was the language. Money was the gesture and the gesture came as a blow."[19] King was reportedly looking for at least $17 million upfront for the book, and one publisher who submit-ted a bid and met with Greene said, "'There was an air of unreality to the meeting.'... [H]e left feeling like the imprisoned character in the Stephen King book *Misery*."[20] In the end King did find a new publisher, Simon & Schuster, but the contract that he signed did not bring him the huge ad-vance that he sought. Rather, he signed a three-book deal worth $2 million in advance per book. In exchange for giving up a large advance, King got 50 percent royalties on all profits. Some believed King got nervous when publishers did not immediately grant him what he wanted, but the royalty deal that had been negotiated was likely to earn him more money from each novel, assuming that his sales numbers remained steady, than he had ever made from a single book.

NOTES

1. Mary B. W. Tabor, "Stephen King on the Installment Plan," *New York Times* (November 11, 1995), sec. 1, p. 39, http://www.lexis-nexis.com/.

2. Ibid.

3. Stephen King, *The Green Mile: The Complete Serial Novel* (New York: Scribner, 2000), p. 16.

4. Quoted in Dana Kennedy, "Going for Cheap Thrills," *Entertainment Weekly* (February 23, 1996–March 1, 1996), p. 60, http://www.lexis-nexis.com/.

5. Quoted in Sherryl Connelly, "King Makes Serial Killing," (New York) *Daily News* (April 3, 1996), p. 29, http://www.lexis-nexis.com/.

6. Quoted in Paul D. Colford, "INK / Suspense as a Marketing Tactic," (New York) *Newsday* (February 8, 1996), Part II, p. B2, http://www.lexis-nexis.com/.

7. Matt Roush, "*Green Mile* Finds Stephen King in Stride," *USA Today* (March 25, 1996), p. 6D, http://www.lexis-nexis.com/.

8. Ted Anthony, "Real Horror: Stephen King's Scary Stories Ring Eerily True," *Chicago Sun-Times* (October 27, 1996), p. NC25, http://www.lexis-nexis.com/.

9. Michael A. Morrison, "Twisted Sister Cities," *Washington Post* (September 22, 1996), p. X5, http://www.lexis-nexis.com/.

10. "Editor's Note," *The Regulators* by Richard Bachman (New York: Signet, 1997 [1996]), unnumbered page.

11. Quoted in "AOL Interview 1996," http://www.stephen-king.de/interviews/aol96.html.

12. Quoted in Richard Helm, "King Promises to Scare All with His TV *Shining*," *Calgary Herald* (January 12, 1997), p. E4, http://www.lexis-nexis.com/.

13. Quoted in Mark Lorando, "*Shining* Suffers a Dull Waxy Buildup," *Times-Picayune* (April 27, 1997), p. T4, http://www.lexis-nexis.com/.

14. Hal Boedeker, "*Shining* Loses Its Luster over 6 Hours," *Orlando Sentinel* (April 27, 1997), p. F1, http://www.lexis-nexis.com/.

15. Stephen Holden, "Draculian Gore, Sound and Fury," *New York Times* (February 6, 1998, Friday), p. E10, http://www.lexis-nexis.com/.

16. Alicia Anstead, "Fly by Night: New Stephen King Thriller Satisfies Craving for Gore, Suspense," *Bangor Daily News* (February 6, 1998), http://www.lexis-nexis.com/.

17. Quoted in "King's Ransom?," *Newsweek* (October 27, 1997), p. 8, http://www.lexis-nexis.com/.

18. Quoted in Doreen Carvajal, "Stephen King Unleashed," *New York Times* (November 9, 1998), p. C1, http://www.lexis-nexis.com/.

19. Ibid.

20. Doreen Carvajal, "Who Can Afford Him?: Stephen King Goes in Search of a New Publisher," *New York Times* (October 27, 1997), p. D1, http://www.lexis-nexis.com/.

Chapter 17

NEW RETIREMENT RUMORS
ALMOST BECOME REAL

King's exploration of different media was again brought to the fore at the beginning of 1998. An episode of *The X-Files*, a show King had not watched until David Duchovny, who plays Agent Mulder and whom King met on *Celebrity Jeopardy*, suggested King write an episode. King found the show to be "like a virus that gains in people's systems, slowly but surely. I love the chemistry between the characters and the reverse psychology. Mulder has the feminine characteristics, and (Agent) Scully (Gillian Anderson) is the tough male."[1] Chris Carter, the show's creator, agreed to the idea. King was not new to television, as he had both adapted his fiction and written original material, but *The X-Files* episode was unlike his other TV projects. He had never worked with another's characters, and even though he said he "had a great time playing with Chris' toys,"[2] he did not find doing so easy. Indeed, his first attempt proved unsuccessful. Carter, King revealed, "came back to me (after the first draft) and said, 'This isn't what we wanted.'"[3] King went back to work but still failed to meet Carter's expectations. Carter then rewrote the screenplay, refashioning King's story, which involves agent Scully, who, while vacating in Maine, finds herself in a community whose inhabitants mutilate themselves, perhaps because they are being controlled by an evil doll.

During the summer *Bag of Bones* was published in Great Britain. The book features a writer, Mike Noonan, who is a resident of Derry with a summer home in the lake region of Maine. He loses his wife, Jo, as the novel opens and, as a result, begins to suffer from writer's block and to have strange dreams about Dark Score Lake, Maine, next to which is his summer home, which is locally known as "Sara Laughs"—a name taken from a blues singer who lived and died there at the beginning of the 20th century. Noonan feels compelled to move there and is contacted by ghostly presences, through which he will discover that Sara had been murdered and buried in a bag next to the lake. He also becomes involved with a local young widow named Mattie. She is being persecuted by her wealthy father-in-law, who wants to take custody of her child. "I wanted to write a gothic novel. For me what that means is a novel about secrets, about things that have happened in the past, that have been buried and stay quiet for a while and then, like a buried body, they start to smell bad."[4]

King successfully weaves the numerous plot elements into his narrative, but their sheer number, some British critics felt, hurt the novel's power. "An awful lot goes on in *Bag of Bones*, which prevents it from achieving the elegant impact of its avowed models (Shirley Jackson's *The Haunting of Hill House*, Daphne du Maurier's *Rebecca*) or even King's own high water mark, *Misery*," Kim Newman wrote, but she went on to observe, "This may be deliberate since, thanks to our bag-of-bones narrator, it has to feel rather like a Mike Noonan book. The final chapter, after all the plot threads have been tied away, seems to offer a naked promise to write no more, that it is impossible to continue with imagined horrors after having experienced real ones. Who knows whether this comes from Mike Noonan or from Stephen King?"[5] King fostered the idea that Noonan's decision might be a reflection of one he had made, telling reporters, during his English book tour, "A writer has only a finite number of stories to write. I think I'm very near the end of publishing my work...I don't want to descend into self-parody. I've written most of the things people are going to appreciate. After this, it might just be the blabberings of a tiresome old uncle. I don't want to become Harold Robbins."[6]

King was back in the United States in September, doing a U.S. book tour. American critics gave *Bag of Bones* rave reviews. "*Bag of Bones* is a Kingian tour de force, a Gothic romance that slowly ensnares the reader in an intricately constructed web of very human emotions (love, grief, desire, regret, frustration, joy) amid a small-town setting,"[7] John Marshall proclaimed. King's wife had told King as much when she read the manuscript for him, while he recalled, "I knew when I was working on it that it was better in a lot of ways than a lot of my other stuff."[8] However, some dismissed the book, treating King with the same disrespect that he felt he had been fighting against his entire career. David Edelstein and Michael Wood, writing for *Slate*, proclaimed it a "bag of old rubbish," for instance.[9] Such dismissals did not deter King's readers, and the book was a big seller, validating his displeasure with the contract Viking had been offering the previous year. "This is psychological," King said. "I would like to sell. I wanted to have one more book that was big, that felt like I was running the tables in terms of sales. I wanted to knock Tom Clancy out of the No. 1 spot. Like Leonardo DiCaprio, I'm king of the world, even if it's only for two weeks, whatever. I wanted those things."[10]

Despite the success of the novel, King's year ended on a sour note, with the release of the film adaptation of "Apt Pupil," the third movie to be made from the novellas that appeared in *Different Seasons*. The first two had proved wildly successful. *Apt Pupil* did not join those successes. It had faced trouble almost from the start. After the attempt to film it failed in the eighties, the rights for the story reverted back to King, and in the 1990s Bryan Singer pursued them, sending King an unreleased version of his *The Usual Suspects*, a movie that would earn accolades in 1995. King liked the film and sold the rights to his novella for $1. The project then got stalled because Spelling Films and Paramount, with whom Singer had agreed to make the film, pulled out of the deal, and a new production company had to be found. Phoenix Pictures stepped in. The movie was shot in 1997 and set for release in early 1998, but a lawsuit, which claimed that adolescent boys were forced to film a shower scene without their parents' permission, delayed the release until October, when the film died at the box office, taking in less than $10 million.

King had other problems to deal with at the time. The explosion of the Internet as a media resource had spawned myriad unofficial King Web sites, which were spreading rumors at an alarming rate. To correct those rumors King launched, at the beginning of January 1999, the Official Stephen King Web site, a sort of electronic *Castle Rock*. ABC then began heavily promoting *Storm of the Century*, a six-hour miniseries about a small town in Maine that suffers through a huge snowstorm and the arrival of a mysterious stranger who seems to know everyone's secrets and begins killing people. King had written the screenplay between December 1996 and February 1997, and filming took place in Southwest Harbor, Maine, and at a set in Toronto, during the first half of 1998. When it aired on February 14, 15, and 18 of February 1999 and the screenplay was published in a paperback edition, the *Storm* proved successful: the movie, while the ratings were not among the best for a King miniseries, found critical acclaim, and the book reached bestseller lists. Calling it "a morality play disguised as horror," Laura Fries, for example, wrote "this three-part miniseries should win over a few remaining Stephen King holdouts while reinforcing the devotion of legions of fans. Taken as allegory, *Storm of the Century* is one of the more philosophical and humanistic of his tales; while the all-too-familiar elements (the snowy isolation of *The Shining*, the prophetic and mysterious newcomer of *Needful Things*, the community spirit of *The Stand*) may be tiring, King has peppered his script with new influences such as Sheila Jackson's 'The Lottery' and even *12 Angry Men* to pose some interesting philosophical questions: What serves the greater good and at what cost would you sacrifice decency? And how does the devil talk you into selling your soul?"[11] The series also pulled in enough viewers, even though the last part was up against George Clooney's exit from the television hospital drama *E.R.*, to please ABC executives, who immediately began negotiations with King for another miniseries.

King's next book, *The Girl Who Loved Tom Gordon*, a novel that King had completed on February 1 and that, a surprise to his publisher, he asked to have in bookstores by April for the beginning of the baseball season, was being prepared for publication. King wanted the games to which his main character was listening "to be the most recent ones on record,"[12] Susan Moldow, the head of Scribner, told reporters. The book was, in a way, a serious response to a question that King had been asked at a press conference in 1994, about whether or not he was going to write a baseball book. "Well, yeah," King replied. "As a matter of fact I have an idea about—well, I don't want to give the whole thing away, but it's about a major-league pitcher who's in the witness-protection program because he's in on fixing the World Series and these guys come up to him and break his pitching hand."[13] Such a book never appeared, and King probably had long forgotten his offhand remark. Nonetheless, *The Girl Who Loved Tom Gordon*—which coincidentally was published on the 25th anniversary of the publication of *Carrie*, when King held a party at which he handed out copies of *The New Lieutenant's Rap*, a chapbook published by the Philtrum Press that contained an unedited part of *Hearts in Atlantis*, the novel King released later in the year—was in its own way a baseball book. Indeed, the story is organized like a baseball game, divided into innings, with a pre-game and a seventh inning stretch, and built around the Red Sox's 1998 season, although King took small liberties with the Sox's schedule.

The story, conceived at a 1998 baseball game at Boston's Fenway Park, is, as King describes it, a "Hansel and Gretel" story without Hansel. Trisha McFarland—a nine-year-old girl who is lost in the woods and begins to imagine that Tom Gordon, an actual relief pitcher for the Boston Red Sox and her favorite baseball player, is with her—takes the place of Gretel. A small book by King's standards, with only 219 pages, it earned critical, as well as popular, success. "Stephen King's new novel," Sheryl Connelly proclaimed in a typical review, "expertly stirs the major ingredients of the American psyche—our spirituality, fierce love of children, passion for baseball and collective fear of the bad thing we know lurks on the periphery of life." She concluded, "King said that in writing this novel he was taken with the notion of 'saves,' of stepping into the final innings and pulling it out. It's an analogy he works through to the last page in what is—and this is an odd adjective to use in relation to King—a lovely book."[14]

King's spring surprise was followed by two other projects later in the year: *Hearts in Atlantis* was released in September, and *Blood and Smoke*, an audio book containing previously unpublished stories, came out in November. The year didn't quite turn out as well as King had hoped, however. Indeed, he almost didn't live to see it end. In June he was spending time with his family at his summer house in Lovell, and after dropping his youngest son off at the airport on the 19th, he went for a walk, as he tried to do everyday when he was in the area. He did not make it back home. While walking on Route 5 in North Lovell, Bryan Smith was driving toward him. Distracted by a Rottweiler, which was trying to get some meat from a cooler, Smith wasn't watching where he was going and struck King, throwing him about fourteen feet. King's right leg suffered multiple fractures. His hip, as well as four ribs, were broken. His lung was punctured, and his spine was chipped. The following day, after surgery, King was alert and was expected to recover, but he would not walk for sometime. King returned home after about five weeks and began writing. "His wife, Tabitha, who is his rock and his redeemer, set him up at a makeshift desk in the back hallway of their Victorian sprawl in Bangor. It reminded him of the laundry room in their old trailer, where he wrote *Carrie*."[15] Still, writing wasn't easy: "That first writing session lasted an hour and forty minutes, by far the longest period I'd spent sitting upright since being struck by Smith's van. When it was over, I was dripping with sweat and almost too exhausted to sit up straight in my wheelchair. The pain in my hip was just short of apocalyptic. And the first five hundred words were uniquely terrifying—it was as if I'd never written anything before them in my life."[16]

In September *Hearts in Atlantis* appeared in bookstores as scheduled. A sequence of five interlocking stories—"Low Men in Yellow Coats," "Hearts in Atlantis," "Blind Willie," "Why We're in Vietnam," and "Heavenly Shades of Night are Falling"—the book follows the lives of a group of characters from their childhood in 1960 to their adult lives, exploring the legacy of Vietnam as it does so, illustrating King's continued interest in engaging social issues in the context of his supernatural tales. The first of the stories, set in 1960, links the novel to The Dark Tower series, as Bobby Garfield, one of the two characters that tie the stories together, becomes involved with Ted Brautigan, who is staying in the boardinghouse in which Bobby lives with his mom. Brautigan is hiding from the low men, supernatural beings working for the Crimson King, the figure of chaos in the world of The Dark Tower. The other main figure in the tale is Carol Gerber, Bobby's first love.

Critics found themselves more drawn to the stories' realistic elements. Ray Olson, for example, after noting the connection between the novel and The Dark Tower books, observed, "Primarily, however, this is a rich, engaging, deeply moving generational epic, something of a baby boomer's equivalent to Vance Bourjaily's great Korean War-generation novel, *The Violated* (1958)."[17] Phil Kloer was more emphatic in his dismissal of the supernatural elements, writing, "King's growing stature hides a dirty little secret: The most popular horror writer ever has outgrown horror....King's characters are so extensively rooted, his voice so authentic and persuasive (whether first or third person), his emotional depth so resonant, his narrative pacing so pitch-perfect, that the spooky stuff now frequently seems to get in the way....So it is with *Hearts in Atlantis*, King's latest, which is most engaging when there isn't a boogeyman for miles, when a boy and a girl in college make bittersweet love in a parked car with the radio playing, knowing it's their last night together, or two old friends meet unexpectedly after the funeral of a third."[18]

Blood and Smoke appeared in November, an audio book that King had made after recording *Bag of Bones*. It was packaged to look like a box of cigarettes and contained the warning, "Listening after dark may cause fear, trembling, and lead to acute paranoia."[19] Included were two previously unpublished stories, "1408" and "In the Deathroom," and one that had appeared in *Dark Love* in 1995, "Lunch at the Gotham Café." They took up "where [two earlier stories] 'Quitters Inc.' and 'The 10 O'clock People' leave off and focus on 'the horror of the evil weed, tobacco. 'There are stories here that scared even me—psychopathic killers, torture chambers, haunted hotel rooms...and wafting through each story, the deadly, seductive scent of tobacco,'"[20] King said.

December saw another King inspired project brought to its conclusion with the arrival of the more than three hour movie adaptation of the *Green Mile*, starring Tom Hanks and directed and written by Frank Darabont, who had so successfully done the other King-based prison movie, *The Shawshank Redemption*, a fact that led King to observe that Darabont had "the world's smallest specialty—Stephen King prison movies set in the past."[21] Having run $10 million dollars over budget, those financing the film may have been nervous, but the reviews were extraordinarily positive, and the movie took in $120 million in the two months after its release, making it by far the most successful King movie to date.

During the fall months King and Tabitha had taken up residence in Boston, where their son Joe was living with his wife and son, Ethan. Once the weather got colder, they headed off to Florida, where their daughter, Naomi has a home. "Stephen can get more exercise there and not worry about falling on ice," Warren Silver, King's lawyer, said. "He's going to try to start putting weight on that leg to see how well it holds up. He's far from out of the woods yet."[22] King would buy a house in Sarasota, Florida, where he would begin to spend the winter months.

NOTES

1. Quoted in Jefferson Graham, "King Game for Another *X-Files:* Horror Master Sends Scully on Maine Vacation," *USA Today* (February 6, 1998), p. 3D, http://www.lexis-nexis.com/.

2. Quoted in "Stephen King Meets *The X-Files,*" *Portland Press Herald* (January 26, 1998,), p. 2C, http://www.lexis-nexis.com/.

3. Quoted in James MacGowan,"*X-Files* Guru Rewrites Script from Stephen King," *Orlando Sentinel* (February 1, 1998), p. A2, http://www.lexis-nexis.com/.

4. Quoted in John Keenan, "King Loves Idea of Secrets," *Omaha World Herald* (June 29, 1998), p. 29, http://www.lexis-nexis.com/.

5. Kim Newman, "Don't Mention the King," (London) *Independent* (August 15, 1998), p. 15, http://www.lexis-nexis.com/.

6. Quoted in Elizabeth Grice, "Horror of Horrors: Stephen King Says He May Start Writing Only for Himself," (Montreal) *Gazette* (August 26, 1998), p. C7, http://www.lexis-nexis.com/.

7. John Marshall, "Feeling Success in His *Bones* King's Back from Near-Death Experience in Book World," *Seattle Post-Intelligencer* (September 29, 1998), p. E1, http://www.lexis-nexis.com/.

8. Ibid.

9. David Edelstein and Michael Wood, "Bag of Old Rubbish," *Slate Magazine* (September 28, 1998), http://www.lexis-nexis.com/.

10. Doreen Carvajal, "Stephen King Unleashed," *New York Times* (November 9, 1998), p. C1, http://www.lexis-nexis.com/.

11. Laura Fries, "*Stephen King's Storm of the Century,*" *Variety* (February 15, 1999–February 21, 1999), p. 48, http://www.lexis-nexis.com/.

12. Quoted in Celia McGee, "Thriller of Pitch from Stephen King," (New York) *Daily News* (February 16, 1999), p. 22, http://www.lexis-nexis.com/.

13. Quoted in Susan Bickelhaupt, "King's Game Remains Horror," *Boston Globe* (January 14, 1994), Living, p. 36, http://www.lexis-nexis.com/.

14. Sheryl Connelly, "Thrills, Chills & Baseball: King Blasts a Homer," (New York) *Daily News* (April 4, 1999), p. 18, http://www.lexis-nexis.com/.

15. Stephen J. Dubner, "Being Stephen King: It Isn't the Money. It isn't the Fans. It Certainly isn't the Reviews. He Writes to Stay Alive," *Ottawa Citizen* (August 20, 2000), p. C15, http://www.lexis-nexis.com/.

16. Stephen King, *On Writing: A Memoir of the Craft* (New York: Scribner, 2000), p. 268.

17. *Booklist* (July 1999), p. 1,893, http://vnweb.hwwilsonweb.com/.

18. Phil Kloer, "Latest Work Shows Stephen King is Becoming More Than Just a Horror Storyteller," *The Atlanta Journal and Constitution* (September 12, 1999), p. L7, http://www.lexis-nexis.com/.

19. Quoted in Bob Minzesheimer, "King Packs Audio Tales with Blood," *USA Today* (November 22, 1999), p. D4, http://www.lexis-nexis.com/.

20. Quoted in Don O'Briant, "Scent of Terror Wafts through King Audio Book," *Atlanta Journal and Constitution* (November 18, 1999), p. D2, http://www.lexis-nexis.com/.

21. Quoted in Gregory Weinkauf, "Instant Karma," *SF Weekly* (December 8, 1999), http://www.lexis-nexis.com/.

22. Quoted in Paula Chin and Eric Francis, "Beyond Misery," *People* (January 24, 2000), p. 125, http://www.lexis-nexis.com/.

Chapter 18

THE LONG RECOVERY

At the end of 1999, King was finding that recovering from his injuries made writing difficult and questioned whether he would continue publishing. His actions, however, belied his statements. He and Peter Straub had already agreed to do a sequel to *The Talisman*, the idea for which had been sketched out in April 1999. The two began writing in February 2000, working on the novel for a little over a year. "It was my job to begin the story, because the part outside The Territories is set in an area of Wisconsin I'm familiar with," Straub recalled. "We alternated sections, working by phone and e-mail. Sometimes we'd take turns beginning new chapters, sometimes not. We might alternate paragraphs. It just depended."[1] Another project more than two years in the making was also about to become available. Late in 1997 King signed a deal with HyperBole Studios and Mainstream Software to develop an interactive companion for computer desktops, which would include games and screensavers based on King's short stories, as well as an unpublished story. It was to be called "Stephen King Desktop Companion," but by the time it was ready for release, at the beginning of 2000, it had been renamed *Stephen King's F13*, and the story turned out to be the novella "Everything's Eventual," which had appeared, in 1997, in the October–November issue of *Fantasy and Science Fiction* and was later released with 13 other short stories in the collection *Everything's Eventual: 14 Dark Tales* (2002).

King, in fact, had a number of projects lined up for the coming year. He was working on his memoirs and the novel *Dreamcatcher* (2001), under the working title "Cancer": he would finish the first draft in May. Writing was helping him escape the pain that his injuries were causing, as he noted in an author note accompanying *Dreamcatcher*, "I was never so grateful to be writing as during my time of work on *Dreamcatcher*. I was in a lot of physical discomfort during those six and a half months, and the book took me away."[2] King was also getting ready to release, in March 2000, "Riding the Bullet," a 16,000-word novella that he had also written during his recovery and that he had decided to issue electronically through Simon & Schuster and the Philtrum Press. The experiment, which got King's face onto the cover of *Time* magazine, was inspired by an online experiment by Arthur C. Clark, who had published a short story through Fatbrain.com, an e-book seller. King had thought, he recalled, "This is good, but it's too small. It isn't a fair test of what the market is about. What Arthur Clarke did, which was a six-page thing, was like a kiss goodnight. The 'Riding the Bullet' experience is more like heavy petting. But you talk about a novel, a full-length novel that would come out in installments and might total 700 or 800 pages—then you're talking about full intercourse."[3] The experiment was wildly successfully, with over 400,000 copies downloaded the day it went online and demand remained steady, if not as high, in the following weeks, making the novella the first book distributed online to become a bestseller and earning King, he estimated, around $450,000, rather than the $10,000 or $20,000 that he might have earned if he had sold the piece to a major magazine such as *Playboy* or the *New Yorker*.

The experiment worked so well for King—even though the copy-protection mechanism was quickly hacked and free copies popped up all over the Web—that he decided to take the next step and publish a full length novel, reviving and revising the story that he issued in three parts through the Philtrum Press, *The Plant*, which told the story of a vampire vine that takes over a publishing office and gives out financial incentives for those who commit human sacrifices. He released it in serial form through the Philtrum Press without going through a traditional publisher. Readers were able to download each approximately 5,000-word chapter from King's official Web site each month and pay afterward, an idea inspired by a fan's mailing him $2.50 after downloading "Riding the Bullet" from an unauthorized Web site for free. "Being something of an optimist about my fellow creatures, I have the idea that most people are honest and will pay for what they get,"[4] King wrote but warned that if enough readers failed to pay, he would cease releasing chapters.

The first chapter appeared in July, and more than 100,000 copies were downloaded; about two thirds of those were paid for. Over the next five months, five more chapters were made available. Readers dwindled, however, and so did those who were paying. King then said that if at least 75 percent of readers failed to pay, the project would be scrapped. Fans started to send King extra money, $5, $10, and $20 payments, to make up for those reading for free, and King continued releasing chapters. By the fourth chapter, however, only about 40,000 people were still download-ing the installments: about half of those paid. King thus announced that he would not complete the project, though his spokesperson said, "We decided to continue, though, because both part five and six were already written."[5] When the fifth part was made available, readers were asked to pay $2, the same amount for which they were asked for the fourth part, while no payment was asked for the sixth part, which appeared online in December. The experiment was widely described as a failure, but King had received $721,448 for the chapters he had posted, earning him, after expenses, $463,832. King has promised to complete the story, saying. "*The Plant* is not finished online. It is only on hiatus. I am no more done than the producers of *Survivor* are done. I am simply in the process of fulfilling my other commitments,'"[6] that is, working on *Black House*, the novel that he was writing with Straub; *Dreamcatcher*; and The Dark Tower series.

As King was winding up his work on *The Plant*, he published two other books, *On Writing: A Memoir of the Craft* and *Secret Windows: Essays and Fiction on the Craft of Writing*, a collection of previous published material, mostly nonfiction, with an introduction by Straub, that complemented the memoir and was only available from the Book-of-the-Month Club. King had begun the memoir in December 1997, but he had found writing it tortuous and put the manuscript down in despair, having drafted the part that was straight memoir, after two or three months, the length of time it usually takes him to finish a first draft of one of his massive novels. He picked it up again in June 1999, deciding to finish it over the summer and let the editors at Scribner's decide if it was any good. Two days after he had begun, his life collided with that of Smith. When he arrived back home from the hospital at the end of July and decided that he had to do his best to write something, King picked it up again, finishing the sec-tion on becoming a writer and adding a postscript that gives an account of his accident and the initial stages of his recovery.

King was still recovering, though no longer considering retiring, when *On Writing* arrived in stores in October to the usual mixture of positive and negative reviews. Critics did lean more toward the positive. Jonathan V. Last, for example, wrote: "His early works, such as *Carrie* and *'Salem's Lot*, were raw, pulpy stuff. But today Mr. King is on the level of Cormac McCarthy and Elmore Leonard. He may not be Shakespeare, but he has made himself into a fine writer through, it seems, sheer force of will. In many ways, this progression makes him a more admirable figure than the uber-talented literary greats. It certainly makes him a fine subject of study.

Young writers should know that Stephen King is an everyday player who reveres Strunk and White and treats writing like the job it is."[7]

King returned to the stage with The Rock Bottom Remainders in 2001, for the first time since his accident; released an audio only book, *LT's Theory of Pets,* which had been recorded in front of an audience and is related to *Pet Sematary* in that it illustrates his "interest in the horror of the beloved pet" and the making of which, King said, "was particularly enjoyable for me since I was able to experience the reactions of my listeners firsthand"[8]; and entered into a collaboration with the pop star John Mellencamp, who came up with an idea for an opera and presented it to King. "I was in Florida, so John came down and told me the plot. It was kind of a ghostly thing, which is why he thought of me, I guess. I liked the story."[9] The project took seven years to complete. Called "Ghost Brothers of Darkland County," the musical is set in a small Mississippi town and is scheduled to open at the Alliance Theater in Atlanta in April 2009.

The novel *Dreamcatcher,* in which four friends from Derry catch a virus from alien visitors while on a hunting trip in the Maine woods, was scheduled for publication in March 2001. Excerpts from the book appeared in 2,000-word installments on the Web site of *Time* magazine on March 5, 12, and 19, and the entire work arrived in bookstores on the 20th. The book revisited King's brush with death; the novel's main character, Gary Jones, or Jonesy as his friends call him, is severely injured when he is run down by a car. "Everything [Jonesy] thinks, I thought about [my accident]," King told Dale McGarrigle. "The circumstances were different, but I too was hit by somebody who didn't mean to hit me. I was left to cope with feelings, to integrate it into my philosophy of life, and to deal with the pain on some level. But this was a chance to exorcise some of my feelings."[10] The entire book, in fact, had been influenced by King's accident. "To be sure, in *Dreamcatcher,* Mr. King supplies enough spooky effects and space aliens to meet his usual quota of weird frissons and throws in enough messy gastrointestinal side effects to keep this book from seeming to have gone soft," Janet Maslin wrote. "But beneath all that, there is also a new urgency. In this craftily phantasmagoric story about dreams, telepathy and extraterrestrials, the emphasis is less on fear than on the shared will and capacity to survive."[11]

King and Straub released *Black House* on September 15, exactly 20 years to the day from the beginning of the events that take place in the *Talisman.* The new novel revived the character Jack Sawyer, who has recently quit his job as a detective in Los Angeles and moved to a small town in Wisconsin, where children are being killed and partially devoured by a serial killer dubbed The Fisherman by locals. Sawyer is reluctantly drawn into the investigation. Debuting on every bestseller list in the United States, *Black House*, the title of which alludes to Charles Dickens's *Bleak House*, was positively received, earning praise for its drawing on authors who have both popular and critical support. Kevin Bicknell, for instance, observed, it "is almost entirely self-contained, and it owes less to *The Talisman* than it does to Dickens, Poe, William Hope Hodgson's *The House on the Borderlands* and David Lynch's *Twin Peaks*. It is a return to pure gothic horror for both authors, and it's the best thing either has written in years."[12] Similarly, Neil Gaiman wrote, "Initially, I found Jack Sawyer as uncomfortable in his role as the book's hero as he is in his retirement. Surrounded by a magnificent supporting cast of colorful characters, Jack comes off as almost too pure, too perfect; he might have wandered into this Upper Midwestern Hell on Earth from a better place. But as I read on, I began to realize that in many ways *Black House* (only one vowel away from *Bleak House*, the foggy opening of which is quoted in the text) is a Victorian novel. The authors cited, quoted from, glossed in the book are popular writers who once were read and are now both read and respected, particularly Dickens, Twain and Poe."[13]

The same month that the King-Straub book appeared, the film *Hearts in Atlantis* was released. The movie was adapted for the screen by William Goldman, who is best known for writing *Butch Cassidy and the Sundance Kid* (1969); directed by Scott Hicks; and starred Anthony Hopkins as Ted Brautigan. While critics acknowledge the quality of the film, there were questions about its freshness. "The whole thing adds up to a moviegoing experience so familiar as to blunt its moments of shock and dull its flashes of suspense. You've experienced *Hearts in Atlantis*' thrills and emotions before; you know how to feel before the movie tells you. And yet *Hearts in Atlantis*, based on two stories lifted from King's same-titled 1999 bestseller, is as stirring as it is slight, as effective as it is familiar. It is like a great cover version of a song you once hated, a hackneyed ballad made somehow moving in the right hands,"[14] Robert Wilonsky noted. The public was indifferent, as the movie earned less at the box office than it had cost to produce. King was not involved in the production, so except for his usual desire to see projects with his name on them succeed, his interest was limited.

The movie that King was more intimately connected with was *Rose Red*, an ABC miniseries that aired on January 27, 28, and 31, 2002. King had written the screenplay back in 1995, when he and Steven Spielberg had gotten together to collaborate on a haunted house movie. Spielberg continually found problems with King's script and asked for revisions. "It's hard to work with Steven," King recalled. "He had so many good ideas, and I incorporated quite a few of them. But in the end, we had to ask, 'Is this going to be a Steven Spielberg picture or a Stephen King picture?'"[15] The collaboration was thus abandoned. Spielberg made *The Haunting* (1999) but still owned the rights to King's work. Based on the story of Winchester House—a mansion in San Jose, California, built by the woman who inherited the Winchester rifle fortune and that was said to be haunted by the ghosts of the Indians whom her family's rifles killed and who threatened to kill her if she ever finished the house—King's tale is about a house built in 1907 by John P. Rimbauer, an oil magnate, whose wife, Ellen, continuously makes additions to it, until she disappeared in 1952, some say when she was absorbed by the house. Now Joyce Reardon, a professor of paranormal studies, seeks to wake the house and assembles a group to help her.

After King regained control of the rights to his script in 1999, he convinced ABC to produce the idea, finishing up discussions on June 18 of that year, the day before his accident. Once he was able to write again, he expanded the original screenplay to six hours, and the movie was filmed, with King serving as an executive producer and making a cameo as a pizza delivery guy, in the later months of 2000, during which David Dukes, who played Professor Carl Miller, a colleague of Reardon, died. "On a personal level, it was terrible," King remembered. "He was a great guy to work with, a consummate professional. First was the shock. Second, we thought, we've got to do something about it. Craig [R. Baxley, the director,] thought he could use a photo double for some of the shots of him running through the foliage. I rewrote some scenes, so that others could fill in for David."[16] Critics, finding the movie overlong, considered it a failure, as did the executives at ABC, who played it outside a sweeps period. "All of the elements that make a King story so accessible and entertaining are missing from this production," Laura Fries complained. "The working-class bravado of an unlikely hero, the rich character development and remote setting are displaced in favor of a downtown haunted house explored by a bunch of opportunists and outcasts. Filled with a few minor jolts and jumps, *Rose Red* actually loses a good deal of tension and credibility with each passing hour."[17] Viewers, however, were interested, and the miniseries pulled in adequate ratings with around 20 million viewers.

King's next book was *Everything's Eventual: 14 Dark Tales*, a collection of previously published stories including four that were published in the *New Yorker*, "The Man in the Black Suit," "That Feeling, You Can Only Say What It is in French," "All That You Love Will be Carried Away," and "The Death of Jack Hamilton"; two stories that were originally released in audio format, "1408" and "In the Deathroom," the latter of which had also been published in *Secret Windows;* the e-novella, "Riding the Bullet"; the title story; "The Road Virus Heads North," which had appeared in *999,* a 1999 anthology of stories; and the six stories from King's 1997 Philtrum Press collection. Discussing the shrinking short-story market, King wrote in the introduction that he continued to practice the craft of the short story "because it's the way I affirm, at least to myself, the fact that I haven't sold out."[18] Unlike other writers' short story collections, which often end up in remainders' bins, King's, as two of the previous three he had released, ended up on the top spot in the *New York Times* bestseller list.

King's last work to appear in 2002 was *From a Buick 8*—the title of which alludes to Bob Dylan's 1960s song "From a Buick 6"—a novel King had drafted at the beginning of 1999 about an abandoned car with deadly properties, though in a much different fashion than King's earlier evil car, *Christine.* The Buick, rather than running down victims, provides a doorway into another dimension, linking the book to The Dark Tower series, as King would explicitly state a couple of years later. The novel, John Dugdale wrote, "finds the doyen of dread in unusually philosophical mood, more occupied with time, mortality and the nature of the universe."[19] Three years after his accident, it was continuing to influence his fiction, and it would continue to do so for many more years.

NOTES

1. Quoted in Jeff Guinn, "Two Horror Writers in One *Black House,*" *Fort Worth Star-Telegram* (September 6, 2001), Life & Arts, p. 1, http://www.lexis-nexis.com/.

2. Quoted in Stephen Finucan, "So Much Roadkill Fiction," *Toronto Star* (March 25, 2001), http://www.lexis-nexis.com/.

3. Andrea Sachs, "Boo! How He Startled the Book World," *Time* (March 27, 2000), p. 76, http://www.lexis-nexis.com/.

4. Quoted in Ray Routhier, "King Seeks to Gauge Web Honesty," *Portland Press Herald* (June 14, 2000), p. B1, http://www.lexis-nexis.com/.

5. Quoted in Stephan Williams, "King Suspends E-Book Venture," (New York) *Newsday* (November 29, 2000), p. A66, http://www.lexis-nexis.com/.

6. Quoted in Linda Harrison, "Stephen King Reveals *The Plant* Profit," *Register* (February 7, 2001), www.theregister.co.uk/2001/02/07/stephen_king_reveals_the_plant/.

7. Johnathan V. Last, "Serial Killers, '70s Films and Stephen King Tips," *Washington Times* (November 12, 2000), p. B6, http://www.lexis-nexis.com/.

8. Quoted in http://archive.salon.com/audio/fiction/2001/07/17/king_live/index.html.

9. Melinda Newman, "A Musical Ghost Story from Mellencamp & King," *Billboard* (October 28, 2000), http://www.lexis-nexis.com/.

10. Quoted in Dale McGarrigle, "Accident Fodder for King Novel *Dreamcatcher*: Character Shares Author's Thoughts," *Bangor Daily News* (March 22, 2001), p. C1, http://www.lexis-nexis.com/.

11. Janet Maslin, "A Fateful Step off a Curb and into Alien Territory," *New York Times* (March 15, 2001), p. E9, http://www.lexis-nexis.com/.

12. Kevin Bicknell, "*House* Finds King and Cohort in Credibly Creepy Form," *Atlanta Journal-Constitution* (September 15, 2001), p. D5, http://www.lexis-nexis.com/.

13. Neil Gaiman, "Night Crawlers," *Washington Post* (September 16, 2001), p. T2, http://www.lexis-nexis.com/.

14. Robert Wilonsky, "Stand by Them," *Dallas Observer* (September 27, 2001), http://www.lexis-nexis.com/.

15. Quoted in Dale McGarrigle, "The Haunted House that Could," *Bangor Daily News* (January 4, 2002), p. C5, http://www.lexis-nexis.com/.

16. Ibid.

17. Laura Fries, "Stephen King's *Rose Red*," *Daily Variety* (January 24, 2002), p. 15.

18. Stephen King, "Introduction: Practicing the Almost Lost Art," *Everything's Eventual: 14 Dark Tales* (New York: Pocket Books: 2007 [2002]), p. xvi.

19. John Dugdale, "The Supernatural Highway," (London) *Sunday Times* (August 18, 2002), Culture, p. 44, http://www.lexis-nexis.com/.

Chapter 19

RETIRING, AGAIN

King again raised the issue of retirement in 2002, promising to finish The Dark Tower series, fulfill a commitment that he had made to ABC to write a 15-part series called *Kingdom Hospital,* and then quit publishing. "I see myself repeating phrases," he explained. "There are only so many ways to describe someone pulled screaming into the drain. My No. 1 critic is my wife. She'll read something and say, 'Oh, Stephen, this is s____.' Whereas a publisher will think that, while it might be s____, they could sell a lot of them. So I'd like to stop while I'm at the top of my game. Ted Williams ended his career by hitting a home run. I'd be happy with a wall-ball double...."[1] At the same time he vowed never to quit writing: "I love to write. I don't know what I would do with those hours."[2] King again found himself playing with the idea of publishing new material in 2003, saying that if he found he had written something really good at some point, he would likely publish it. He, nonetheless, seemed to be honoring his retirement, limiting his book releases to a heavily revised version of the first volume of The Dark Tower series, as well as *The Dark Tower V: Wolves of the Calla* (2003). Those books were followed, in 2004, with *The Dark Tower VI: Song of Susannah* and *The Dark Tower VII: The Dark Tower.*

Of course, King had other projects, which didn't have anything to do with forthcoming books, in the pipeline. The first of these was Castle Rock's adaptation of *Dreamcatcher,* the rights for which King had sold for $1. King was so happy with the movie that he agreed to actively promote it, even though his involvement had been limited to approving the script, cast, and director—something he had been doing for most of the film adaptations of his work for about 10 years—and suggesting how to redo the ending, when the original one proved problematic. "This movie is amazingly faithful to the book. I haven't seen it in the theater yet.... I looked at it [before the revised ending had been shot], and when I finished it, I looked at my wife and I said, 'I don't know how they did this, but it's my book to the corners.'"[3] Critics, however, were not as enthusiastic about the writer William Goldman and director Lawrence Kasdan's condensing of a more than 600-page novel into a two-hour movie. In a representative review Moira McDonald observed: "*Dreamcatcher* the movie keeps all of [the book's] plot elements, but takes out all the character development and explanations. What's left is a head-scratchingly silly B-movie, blending boyish sentiment and cheesy creature effects, that even Morgan Freeman [who starred as the alien-hunter Kurtz] can't save."[4]

During the summer of 2003, King began to show that the idea of retiring was difficult for him: he agreed to do a monthly column on pop culture called "The Pop of King," which he continues to write, for *Entertainment Weekly*. "A couple of months back," he wrote for his first column, "the editors at *Entertainment Weekly* asked me to review *Harry Potter and the Order of the Phoenix* and either they liked the review itself or liked the fact that it was written in longhand. (For all I know, they might have thought it would be good to have at least one writer on tap who could turn in copy even after a nuclear pulse wiped out the hard drives on all the laptops.) Whatever the reason, they came back and asked me if I'd like to write a column once a month, a thing that I haven't done since college. I decided I'd like to give it a try."[5] The man whose job King took, Joel Stein, would later write: "Two years ago, I lost a job writing a weekly column on the back page of *Entertainment Weekly* to Stephen King. Sure, writing a column isn't all that hard, but I thought I was better at it than King, if only because he covers movies when they open in Maine. Still, I think his columns are more interesting than mine because he gets to report the thoughts of Stephen King."[6]

The summer, in preparation for the release of the last three volumes of The Dark Tower series, which King had revealed were finished, also saw the reissuing of the first four Dark Tower books in hard cover; the revised version of *The Gunslinger* was among them. King could no longer allow the inconsistencies, both within the book and in its relation to the later volumes, to stand, nor could he let what he realized were overwritten passages remain. King took the opportunity to discuss his hopes for the books in a new introduction, explaining, as Charles Coleman Finlay observed, "his desire to fashion an epic novel deeply rooted in the American landscape," something that illustrated Whitman's influence on King's idea." Thus, Finlay continued, "it's no coincidence that an important revelation at the climax of *The Gunslinger* revolves around the image of a single blade of grass,"[7] as the title of Whitman's great book is *Leaves of Grass*. "This is a better version of what always has been one of the better titles in the King *oeuvre*,"[8] John Mark Eberhart observed.

The first of the last volumes, *Wolves of the Calla*, appeared in November, the same month that King received the Medal for Distinguished Contribution to Arts and Letters from the National Book Foundation, confirming, many felt, King's place among the great writers of our age, although granting the award to someone that many high-brow literary critics regard as a hack was controversial. King, who was overcoming pneumonia, addressed the controversy in his acceptance speech, scolding those who condemned his being awarded anything and suggesting that what is considered literature isn't really relevant to contemporary culture. Shirley Hazzard, who won the fiction prize for her novel *The Great Fire*, addressed his remarks: "I want to say in response to Stephen King that I do not—as I think he a little bit seems to do—I don't regard literature, which he spoke of perhaps in a slightly pejorative way, . . . as a competition."[9]

Song of Susannah, the sixth Dark Tower book, was due out the next summer, while the final book, *The Dark Tower*, would be released on King's birthday, September 21, 2004, but first *Kingdom Hospital*—an adaptation of the famed director Lars von Trier's Danish miniseries *Riget* ("Kingdom") that King had first considered working on in 1996, when he saw a video of the original with English subtitles—appeared on television. Negotiations for King to adapt the work had been underway in the late 1990s, but von Trier wanted a big screen version, and, in 1999, discussions with ABC were interrupted by King's accident. Columbia Pictures then won the rights to the work. King's accident changed his approach to the story, and King wrote, in 2000, a version that he hoped would become a miniseries, even though no deal was in place with either ABC or Columbia. His new version incorporated his hospital experience into it, thereby turning the original into a commentary on the U.S. healthcare system. "He was so moved and driven by what he had experienced in the hospital," Mark Carliner, the executive producer of the series, told a press conference. "He came out of the hospital, and he sat down and wrote."[10]

When executives at ABC saw the script, they were enthralled, and they negotiated a deal with Columbia Pictures, who got the rights to adapt "Secret Window, Secret Garden" in the agreement. King, therefore, went back to his script, completing what was now to be a series, in May 2003. "We really sort of backed into [the idea of making a series]; it started out as one of those miniseries things," King told Ray Routhier, whose name King used for the byline of the fictional King obituary in the *Song of Susannah*.

"I didn't really want to do it as a series, but I said maybe I'd do a limited series (13 episodes this year) like *The Sopranos*."[11] The first episode, a two-hour premier that was followed by 11 one-hour episodes and a two-hour conclusion, aired at the beginning of March. Critics were treated to a preview in January, though King was absent from the press conference as he was still recovering from his bout with pneumonia in his Florida home. In his stead was Carliner, who had also worked with King on the remake of *The Shining*. He explained, "What you're seeing here is Lars von Trier as interpreted by Stephen King."[12]

King, although ill and unable to be in Vancouver, where the series was filmed, had remained involved, getting daily footage and offering advice to Carliner, something ABC executives, according to the contract King negotiated, were unable to do. King also served as the narrator in the opening two-hour episode and had control over casting, in which he took a personal interest, for example, helping Bruce Davison get a major part. Davison had worked on the audio version of *From a Buick 8* and impressed King so much that King wrote him a letter that said, "You did a great job. Anytime you want to do something, you are the man."[13] Davison had kept the letter, and when he saw the script for *Kingdom Hospital*, he decided to see if he could use it to get the part of Dr. Stegman, the hospital's chief neurologist. To his surprise King called, asking him, " 'Why do you want to do this?' I said," Davidson recalled, " 'I think the part can really work if it had a kind of vulnerability to carry off all the evil, and I can do that.' He said, 'Well, you go in and do what you can. I'll do what I can.' And he put his head down and he got me the part, finally, after reading and auditioning and everything else. It's not something I'm usually cast as. [Dr. Stegman] is bombastic. He's big and arrogant and totally self-involved."[14]

The series, which cost $37.5 million to produce, premiered a week after ABC aired a pseudo-documentary about the hospital and featured a fictional recreation of King's accident: Peter Rickman, an artist, is hit by a van while jogging because the van driver is distracted by a dog that is trying to get to his steak dinner. Rickman is taken to Kingdom Hospital, which was built on the site where, in 1869, a mill burned, killing a number of children who, it is rumored, haunt the building. The show turned out to be both a critical and ratings disaster "Aside from a few tremors and power outages, nobody seems to think anything's particularly weird about the hospital. Two hours after the thing begins, neither will you," Melanie McFarland wrote. "*Kingdom Hospital* has scant moments that work; Rickman's point of view on his emergency surgery is especially effective, and captures everything we fear about being on the table. For all its attempted nightmare scenarios and spookery, there isn't a single element in the premiere that makes it necessary for you to return next week, let alone 12 more episodes."[15]

Ten days after *Kingdom Hospital* debuted, *Secret Window*, the David Koepp adaptation of "Secret Window, Secret Garden" that starred Johnny Depp, was released. Depp worked with both Koepp and King to develop his interpretation of the role of Mort Rainey, the writer who is suffering writer's block and who is accused of plagiarism by a crazed fan. The movie was one of the more successful King-inspired movies, taking in over $18 million in its first weekend and remaining in theaters for three months, though King's name had not been used as a promotional tool. Depp's star-power, in fact, was the draw that brought audiences to the theaters, and he, in the minds of critics, saved the film. Koepp, Austin O'Connor wrote in a representative review, "knows how to build suspense, appreciates how odd angles can throw an audience off balance, understands how to provide key details without blowing his movie's cover. Skillfully done but a tad too predictable, *Secret Window* works far better than it has any right to. That's thanks mostly to Depp."[16]

King, by the time his television series was being promoted, was again raising questions about his retired status. He had indicated that if *Kingdom Hospital* was popular enough, he could have—with the help of the novelist Richard Dooling, who had also worked with King on the first 15 hours—13 new episodes written by the summer. The series' failure put an end to any speculation that another 13 episodes would be made, but King's work did return to television soon afterwards. A remake of *Salem's Lot*, with a script written by Peter Filardi and starring Rob Lowe as Ben Mears, was aired over two nights on TNT in June. "TV producers have bungled so many attempts to adapt Stephen King novels—including a criminally tedious *Salem's Lot* miniseries in 1979—that I didn't dare get my hopes up for TNT's two-part, four-hour remake," Noel Holston observed. "But screenwriter Peter Filardi (*The Craft*) and director Mikael Salomon (HBO's *Band of Brothers*) have defied the odds, delivering a four-hour, two-night version of King's vampire-infestation parable that ranks with the best filming of his work. It has genuinely scary parts, which is rare enough in video-King, but it's also perfectly in tune with his mordant sense of humor."[17]

Song of Susannah, the penultimate volume in the Dark Series, then appeared. King, as he had done earlier in the series as well as in other novels, linked Roland's realm with our own. This time he did so by inserting himself into the story and then killing himself off in his real-life 1999 accident. The work landed on bestseller lists and reviewed positively. "King gives enough to fascinate our attention, cranking it to fever pitch then dropping us with a curious and vital ending that whips up a frenzy for the final installment. King is as perennial as his story, always pulse-poundingly engaging. He once again proves himself a true master of suspense in a truly monolithic tale,"[18] Sarah Jane Downing observed. Ben Sisario was less impressed, deriding King's fashioning of the other world but pointing out, "King's prose crystallizes whenever he leaves the netherworld; this suggests that his favorite fantasy is not the Byzantine cosmology of another world but a skewed version of our own."[19]

More indicative of King's inability to retire was that he was working on a new book, a work of nonfiction that he had agreed to write with Stewart O'Nan, another novelist who is a Red Sox fan. They had decided to chronicle the Red Sox's season from the perspective of two fans, an aspect of the book that annoyed some reviewers. For example, David King, echoing a number of others, wrote about the final product, "Much of it reads like grammatically corrected Web logs, those bastions of millions of so-called experts whose only qualification to talk about a subject is the fact they own a computer."[20] When the Red Sox managed to win the World Series for the first time since 1918, the book came to be called *Faithful: Two Diehard Boston Red Sox Fans Chronicle the Historic 2004 Season* (2004), and while it drew its fair share of bad reviews, it also had its defenders. "For all its nail-biting real-life drama, *Faithful* is yet another testament to the irrational attraction of blind fandom," Sean O'Hagan wrote. "King is the more illuminating, in part because he is a more accomplished writer, gifted in his powers of description and scene-setting and, in part, because he is a diehard Sox fan, born and bred. O'Nan, on the other hand, seems more obsessed with describing the minutiae of the game in true anorak fashion; interestingly, he shifted his allegiances to the Sox—because he lived close to their ground—after growing up a Pittsburgh Pirates fan."[21]

The movie version of "Riding the Bullet" appeared in October. Lambasted by critics and ignored by the public, the film, having taken in only $134,711, disappeared from theaters after only a week. In the meantime King had been contacted by Charles Ardai, the editor of the Hard Case Crime series, which was developed to revive old-fashion pulp noir and crime novels, to write a blurb for the series. King was so taken by Ardai's desire to revive a genre that he had fallen in love with in the fifties that he decided to write a novel for it, and by the end of February 2005, King had signed a contract to publish a mystery called *The Colorado Kid,* which would appear in October. "This is an exciting line of books," King observed, "and I'm delighted to be a part of it. Hard Case Crime presents good, clean, bare-knuckled storytelling, and even though *The Colorado*

Kid is probably more *bleu* than outright *noir,* I think it has some of those old-fashioned kick-ass story-telling virtues. It ought to; this is where I started out, and I'm pleased to be back."[22] King's novel, which was inspired by a news story about a dead woman found on the coast of Maine, is set in a restaurant on the island of Moose-Lookit, Maine, where a 22-year-old intern, Stephanie, at the local paper, *The Weekly Islander,* is told by the paper's elderly editors about a mystery that has troubled the island since 1980. A 40-year-old man who, it was later discovered, came from Colorado was found dead on the beach with a pack of cigarettes and a Russian coin but no identification.

The details of the mystery unfold as the men respond to Stephanie's questions, but a positive solution is never offered, suggesting that King's interest had less to do with reproducing the pulp genre that Ardai's series was started to save than with playing with the pulp style to pursue "a philosophic goal: contemplating the unanswerable," as Adam Parfrey wrote. Parfrey concluded, "*The Colorado Kid* is Stephen King's existential despair, his *Nausea* or *Waiting for Godot,* in which he equates the structural straitjackets of genre fiction with greedy fundamentalism. 'A lot of churches,' King writes in the afterword, 'have what they assure us are the answers, but most of us have a sneaking suspicion all that might be a con-job laid down to fill the collection plates. In the meantime, we're in a kind of compulsory dodgeball game as we free-fall from Wherever to Ain't Got a Clue.'"[23] Other critics were disappointed with King's unwillingness to write an actual hardboiled mystery, something that King had expected, writing in the afterword, "Mystery is my subject here, and I am aware that many readers will feel cheated, even angry, by my failure to provide a solution to the one posed."[24] Thus Bruce Westbrook complains that King's contribution to the series "is no lurid romp but a perversely thin look at a dead-end mystery."[25]

The Colorado Kid was, in a way, a demonstration of King's generosity: his name on one of the books in Ardai's series, after all, brought it attention and an assured profit, since a large number of King's fans—100,000 in fact—would buy the book. King's generous nature was on display in different ways as the year ended. He donated to *Weekly Reader* online an opening for a story called "The Furnace," which American students were encouraged to finish, to help encourage young people to become interested in writing. He also donated, through his foundation, $50,000 to St. Croix Regional Technical Center and the Washington County Community College, both of which are located near Bangor, so that they could build new facilities for their early childhood education programs.

NOTES

1. Quoted in Marshall Fine, "Final," *Journal News* (September 27, 2002), p. E1, http://www.lexis-nexis.com/.

2. Ibid.

3. Quoted in "In Good Faith with the King of Horror," *Chicago Sun-Times* (March 16, 2003), Show, p. 1, http://www.lexis-nexis.com/.

4. Moira McDonald, "*Dreamcatcher:* Run, Before It's Too Late," *Seattle Times* (March 21, 2003), p. H19, http://www.lexis-nexis.com/.

5. Quoted in Dale McGarrigle, "King to Take up Pen for Magazine," *Bangor Daily News* (August 5, 2003), p. C1, http://www.lexis-nexis.com/.

6. Joel Stein, "Celebrity Bloggers? That's Stephen King-Scary," *Los Angeles Times* (May 15, 2005), p. M2, http://www.lexis-nexis.com/.

7. Coleman Finlay, "Author Finishes Dark Tower Series, Revises First Volume," *Columbus Dispatch* (June 23, 2003), p. D8, http://www.lexis-nexis.com/.

8. John Mark Eberhart, "Newly Remodeled: Stephen King Shores up First Book in Dark Tower Series," *Kansas City Star* (June 29, 2003), Arts, p. 16, http://www.lexis-nexis.com/.

9. Quoted in Colette Bancroft, "The Great Divide between Popular and Literary Narrows," *Pittsburgh Post-Gazette* (January 29, 2004), p. D4, http://www.lexis-nexis.com/.

10. Quoted in Hal Boedeker, "ABC Hopes King Can Cure Its Misery," *Orlando Sentinel* (January 17, 2004), p. E1, http://www.lexis-nexis.com/.

11. Quoted in Ray Routhier, "TV's *Kingdom Hospital* Premieres Wednesday," *Portland Press Herald* (February 29, 2004), p. E1, http://www.lexis-nexis.com/.

12. Quoted in Hal Boedeker, "ABC Hopes King Can Cure Its Misery."

13. Quoted in Alex Ben Block, "Bruce Davison: Character Counts," *Television Week* (February 23, 2004), p. 10, http://www.lexis-nexis.com/.

14. Ibid.

15. Melanie McFarland, "*Kingdom Hospital* Offers a Fear Factor of Zilch," *Seattle Post-Intelligencer* (March 2, 2004), p. E1, http://www.lexis-nexis.com/.

16. Austin O'Connor, "Depp Suffers Scary Writer's Block in *Secret Window*," *Lowell Sun* (March 11, 2004), http://www.lexis-nexis.com/.

17. Noel Holston, "Vampires with Biting Humor: The Best of the *Lot*," (New York) *Newsday* (June 20, 2004), p. 11, http://www.lexis-nexis.com/.

18. Sarah Jane Downing, "Fantasy World of the Lord of Dark, Magical Frenzies," *Sunday Express* (June 27, 2004), p. 68, http://www.lexis-nexis.com/.

19. Ben Sisario, "Books in Brief," *New York Times* (June 20, 2004), sec. 7, p. 16, http://www.lexis-nexis.com/.

20. David King, "*Faithful* Will Appeal Only to Die-Hard Boston Red Sox Fans," *San Antonio Express-News* (December 19, 2004), p. 71, http://www.lexis-nexis.com/.

21. Sean O'Hagan, "Who Needs Babe Ruth?: When the Boston Red Sox at Last Reigned Supreme, Two Fans Recorded Their Finest Hour," *Observer* (January 16, 2005), p. 15, http://www.lexis-nexis.com/.

22. Quoted in Business Wire (February 28, 2005), http://www.lexis-nexis. com/.

23. Adam Parfrey, "Stephen King Serves up Pulp Softly Boiled," *Los Angeles Times* (October 5, 2005), p. E9, http://www.lexis-nexis.com/.

24. Stephen King, *The Colorado Kid* (New York: Hard Case Crime, 2005), p. 182.

25. Bruce Westbrook, "Endearing Characters Can't Save Crime Caper," *Houston Chronicle* (October 9, 2005), *Zest,* p. 19, http://www.lexis-nexis.com/.

Chapter 20

HIS BUSY RETIREMENT CONTINUES

Faithful and *The Colorado Kid* may have belied King's apparent intention to retire, but these books were unlike those King wrote for professional reasons. The baseball book, after all, was a one-off nonfiction book, and the short novel was more akin to the collectors' editions that he had published for his own pleasure. In between the release of these two books, however, King fully abandoned the idea of just writing for the sake of writing, signing contracts to publish two new novels, *Cell*, which would be released early in 2006 and which he said would be "like cheap whisky . . . very nasty and extremely satisfying,"[1] and *Lisey's Story*, for which King would revive Castle Rock and which would be released in the fall of 2006. In fact, other projects with King's name on them, some of which King had written original material for, were made available in 2006, including the television adaptation of *Desperation*, the script for which was King's; an eight-episode series containing made-for-TV adaptations of King short stories; a new book of short stories called *The Secretary of Dreams*; and an audio book called *Stationary Bike*.

In a move that served his philanthropic spirit and helped to promote *Cell*, King participated with 15 authors, including John Grisham and Amy Tan, in an eBay auction. For sale was the right to name a character in a forthcoming book. The auction for the King character became the most watched auction on eBay, and in September 2005 Pam Alexander of Fort Lauderdale, paid $25,100 for the right to name a character after her brother, Ray Huizenga, whose fictional persona, before shooting himself, helps the novel's hero, Clayton Riddell—a comic book artist who serves as King's mouthpiece. The proceeds from the auction went to support a

Californian non-profit group called the First Amendment Project that promotes free speech.

Four months later *Cell*—in which a signal, the Pulse, is sent through cell phones, turning those who have them into zombies and leaving those without them as normies—arrived in bookstores. The same day a text message appeared on 100,000 cell phones that read: "The next call you take may be your last....Join the Stephen King VIP Club at http://www.cellthebook.com."[2] King also provided his voice for ring tones, which said: "Beware. The next call you take may be your last" and "It's okay, it's a normie calling."[3] The book marked King's return to the brand of horror with which he had made his name. Brendan O'Neill thus observed, "For this King fan, *Cell* represents a welcome return to form...[King is] back where he belongs, in the real world, doing what he does best: making the real world seem like a totally freaky place."[4] Indeed, the horror element of the tale brought King the most positive attention. Dave Itzkoff, for example, called that aspect of the novel the most satisfying, writing, "As you may recall from Aristotle's discussion of the form in the *Poetics*, an effective zombie apocalypse story should satisfy two conditions. First, it should fulfill an audience's desire to see aberrant acts of violence triggered by civilization's collapse, and in this respect *Cell* does not disappoint: there's still no other writer who takes as much delight as King does in rendering the sight of a soccer field's worth of zombies being charbroiled out of existence, or a poodle getting run over by a car ('Fluff at one moment; guts at the next')." He concluded, "Second, a good zombie tale should offer some fresh insights about basic human nature, if only to pass the time between episodes of cannibalism, and it's in this capacity that *Cell* turns out to be a bit brain-dead."[5]

Cell was a huge success for King, but *Desperation*, which was filmed at the end of 2005 and aired on ABC on May 23, turned out to be one of the lesser King adaptations. "Veteran best-selling novelist John Edward Marinville, titular head of Stephen King's latest TV opus, devotes his last breath to bellowing 'I hate critics!' OK, be that way," Ed Bark quipped. "But hey, King Stephen, we're not the ones grinding this stuff out for the small screen. You are. And frankly, your fastball has long since faded to a batting practice pitch. That leaves ABC on the receiving end of Stephen King's *Desperation*, a three-hour blend of mumbo jumbo and gore galore."[6] Up against that season's penultimate show of the popular series *American Idol*, the movie had little hope of becoming a rating's juggernaut.

Desperation was followed by TNT's *Nightmares & Dreamscapes: From the Stories of Stephen King*, an eight-episode series that presented a different King story each week, most of them from the collection from which the series took its name: "Umney's Last Case," "The End of the Whole Mess," "Crouch End," "The Fifth Quarter," "Autopsy Room Four," "You Know They Got a Hell of a Band," "Battleground," and "The Road Virus Heads North." When it came out on DVD later in the year, T. Michael Testi, giving the collection an overall grade of A-, with "Autopsy Room Four" receiving the lowest individual grade, a C, wrote, "Like any collection, even within a greatest hits collection, some are better than others. And your favorites may not be mine. But overall, I would recommend *Nightmares & Dreamscapes* for anyone who likes their spine tingled and especially those who are Stephen King fans."[7] TNT was pleased enough with the results to seek out more King projects, and in the fall the station announced that King was going to work on "The Talisman" with Spielberg, who has owned the movie rights to the story since the 1980s.

During the summer King released his audio book, *Stationary Bike*, a novella that had previously appeared in the anthology *Borderlands 5* (2004) and in which Richard Sifkitz obsessively exercises on his stationary bike and builds a fantasy world that turns dark. King also released the short-story collection, *The Secretary of Dreams*, with the small fantasy publisher, Cemetery Dance Publications. His next major publication would be *Lisey's Story*, a novel that he had begun in 2003. "The seed of the novel," Motoko Rich wrote, paraphrasing King, "came after he had returned from the hospital and his wife, Tabitha, had started renovating his office. When he walked into the room, in a converted barn, the rugs were gone, and most of his books and papers were boxed up. 'I went in there, and I could barely walk, and I could barely breathe,' he recalled. 'I thought, this is what places look like when somebody's died. I thought to myself, this is what it is like to be a ghost.'"[8] He then started thinking about a book about a widow who was the force behind her famous husband, the Pulitzer Prize–winning novelist Scott Landon. King's own wife served as the model for the principal character, and Nan Graham at Scribner edited the piece, rather than Verrill, as King thought a woman would do a better job on a book narrated by a woman.

The book also marked a major change in King's approach to his art: while writing he concerned himself with his use of language as much as he did with the story, a procedure that he had suggested was wrong-headed earlier in his career. The change in attitude was a result of King's reading more poetry, particularly that of D. H. Lawrence, Richard Wilbur, and James Dickey, and other literary figures. "You get older, you find out time is shorter, and you read stuff that you've missed before. You say, 'I can't wait forever anymore to read Eudora Welty.' I finally got to Eudora Welty, so maybe I'm just meeting a better class of literary person."[9] The new focus made for a powerful book, leading Brent A. Bowles to write, King's "most recent novel, *Lisey's Story*, demonstrates not just his deft use of language and crisp story construction, but also the dizzying blend of fantasy and reality that binds the reader to a rich and magnificent tale."[10] Not everyone, even when they were impressed by the work, appreciated the language, however. "Here is a tender, intimate book that makes an epic interior journey without covering much physical terrain. It can move great distances while traveling no further than from a house (home to lonely Lisey Landon, the widow of a writer à la King) to its neighboring barn," Janet Maslin wrote but went on to observe, "His use of language in *Lisey's Story* is so larded with baby talk that it borders on the pathological. Here is a writer who has a thousand ways of naming a toilet, and whose work can thus be an acquired taste. But *Lisey's Story* transcends the toidy-talk to plumb thoughts of love, mortality and madness—and to deliver them with gale-force emotion. When Mr. King writes in a coda to this blunt but stunning book that 'much here is heartfelt, very little is clever,' he is telling the truth."[11]

Throughout 2006 King was also working on the comic-book version of *The Gunslinger*, a project based on The Dark Tower series that he had agreed to do with Marvel comics in 2005. Originally slated for release in 2006, King and Marvel quickly realized that they had been too optimistic about their ability to complete the project so quickly, and by the end of 2005, they had put back the completion date to 2007. "Given the size of the project and all the creative talent involved, I want to give the Marvel series all the room to breathe it needs and deserves," King said in a statement released on his Web site. "I've got so much else going on in 2006."[12] The seven-issue series *The Dark Tower: The Gunslinger Born*, which was primarily based on the content of the fourth novel in the series, *Wizard and Glass*, thus didn't appear until February 2007. Written, with King's input, by Peter David, a well-known figure in comic book circles, and Robin Furth, who has established himself as an expert on King's series, and illustrated by Jae Lee and Richard Isanove, the comics pleased King. "I had a lot of involvement in casting the course of the narrative," King said. "Beyond that, I wanted to give a lot of control over to these other imaginations, which I had come to respect.... Do I absolutely love everything? Nope. It's a collaboration. But I absolutely love a lot, and in an imperfect world, that's just about Nirvana."[13] Comic book lovers were pleased as well, and in March, Marvel announced that it would produce another set of King comics. The first issue of the second one, *Dark Tower: The Long Road Home*, was released in March 2008.

As the first set of comics were issued, King was working on two novels, revising the manuscript of *Blaze*, which he had drafted in the mid-1970s, and writing *Duma Key* (2008). He was also performing his now usual role—approving scripts, casts, and offering a little input—on two film-adaptations of his work, the TNT miniseries "The Talisman" and the big-screen production, *The Mist*. Explaining his approach to the films that bore his name, he observed, "You just go in there and bang it and see what falls out. Trash or treasure? I almost don't care which. Sometimes good things happen. I really thought Rob Reiner did something exceptional when he turned 'The Body' into *Stand By Me*. I felt the same way about *Shawshank*. But then I thought *Dreamcatcher* would be good, and it wasn't."[14]

Blaze, which tells the story of Clay "Blaze" Blaisdell, a simple-minded giant who, as the sidekick of a conman named George, gets involved in a plot to kidnap the child of a famous tycoon for a $1 million ransom, was finished first. King had recalled the long-forgotten manuscript about a year after completing *The Colorado Kid*, thinking that it might work for a follow up with the Hard Case Crime imprint. When his assistant Marsha DeFilippo dug the manuscript out of a box at the Fogler Library, King found that it did not fit Ardai's needs but "could be rewritten and published without too much embarrassment."[15] King thus set about rewriting the story—stripping "all the sentiment I could" from it with the hope of making "the finished book...as stark as an empty house without even a rug on the floor."[16] He released it as the last posthumous novel of Richard Bachman and donated the royalties to the Haven Foundation, which King had set up after his accident in 1999 to help artists who were down on their luck. "What we get," Jon Courtenay Grimwood explained, "is King's former alter ego channelling John Steinbeck, in a novel that reads like *Of Mice and Men* written as a crime caper. Clay is an honourable man in a dishonourable life, never given a chance and headed for a fate the reader can guess before even opening the book. The kidnapping is doomed, and Clay leaves so many clues it's not a question of whether the police will identify him but of when."[17] No one, including King, claimed that the book showed King at his best, but it nonetheless became a bestseller.

King followed *Blaze* with "The Gingerbread Girl," a 21,000-word story about a woman who flees to Florida after her baby dies and finds herself in the hands of a madman. When it was published in its entirety, in the July issue of *Esquire*, King was compared to such figures as Norman Mailer, who had also published work in *Esquire*. Something else placed King in the company of big-name literary figures later in the year; the *Paris Review*, one of the most respected literary journals in the United States, published a lengthy interview with him and, in the Fall 2007 issue, published a new short story called "Ayana."

1408, a movie based on a short story of the same name, then arrived in theaters. Starring John Cusack as Mike Enslin, a man who makes his living debunking supernatural stories, and Samuel L. Jackson as Gerald Olin, the hotel manager who begs Enslin to stay out of room 1408, the movie made more than $20 million in its opening weekend and remained in theaters until October, even though it "breaks no new ground," as Michael Phillips noted. It did, Phillips went on to write, "plo[w] old ground with style. Bits such as an unkillable clock radio going off at startling moments can work, still, if you do them correctly. There is one aspect that feels abrupt: Enslin's transition from blasé cynic to cold-sweat believer comes rather suddenly at the film's midpoint. Later, some of the more elaborate room-morphing visual touches lack a touch of black magic. But it's a good, solid scare picture, modestly scaled but well-crafted."[18]

The year ended for King with the release of the movie *The Mist*—which had been shot as if it were a documentary by Darabont—in November. Taking in around $9 million in its opening weekend, the movie was a fairly successful film for the King catalogue, receiving its share of positive reviews, though some critics complained that the special effects were cheesy. As if responding to such complaints, Jay Stone observed, "King is talking about a lot of things here, including the thinness of the veneer that keeps us civilized and the brutality of self-preservation when it is pierced.... [T]hat is far more frightening than anything the special effects department can dream up."[19]

King's latest novel, *Duma Key*, his first full-length book set in Florida, arrived in bookstores in January of 2008. It was set on the island, from which the book gets its title, where King now spends the winter months, and once again King found himself exploring the relationship between suffering physical trauma and the redemptive power of creativity, though painting, not writing, is the art that the main character, Edgar Freemantle, takes up after getting into a traffic accident and losing everything that is important to him. "King may be meditating on the diverse powers of the creative soul, but he has in no way lost his unmatched gift for ensnaring and chilling his readers with 'terrible fishbelly fingers.'"[20] Others felt that although the book was well written, King had gone too far. "While the first half of the novel may be the finest prose King has ever written, the author overdoes it a bit in the second half. Even if Edgar knew he was a character in a Stephen King novel, I doubt he would have expected all he ends up having to endure. In fact, it's easy to imagine the Biblical Job reading *Duma Key* and saying, 'Come on, Steve, take it easy on Ed.' But don't imagine for a minute that even Job would have been able to put the book down until he had read the last page. At 60 years old (as of last September 21), King is at the height of his powers as a storyteller here."[21]

King continues to write, publish, and see his work adapted for film. Two miniseries, "The Talisman" and "Faithful: Two Diehard Boston Red Sox Fans Chronicle the Historic 2004 Season" are scheduled to appear over the next two years, as well as three movies, "Creepshow 3," "Cell," and "From a Buick 8." King recently published another short-story collection, *Just After Sunset*, and is planning to release another volume of *The Secretary of Dreams* with Cemetery Dance Publications. He also is working on a novella called "Throttle" with his son, who now publishes horror fiction under the name Joe Hill. It will appear in "He Is Legend: An Anthology Celebrating Richard Matheson" at the beginning of 2009. Retirement, at least for King, is a very busy time.

NOTES

1. Quoted in Garance Burke, "EBay Fictional Character Auction Wins for Charity," *Ventura County Star* (September 20, 2005), p. 3, http://www.lexis-nexis.com/.

2. Quoted in Jeffrey A. Trachtenberg, "Stephen King Tries to Ring up Sales through Text Messages," Associated Press Financial Wire (January 17, 2006), http://www.lexis-nexis.com/.

3. Ibid.

4. Brendan O'Neill, "Wrong Number," *New Statesman* (March 27, 2006), p. 54, http://www.lexis-nexis.com/.

5. Dave Itzkoff, "Dead Ringers," *New York Times Book Review* (February 5, 2006), p. 15, http://www.lexis-nexis.com/.

6. Ed Bark, "Stephen King's Latest Flick a Muddled Creepshow," *Bradenton Herald* (May 21, 2006), p. 6, http://www.lexis-nexis.com/.

7. T. Michael Testi, "DVD Review: *Nightmares & Dreamscapes from Stephen King*," Blogcritics.org Video (November 8, 2006), http://www.lexis-nexis.com/.

8. Motoko Rich, "A King Book that Transcends Horror," *International Herald Tribune* (October 6, 2006), p. 9, http://www.lexis-nexis.com/.

9. Ibid.

10. Brent A. Bowles, "The Examination of a Marriage," *Virginian-Pilot* (November 26, 2006), p. E3, http://www.lexis-nexis.com/.

11. Janet Maslin, "Her Story of Him, Both Tender and Terrible," *New York Times* (October 23, 2006), p. E1, http://www.lexis-nexis.com/.

12. Quoted in Dan Koller, "King's Too Damn Busy," *Dallas Morning News* (December 7, 2005), p. 20, http://www.lexis-nexis.com/.

13. Quoted in "Scene & Heard," (Albany) *Times Union* (December 22, 2006), p. D22, http://www.lexis-nexis.com/.

14. Quoted in Charles McGrath, "A Foggy Reunion with Horror's Master," *New York Times* (November 18, 2007), p. 6, http://www.lexis-nexis.com/.

15. Stephen King, "Full Disclosure," in *Blaze* (New York: Pocket Books, 2007), p. 5.

16. Ibid., p. 6.

17. Jon Courtenay Grimwood, "A Giant, a Kidnap and a Block of Cheese," (London) *Daily Telegraph* (June 9, 2007), p. 26, http://www.lexis-nexis.com/.

18. Michael Phillips, "*1408:* The Room for Quality Chills," *Chicago Tribune* (June 22, 2007), p. C1, http://www.lexis-nexis.com/.

19. Jay Stone, "King Eyes Monsters Within," *Times Colonist* (November 24, 2007), p. D5, http://www.lexis-nexis.com/.

20. Brigitte Weeks, "Stephen King Wields an Artist's Dark Palette," *Washington Post* (January 16, 2008), p. C1.

21. Mark Graham, "King Plot No Accident: Author Shapes Character from His Own Experience in New Novel, *Duma Key*," *Rocky Mountain News* (January 18, 2008), p. 30, http://www.lexis-nexis.com/.

SELECTED BIBLIOGRAPHY

PRIMARY SOURCES
Novels

King, Stephen. *Carrie*. New York: Doubleday, 1974.

———. *'Salem's Lot*. New York: Doubleday, 1975.

———. *The Shining*. New York: Doubleday, 1977.

———. *The Stand*. New York: Doubleday, 1978.

———. *The Dead Zone*. New York: Viking, 1979.

———. *Firestarter*. New York: Viking, 1980.

———. *Cujo*. New York: Viking, 1981.

———. *The Dark Tower: The Gunslinger*. Hampton Falls, NH: Donald M. Grant Publisher, Inc., 1982.

———. *Christine*. New York: Viking, 1983.

———. *Pet Sematary*. New York: Doubleday, 1983.

———. *Cycle of the Werewolf*. Detroit, MI: Land of Enchantment, 1983.

———. *The Talisman*. New York: Viking, 1984.

———. *The Eyes of the Dragon*. Bangor, ME: Philtrum Press, 1984.

———. *Silver Bullet*. New York: Signet, 1985.

———. *It*. New York: Viking, 1986.

———. *The Tommyknockers*. New York: Viking, 1987.

———. *Misery*. New York: Viking, 1987.

———. *The Dark Tower II: The Drawing of the Three*. Hampton Falls, NH: Donald M. Grant Publisher, Inc., 1987.

———. *The Dark Half*. New York: Viking, 1989.

———. *The Stand, The Complete and Uncut Edition*. New York: Doubleday, 1990.

———. *Needful Things*. New York: Viking, 1991.

———. *The Dark Tower III: The Waste Lands*. Hampton Falls, NH: Donald M. Grant Publisher, Inc., 1991.

———. *Gerald's Game*. New York: Viking, 1992.

———. *Dolores Claiborne*. New York: Viking, 1992.

———. *Insomnia*. New York: Viking, 1994.

———. *Rose Madder*. New York: Viking, 1995

———. *The Green Mile 1: "The Two Dead Girls."* New York: Penguin, 1996.

———. *The Green Mile 2: "The Mouse on the Mile."* New York: Penguin, 1996.

———. *The Green Mile 3: "Coffey's Hands."* New York: Penguin, 1996.

———. *The Green Mile 4: "The Bad Death of Edward Delacroix."* New York: Penguin, 1996.

———. *The Green Mile 5: "Night Journey."* New York: Penguin, 1996.

———. *The Green Mile 6: "Coffey on the Mile."* New York: Penguin, 1996.

———. *Desperation*. New York: Viking, 1996.

———. *The Dark Tower IV: Wizard and Glass*. Hampton Falls, NH: Donald M. Grant Publisher, Inc., 1997.

———. *Bag of Bones*. New York: Scribner, 1998.

———. *The Girl Who Loved Tom Gordon*. New York: Scribner, 1999.

———. *Hearts in Atlantis*. New York: Scribner, 1999.

———. *Dreamcatcher*. New York: Scribner, 2001.

———. *Black House* (with Peter Straub). New York: Random House, 2001.

———. *From a Buick 8*. New York: Scribner, 2002.

———. *The Dark Tower V: Wolves of The Calla*. Hampton Falls, NH: Donald M. Grant Publisher, Inc., 2003.

———. *The Dark Tower VI: Song of Susannah*. Hampton Falls, NH: Donald M. Grant Publisher, Inc., 2004.

———. *The Dark Tower VII: The Dark Tower*. Hampton Falls, NH: Donald M. Grant Publisher, Inc., 2004.

———. *The Colorado Kid*. New York: Hard Case Crime, 2005.

———. *Cell*. New York: Scribner, 2006.

———. *Lisey's Story*. New York: Scribner, 2006.

———. *Duma Key*. New York: Scribner, 2008.

Fiction Collections

King, Stephen. *Night Shift*. New York: Doubleday, 1978.

———. *Different Seasons*. New York: Viking, 1982.

———. *Skeleton Crew*. New York: Viking, 1985.

———. *The Bachman Books: Four Early Novels*. New York: New American Library, 1985.

———. *Four Past Midnight*. New York: Viking, 1990.

———. *Nightmares & Dreamscapes*. New York: Viking, 1993.

———. *Six Stories Story*. Bangor, ME: Philtrum Press, 1997.

———. *Everything's Eventual: 14 Dark Tales*. New York: Scribner, 2002.

———. *The Secretary of Dreams*. Forest Hill, MD: Cemetery Dance Publications, 2006.

Non-Fiction

King, Stephen, *Danse Macabre*. New York: Everest House, 1981.

———. *On Writing: A Memoir of the Craft*. New York: Scribner, 2000.

———. *Secret Windows: Essays and Fiction on the Craft of Writing*. New York: Book of the Month Club, 2000.

———. *Faithful: Two Diehard Boston Red Sox Fans Chronicle the Historic 2004 Season*. New York: Scribner, 2004.

As Richard Bachman

Bachman, Richard. *Rage*. New York: New American Library, 1977.

———. *The Long Walk*. New York: New American Library, 1979.

———. *Roadwork*. New York: New American Library, 1981.

———. *The Running Man*. New York: New American Library, 1982.

———. *Thinner*. New York: New American Library, 1984.

———. *The Regulators*. New York: Dutton, 1996.

———. *Blaze*. New York: Scribner, 2007.

Web Sites

http://www.stephenking.com/index_flash.php

http://www.kingclub.ru/e-books/shortstories/rares/eng/htm/Glass-Floor-htm.htm

http://www.nationalbook.org/nbaacceptspeech_sking.html

SECONDARY SOURCES

"2nd Circuit Allows 'Based On' Credit for 'Lawnmower Man': Lanham Act: King v. Allied Vision Ltd." *Entertainment Litigation Reporter* (November 23, 1992), http://www.lexis-nexis.com/.

Ackerman, Forrest J. *Monster's Movie Gold*. Norfolk, VA: Donning Company, 1982.

Anstead, Alicia. "Fly by Night: New Stephen King Thriller Satisfies Craving for Gore, Suspense." *Bangor Daily News* (February 6, 1998), http://www.lexis-nexis.com/.

Anthony, Ted. "Real Horror: Stephen King's Scary Stories Ring Eerily True." *Chicago Sun-Times* (October 27, 1996), p. NC25, http://www.lexis-nexis.com/.

AOL Interview 1996, http://www.stephen-king.de/interviews/aol96.html.

Arkansas Democrat-Gazette (April 26, 1985), http://www.lexis-nexis.com/.

Arkansas Democrat-Gazette (August 22, 1986), http://www.lexis-nexis.com/.

Arnold, Gary. "Kubrick's $12 Million Shiner." *Washington Post* (June 13, 1980), p. E1, http://www.lexis-nexis.com/.

———. "*Cujo*: A Really Bad Dog." *Washington Post* (August 16, 1983), p. B11, http://www.lexis-nexis.com/.

Arnold, William. "Stephen King's *Misery* Never Lets up on the Thrills." *Seattle Post-Intelligencer* (November 30, 1990), p. 5, http://www.lexis-nexis.com/.

Atherton, Tony. "King Novel Wilts in TV Adaptation." *Ottawa Citizen* (May 7, 1994), p. F7, http://www.lexis-nexis.com/.

Bancroft, Colette. "The Great Divide between Popular and Literary Narrows." *Pittsburgh Post-Gazette* (January 29, 2004), p. D4, http://www.lexis-nexis.com/.

Bark, Ed. "Stephen King's Latest Flick a Muddled Creepshow." *Bradenton Herald* (May 21, 2006), p. 6, http://www.lexis-nexis.com/.

Base, Ron. "Toronto Kids Carry King's Werewolf Movie." *Toronto Star* (October 15, 1985), p. B1, http://www.lexis-nexis.com/.

———. "Stephen King Makes the Worst Stephen King Movie Ever Made." *Toronto Star* (July 25, 1986), p. D12, http://www.lexis-nexis.com/.

Beahm, George. *Stephen King from A to Z: An Encyclopedia of His Life and Work.* Kansas City, MO: Andrews and McMeel, 1988.

———. *The Stephen King Story.* Kansas City, MO: Andrews and McMeel, 1992.

———. *Stephen King: America's Best Loved Boogeyman.* Kansas City, MO: Andrews and McMeel, 1998.

———. Ed. *The Stephen King Companion.* Kansas City, MO: Andrews and McMeel, 1995.

Beaulieu, Janet C. "An Interview with Stephen King," http://carolinanavy.com/navy/creativewriting/sking/view.html.

Bickelhaupt, Susan. "King's Game Remains Horror." *Boston Globe* (January 14, 1994), Living, p. 36, http://www.lexis-nexis.com/.

Bicknell, Kevin. "*House* Finds King and Cohort in Credibly Creepy Form." *Atlanta Journal-Constitution* (September 15, 2001), p. D5, http://www.lexis-nexis.com/.

Biederman, Patricia Ward. "On the Road for a Novel Tour: Prolific Author Donald E. Westlake is Now Signing Copies of His Latest Work, *Baby Would I*

Lie?, for Fans at a Bookstore Near You." *Los Angeles Times* (September 23, 1994), *Valley Life*, p. 9, http://www.lexis-nexis.com/.

Bleiler, Everett F. "The Ghosts of Christmas Present." *Washington Post* (December 23, 1984), Book World, p. 11, http://www.lexis-nexis.com/.

Block, Alex Ben. "Bruce Davison: Character Counts." *Television Week* (February 23, 2004), p. 10, http://www.lexis-nexis.com/.

Blonsky, Marshall. "Hooked on Horror." *Washington Post* (August 13, 1989), p. B1, http://www.lexis-nexis.com/.

Bloom, Harold. "Dumbing Down American Readers." *Boston Globe* (September 24, 2003), http://www.boston.com/news/globe/editorial_opinion/oped/articles/2003/09/24/dumbing_down_american_readers.

Bobbin, Jay. "Stephen King: TV with Twist." *St. Louis Post-Dispatch* (July 14, 1991), TV Magazine, p. 5, http://www.lexis-nexis.com/.

Boedeker, Hal. "ABC Hopes King Can Cure Its Misery." *Orlando Sentinel* (January 17, 2004), p. E1, http://www.lexis-nexis.com/.

———. "*Shining* Loses Its Luster over 6 Hours." *Orlando Sentinel* (April 27, 1997), p. F1, http://www.lexis-nexis.com/.

Bohjalian, Chris. "The Ghouls Next Door." *New York Times Book Review* (October 30, 1994), p. 24.

Bokamper, Jerry. "*Sematary* is a Shody Potboiler." *Arkansas Democrat-Gazette* (April 22, 1989), http://www.lexis-nexis.com/.

Bolotin, Susan. "Don't Turn Your Back on This Book." *New York Times* (June 9, 1985), sec. 7, p. 11, http://www.lexis-nexis.com/.

Bowles, Brent A. "The Examination of a Marriage." *Virginian-Pilot* (November 26, 2006), p. E3, http://www.lexis-nexis.com/.

Bruni, Frank. "Human Spirit Triumphs in Prison Drama *Shawshank*." *Detroit Free Press* (September 23, 1994), p. 4D, http://www.lexis-nexis.com/.

"Burglar Armed with Fake Bomb Caught in Stephen King's Home." United Press International (April 20, 1991), http://www.lexis-nexis.com/.

Burke, Garance. "EBay Fictional Character Auction Wins for Charity." *Ventura County Star* (September 20, 2005), p. 3, http://www.lexis-nexis.com/.

Butler, Robert W. "Hello, This is Oscar Calling: It Could Happen." *Kansas City Star* (October 7, 1994), p. H20, http://www.lexis-nexis.com/.

Canby, Vincent. "*Creepshow*, In Five Parts." *New York Times* (November 10, 1982), p. C23, http://www.lexis-nexis.com/.

———. "*Children of the Corn*, Based on King Story." *New York Times* (March 16, 1984), p. C7, http://www.lexis-nexis.com/.

———. "The Screen, *Cat's Eye*." *New York Times* (April 12, 1985), p. C8, http://www.lexis-nexis.com/.

Carr, Jay. "*Pet Sematary*: No Flowers, Please." *Boston Globe* (April 21, 1989), p. 46, http://www.lexis-nexis.com/.

Carvajal, Doreen. "Who Can Afford Him?: Stephen King Goes in Search of a New Publisher." *New York Times* (October 27, 1997), p. D1, http://www.lexis-nexis.com/.

———. "Stephen King Unleashed." *New York Times* (November 9, 1998), p. C1, http://www.lexis-nexis.com/.

Castleman, Riva. *A Century of Artists Books*. New York: Museum of Modern Art, 1994.

Cerone, Daniel. "What Does King Think?" *Los Angeles Times* (November 18, 1990), p. 82, http://www.lexis-nexis.com/.

Chatain, Robert. "King of the Creeps: Four Chilling Tales from Stephen King, Our Modern Master of Suspense." *Chicago Tribune* (August 26, 1990), p. C3, http://www.lexis-nexis.com/.

Chelton, Mary K. "*Pet Sematary* (Book Review)." *Voice of Youth Advocates* v. 7 (April 1984), p. 32, http://vnweb.hwwilsonweb.com/hww.

Chin, Paula, and Eric Francis. "Beyond Misery." *People* (January 24, 2000), p. 125, http://www.lexis-nexis.com/.

Colford, Paul D. "INK / Suspense as a Marketing Tactic." (New York) *Newsday* (February 8, 1996), Part II, p. B2, http://www.lexis-nexis.com/.

Connelly, Sherryl. "King Makes Serial Killing." *Daily News* (April 3, 1996), p. 29, http://www.lexis-nexis.com/.

———. "Thrills, Chills & Baseball: King Blasts a Homer." *Daily News* (April 4, 1999), p. 18, http://www.lexis-nexis.com/.

Cox, Dan. "New Line Raked over *Lawn*." *Variety* (April 4, 1994–April 10, 1994), p. 15, http://www.lexis-nexis.com/.

Dawidziak, Mark. "It Grabs You by the Throat and Refuses to Let Go." *Calgary Herald* (May 8, 1994), p. C4, http://www.lexis-nexis.com/.

Diamant, Tasha. "Supernatural Meanderings." *Maclean's* (December 18, 1989), p. 57, http://www.lexis-nexis.com/.

Downing, Sarah Jane. "Fantasy World of the Lord of Dark, Magical Frenzies." *Sunday Express* (June 27, 2004), p. 68, http://www.lexis-nexis.com/.

Dubner, Stephen J. "Being Stephen King: It Isn't the Money. It Isn't the Fans. It Certainly Isn't the Reviews. He Writes to Stay Alive." *Ottawa Citizen* (August 20, 2000), p. C15, http://www.lexis-nexis.com/.

Dugdale, John. "The Supernatural Highway." (London) *Sunday Times* (August 18, 2002), Culture, p. 44, http://www.lexis-nexis.com/.

Eberhart, John Mark. "Newly Remodeled: Stephen King Shores up First Book in Dark Tower Series." *Kansas City Star* (June 29, 2003), Arts, p. 16, http://www.lexis-nexis.com/.

Edelstein, David and Michael Wood. "Bag of Old Rubbish." *Slate Magazine* (September 28, 1998), http://www.lexis-nexis.com/.

Ellis, Arthur. "Only for Hardy Fans of Stephen King." *Toronto Star* (December 29, 1985), p. E10, http://www.lexis-nexis.com/.

Field, Ben. "Book Reviews." United Press International (October 18, 1985), http://www.lexis-nexis.com/.

Fine, Marshall. "Final." *Journal News* (September 27, 2002), p. E1, http://www.lexis-nexis.com/.

Finlay, Charles Coleman. "Author Finishes Dark Tower Series, Revises First Volume." *Columbus Dispatch* (June 23, 2003), p. D8, http://www.lexis-nexis.com/.

Finucan, Stephen. "So Much Roadkill Fiction." *Toronto Star* (March 25, 2001), http://www.lexis-nexis.com/.

Florio, Gwen. "Turning the Page, 25 Years Later: A Literary Kingmaker—*Antaeus*—Hits the End." *Philadelphia Inquirer* (January 16, 1995), p. A1, http://www.lexis-nexis.com/.

Foltz, Kim, and Penelope Wang. "An Unstoppable Thriller King." *Newsweek* (June 10, 1985), p. 62, http://www.lexis-nexis.com/.

Fries, Laura. "*Stephen King's Storm of the Century*." *Variety* (February 15, 1999–February 21, 1999), p. 48, http://www.lexis-nexis.com/.

Gaiman, Neil. "Night Crawlers." *Washington Post* (September 16, 2001), p. T2, http://www.lexis-nexis.com/.

Gates, David. "The Creature that Refused to Die." *Newsweek* (September 1, 1986), p. 82, http://www.lexis-nexis.com/.

Goldstein, Patrick. "Rob Reiner Takes on *Misery*." *Los Angeles Times* (April 29, 1990), p. 8, http://www.lexis-nexis.com/.

Gourevitch, Philip. *The Paris Review Interviews, II*. New York: Paris Review, 2007.

Graff, Gary. "Stephen King's Short Stories Long on Chills and Thrills." *Ottawa Citizen* (October 30, 1993), p. B7, http://www.lexis-nexis.com/.

Graham, Jefferson. "King Game for Another X-Files: Horror Master Sends Scully on Maine Vacation." *USA Today* (February 6, 1998), p. 3D, http://www.lexis-nexis.com/.

Graham, Mark. "King Plot No Accident: Author Shapes Character from His Own Experience in New Novel, *Duma Key*." *Rocky Mountain News* (January 18, 2008), p. 30, http://www.lexis-nexis.com/.

Gray, Paul. "Master of Postliterate Prose." *Time* (August 30, 1982), p. 87, http://www.lexis-nexis.com/.

Grice, Elizabeth. "Horror of Horrors: Stephen King Says He May Start Writing Only for Himself." (Montreal) *Gazette* (August 26, 1998), p. C7, http://www.lexis-nexis.com/.

Grimwood, Jon Courtenay. "A Giant, a Kidnap and a Block of Cheese." (London) *Daily Telegraph* (June 9, 2007), p. 26, http://www.lexis-nexis.com/.

Guinn, Jeff. "Two Horror Writers in One *Black House*." *Fort Worth Star-Telegram* (September 6, 2001), Life & Arts, p. 1, http://www.lexis-nexis.com/.

Haft, Chris. "Giants Pitcher Attached to Fame at an Early Age." *Contra Costa Times* (September 23, 2005), p. F4, http://www.lexis-nexis.com/.

Hand, Elizabeth. "The Very Picture of Menace." *Washington Post* (June 18, 1995), p. X2, http://www.lexis-nexis.com/.

Harkavy, Jerry. "Horror Film Rooted in Author's Experience." Associated Press (April 21, 1989), http://www.lexis-nexis.com/.

Harmetz, Aljean. "*Pet* Film Rights Sold." *New York Times* (June 8, 1984, Friday), p. C10, http://www.lexis-nexis.com/.

Harrington, Richard. "*Pet Sematary*: King's Crass Menagerie." *Washington Post* (April 22, 1989), p. C1, http://www.lexis-nexis.com/.

———. "*The Dark Half*: The Gory Penalties of Using a Pen Name." *Washington Post* (April 23, 1993), p. D7, http://www.lexis-nexis.com/.

Harrison, Judy. "King to UM Grads: Please Stay in Maine." *Bangor Daily News* (May 9, 2005), p. A1, http://www.lexis-nexis.com/.

Harrison, Linda. "Stephen King Reveals *The Plant* Profit." *Register* (February 7, 2001), www.theregister.co.uk/2001/02/07/stephen_king_reveals_the_plant/.

Hartl, John. "Thin Script, Uninteresting Characters Help Bury *Graveyard Shift*." *Seattle Times* (October 27, 1990), p. C3, http://www.lexis-nexis.com/.

———. "*Dark Half*: Hutton's Double Duty." *Seattle Times* (April 22, 1993), p. D4, http://www.lexis-nexis.com/.

Helm, Richard. "King Promises to Scare All with His TV *Shining*." *Calgary Herald* (January 12, 1997), p. E4, http://www.lexis-nexis.com/.

———. "Stephen King Taking Another Run at *Shining*." *Toronto Star* (February 8, 1997), p. M4, http://www.lexis-nexis.com/.

Herbert, Frank. "When Parallel Worlds Collide." *Washington Post* (October 14, 1984), Book World, p. 1, http://www.lexis-nexis.com/.

"Here Comes the Fall!" *People* (August 29, 1983), p. 75, http://www.lexis-nexis.com/.

Holden, Stephen. "Draculian Gore, Sound and Fury." *New York Times* (February 6, 1998), p. E10, http://www.lexis-nexis.com/.

Holston, Noel. "Vampires with Biting Humor: The Best of the *Lot*." (New York) *Newsday* (June 20, 2004), p. 11, http://www.lexis-nexis.com/.

Horowitz, Lois. "Books/Writers." *San Diego Union-Tribune* (November 6, 1984), p. 5, http://www.lexis-nexis.com/.

Howard, Judith Lynn. "Stephen King Eases the Misery." *Dallas Morning News* (February 27, 1994), p. A33, http://www.lexis-nexis.com/.

"IATSE, Laurel King Near Agreement on Stand Off." *Daily Variety* (July 9, 1993), p. 6, http://www.lexis-nexis.com/.

"In Good Faith with the King of Horror." *Chicago Sun-Times* (March 16, 2003), *Show*, p. 1, http://www.lexis-nexis.com/.

Itzkof, Dave. "Dead Ringers." *New York Times Book Review* (February 5, 2006), p. 15, http://www.lexis-nexis.com/.

James, Rebecca. "Stephen King Says He Sometimes Scares Himself." *Post-Standard* (October 7, 1994), p. D1, http://www.lexis-nexis.com/.

Jennings, Gary. "King, Haunted by His Past." *Washington Post* (August 26, 1988), p. B3, http://www.lexis-nexis.com/.

Joffee, Linda. "Terry Hands Explains Interest in *Carrie*." *Christian Science Monitor* (May 6, 1988), p. 21, http://www.lexis-nexis.com/.

Johnson, Peter, and Brian Donlon. "Screenwriting *The Stand* a Horror for Stephen." *USA Today* (February 18, 1993), p. 3D, http://www.lexis-nexis.com/.

Jones, Stephen. *Creepshows: The Illustrated Stephen King Movie Guide*. New York: Billboard Books, 2002.

Kasdan, Lawrence. "*Dreamcatcher*: Run, Before It's Too Late." *Seattle Times* (March 21, 2003), p. H19, http://www.lexis-nexis.com/.

Katzenbach, John. "Summer Reading." *New York Times* (May 31, 1987), p. 20, http://www.lexis-nexis.com/.

Keenan, John. "King Loves Idea of Secrets." *Omaha World Herald* (June 29, 1998), p. 29, http://www.lexis-nexis.com/.

Kempley, Rita. "*Creepshow* is the Word." *Washington Post* (November 12, 1982), p. 17, http://www.lexis-nexis.com/.

Kendrick, Walter. "Pacts with the Devil." *Washington Post* (September 29, 1991), p. X9, http://www.lexis-nexis.com/.

Kennedy, Dana. "Going for Cheap Thrillers." *Entertainment Weekly* (February 23, 1996–March 1, 1996), p. 60, http://www.lexis-nexis.com/.

Kernan, Michael. "Kindred Spirits." *Washington Post* (November 27, 1984), p. C1, http://www.lexis-nexis.com/.

Kiely, Robert. "Armageddon, Complete and Uncut." *New York Times* (May 13, 1990), sec. 7, p. 3, http://www.lexis-nexis.com/.

King, David. "*Faithful* Will Appeal Only to Die-Hard Boston Red Sox Fans," *San Antonio Express-News* (December 19, 2004), p. 71, http://www.lexis-nexis.com/.

King, D. Brett, and Michael Wertheimer. *Max Wertheimer and Gestalt Theory*. New Brunswick: Transaction Publishers, 2005.

"King's Ransom?" *Newsweek* (October 27, 1997), p. 8, http://www.lexis-nexis.com/.

Klinghoffer, David. "High-School Bullies Are Real Ghouls in King Tale." *Washington Times* (May 7, 1991), p. E1, http://www.lexis-nexis.com/.

Kloer, Phil. "Latest Work Shows Stephen King is Becoming More Than Just a Horror Storyteller." *Atlanta Journal and Constitution* (September 12, 1999), p. L7, http://www.lexis-nexis.com/.

Kogan, Rick. "Come and Get It—Stephen King on TV." *Chicago Tribune* (November 16, 1990), p. C1, http://www.lexis-nexis.com/.

Koller, Dan. "King's Too Damn Busy." *Dallas Morning News* (December 7, 2005), p. 20, http://www.lexis-nexis.com/.

Krebs, Albin, and Robert McG. Thomas Jr. "Dreaming up a Book." *New York Times* (September 21, 1981), p. A18, http://www.lexis-nexis.com/.

Lacey, Liam. "Young Star Saves *Firestarter*: Barrymore a Hot Property." *Globe and Mail* (May 14, 1984), http://www.lexis-nexis.com/.

Lannon, Linnea. "Stephen King: Too Many Books, Not Enough Awards?" *Oregonian* (June 19, 1991), p. D5, http://www.lexis-nexis.com/.

LaSalle, Mick. "The Naughty *Sleepwalkers*." *San Francisco Chronicle* (April 11, 1992), p. C3, http://www.lexis-nexis.com/.

———. "*Needful Things*: High Budget but Still Low Grade." *San Francisco Chronicle* (August 27, 1993), p. C4, http://www.lexis-nexis.com/.

Last, Johnathan V. "Serial Killers, '70s Films and Stephen King Tips." *Washington Times* (November 12, 2000), p. B6, http://www.lexis-nexis.com/.

Lehmann-Haupt, Christopher. "Books of The Times." *New York Times* (September 8, 1980), p. C15, http://www.lexis-nexis.com/.

———. "Books of the Times." *New York Times* (August 14, 1981), p. C21, http://www.lexis-nexis.com/.

———. "Books of the Times." *New York Times* (July 11, 1985), p. C21, http://www.lexis-nexis.com/.

———. "Books of the Times." *New York Times* (October 21, 1983), p. C31, http://www.lexis-nexis.com/.

———. "Books of the Times." *New York Times* (June 29, 1992), p. C13, http://www.lexis-nexis.com/.

Lint, Charles de. "King Has Us Gasping for More." *Ottawa Citizen* (October 12, 1991), p. 13, http://www.lexis-nexis.com/.

Lorando, Mark. "*Shining* Suffers a Dull Waxy Buildup." *Times-Picayune* (April 27, 1997), p. T4, http://www.lexis-nexis.com/.

Lyall, Sarah, and Marjorie Williams. "*Dreamcatcher*." *Slate Magazine* (April 4, 2001), http://www.lexis-nexis.com/.

MacGowan, James. "*X-Files* Guru Rewrites Script from Stephen King." *Orlando Sentinel* (February 1, 1998), p. A2, http://www.lexis-nexis.com/.

Magistrale, Tony. *Hollywood's Stephen King*. New York: Palgrave Macmillan, 2003.

Marshall, John. "Feeling Success in His Bones King's Back from Near-Death Experience in Book World." *Seattle Post-Intelligencer* (September 29, 1998), p. E1, http://www.lexis-nexis.com/.

Maslin, Janet. "*Dead Zone*, From King Novel." *New York Times* (October 21, 1983), p. C8, http://www.lexis-nexis.com/.

————. "*Christine*, A Car." *New York Times* (December 9, 1983), p. C10, http://www.lexis-nexis.com/.

————. "Prison Tale by Stephen King Told Gently, Believe It or Not." *New York Times* (September 23, 1994), p. C3, http://www.lexis-nexis.com/.

————. "A Fateful Step off a Curb and into Alien Territory." *New York Times* (March 15, 2001), p. E9, http://www.lexis-nexis.com/.

————. "Her Story of Him, Both Tender and Terrible." *New York Times* (October 23, 2006), p. E1, http://www.lexis-nexis.com/.

McClurg, Jocelyn. "With 3 Books Due, Guess Who's King of Book Convention?" *Hartford Courant* (June 16, 1991), p. G3, http://www.lexis-nexis.com/.

McDowell, Edwin. "Behind the Best Sellers." *New York Times* (September 27, 1981), sec. 7, p. 40, http://www.lexis-nexis.com/.

————. "Book Notes." *New York Times* (March 22, 1989), p. C.25, http://www.lexis-nexis.com/.

Mcfarland, Melanie. "*Kingdom Hospital* Offers a Fear Factor of Zilch." *Seattle Post-Intelligencer* (March 2, 2004), p. E1, http://www.lexis-nexis.com/.

McGarrigle, Dale. "Accident Fodder for King Novel *Dreamcatcher*." *Bangor Daily News* (March 22, 2001), p. C1, http://www.lexis-nexis.com/.

————. "The Haunted House that Could." *Bangor Daily News* (January 4, 2002), p. C5, http://www.lexis-nexis.com/.

————. "King to Take up Pen for Magazine." *Bangor Daily News* (August 5, 2003), p. C1, http://www.lexis-nexis.com/.

McGee, Celia. "Thriller of Pitch from Stephen King." *Daily News* (February 16, 1999), p. 22, http://www.lexis-nexis.com/.

McGrath, Charles. "A Foggy Reunion with Horror's Master." *New York Times* (November 18, 2007), p. 6, http://www.lexis-nexis.com/.

McQueen, Max. "Horror Hits Music World: King's Rocking with Novel Band." *Gazette* (November 10, 1992), p. G7, http://www.lexis-nexis.com/.

Mietkiewicz, Henry. "King of the Horror Novels Has Light Touch in Fairytale, *The Eyes of the Dragon*." *Toronto Star* (February 22, 1987), p. A18, http://www.lexis-nexis.com/.

Minzesheimer, Bob. "King Packs Audio Tales with Blood." *USA Today* (November 22, 1999), p. D4, http://www.lexis-nexis.com/.

Mitchell, Sean. "Rob Reiner in Hollywood: The Sweet *Misery* that Fame Brings." *Los Angeles Times* (November 25, 1990), p. 5, http://www.lexis-nexis.com/.

Mobilio, Albert. "Dark Nights of the Soul." *New York Newsday* (June 28, 1992), p. 36, http://www.lexis-nexis.com/.

Montgomery, M. R. "King of Fear—and Philanthropy." *Boston Globe* (November 22, 1991), Metro, p. 1, http://www.lexis-nexis.com/.

Morrison, Michael A. "Stephen King: Time Out of Joint." *Washington Post* (August 26, 1990), p. X9, http://www.lexis-nexis.com/.

———. "Twisted Sister Cities." *Washington Post* (September 22, 1996), p. X5, http://www.lexis-nexis.com/.

Murphy, Ray. "Stephen King's 'New' *Stand*." *Boston Globe* (May 16, 1990), p. 73, http://www.lexis-nexis.com/.

"Names in the News." Associated Press (July 25, 1980), http://www.lexis-nexis. com/.

"Names in the News." Associated Press (May 27, 1983), http://www.lexis-nexis. com/.

"Names in the News," Associated Press (May 5, 1990), http://www.lexis-nexis. com/.

"New Book by Stephen King to Kick off Hard Case Crime's Second Year." Business Wire (February 28, 2005), http://www.lexis-nexis.com/.

Newman, Kim. "*Misery* (Book Review)." *New Statesman* v. 114 (September 11, 1987), p. 30, http://vnweb.hwwilsonweb.com/hww.

———. "Don't Mention the King." (London) *Independent* (August 15, 1998), p. 15, http://www.lexis-nexis.com/.

Newman, Melinda. "A Musical Ghost Story from Mellencamp & King." *Billboard* (October 28, 2000), http://www.lexis-nexis.com/.

"New Stand on *The Stand*." *Sun-Sentinel* (January 15, 1994), p. A2, http://www. lexis-nexis.com/.

Nicholls, Peter. "*Skeleton Crew*." *Washington Post* (June 16, 1985), Book World, p. 1, http://www.lexis-nexis.com/.

Nicholls, Richard E. "Avaunt Thee, Recreant Cyborg!" *New York Times* (September 29, 1991), sec. 7, p. 14, http://www.lexis-nexis.com/.

Nicholson, David. "Stephen King and Strange Happenings in Haven, Maine." *Washington Post* (November 29, 1987), p. X9, http://www.lexis-nexis. com/.

North, John. "This King Can't Win Them All." *Toronto Star* (December 30, 1989), p. M11, http://www.lexis-nexis.com/.

O'Briant, Don. "Scent of Terror Wafts through King Audio Book." *Atlanta Journal and Constitution* (November 18, 1999), p. D2, http://www.lexis-nexis. com/.

O'Connor, John J. "An Eerie Plane Trip, Piloted by Stephen King." *New York Times* (May 12, 1995), p. D18, http://www.lexis-nexis.com/.

O'Hagan, Sean. "Who Needs Babe Ruth?: When the Boston Red Sox at Last Reigned Supreme, Two Fans Recorded Their Finest Hour." *Observer* (January 16, 2005), p. 15, http://www.lexis-nexis.com/.

Ollove, Michael. "Typhoid Stevie." (Baltimore) *Sun* (October 27, 1996), p. J1, http://www.lexis-nexis.com/.

Olson, Ray. "*Insomnia* (Book Review)." *Booklist* v. 90 (August 1994), p. 1,988, http://vnweb.hwwilsonweb.com.

————. "*Hearts in Atlantis* (Book Review)." *Booklist* v. 95 (July 1999), p. 1,893, http://vnweb.hwwilsonweb.com/.

O'Neill, Brendan. "Wrong Number." *New Statesman* (March 27, 2006), p. 54, http://www.lexis-nexis.com/.

Parfrey, Adam. "Stephen King Serves up Pulp Softly Boiled." *Los Angeles Times* (October 5, 2005), p. E9, http://www.lexis-nexis.com/.

"People in the News." Associated Press (November 22, 1993), http://www.lexis-nexis.com/.

Perry, Vern. "Fantasy Failures: Snail Could Outrun Pace of King's *Eyes of the Dragon.*" *Orange County Register* (February 1, 1987), p. L8, http://www.lexis-nexis.com/.

Phillips, Michael. "*1408*: The Room for Quality Chills." *Chicago Tribune* (June 22, 2007), p. C1, http://www.lexis-nexis.com/.

Piccoli, Sean. "King's Newest Horror Tale is Decidedly This-Worldly: *Dolores* Doesn't Need Supernatural." *Washington Times* (January 11, 1993), p. D2, http://www.lexis-nexis.com/.

Quarnstrom, Lee. "All This for *Insomnia*: Author Ends Tour in Santa Cruz." *San Jose Mercury News* (October 25, 1994), p. B1, http://www.lexis-nexis.com/.

Queenan, Joe. "And Us without Our Spoons." *New York Times* (September 29, 1991) sec. 7, p. 13, http://www.lexis-nexis.com/.

Rich, Motoko. "A King Book That Transcends Horror." *International Herald Tribune* (October 6, 2006), p. 9, http://www.lexis-nexis.com/.

Rodriguez, Rene. "King of Horror." *Hamilton Spectator* (October 29, 1992), p. 5, http://www.lexis-nexis.com/.

————. "After Rosie Walked Out, Norman Got Madder." *Miami Herald* (June 11, 1995), p. 31, http://www.lexis-nexis.com/.

Roush, Matt. "*It* Calms King's Fear of TV." *USA Today* (November 16, 1990), p. D3, http://www.lexis-nexis.com/.

————. "*Green Mile* Finds Stephen King in Stride." *USA Today* (March 25, 1996), p. 6D, http://www.lexis-nexis.com/.

Routhier, Ray. "King Seeks to Gauge Web Honesty." *Portland Press Herald* (June 14, 2000), p. B1, http://www.lexis-nexis.com/.

————. "TV's *Kingdom Hospital* Premieres Wednesday." *Portland Press Herald* (February 29, 2004), p. E1, http://www.lexis-nexis.com/.

Russell, Sharon A. *Stephen King: A Critical Companion*. Westport: Greenwood Press, 1996.

Sachs, Andrea. "Boo! How He Startled the Book World." *Time* (March 27, 2000), p. 76, http://www.lexis-nexis.com/.

Salem, Rob. "*Creepshow 2* Really a Monster Bore!" *Toronto Star* (June 3, 1987), p. C3, http://www.lexis-nexis.com/.

"Scene & Heard." (Albany, New York) *Times Union* (December 22, 2006), p. D22, http://www.lexis-nexis.com/.

Schleier, Curt. "Stephen King's Stories Offer Evidence of Pact with the Devil." *Chicago Tribune* (June 9, 1985), p. C35, http://www.lexis-nexis.com/.

Scott, Jay. "Stephen King's *Danse Macabre*." *The Globe and Mail* (May 2, 1981), http://www.lexis-nexis.com/.

Scott, Vernon. "King Takes Wheel on His Vehicle." *Chicago Tribune* (July 24, 1986), p. B15, http://www.lexis-nexis.com/.

Seymour, Gene. "Reigning Cats in King Country." *New York Newsday* (April 11, 1992), Part II, p. 23, http://www.lexis-nexis.com/.

Shales, Tom. "Small Town Vampire: Gruesome Fun in *Salem's Lot*." *Washington Post* (November 17, 1979), p. B1, http://www.lexis-nexis.com/.

Sisario, Ben. "Books in Brief," *New York Times* (June 20, 2004), sec. 7, p. 16, http://www.lexis-nexis.com/.

Skow, John. "Monstrous: *The Talisman*." *Time* (November 5, 1984), p. 88, http://www.lexis-nexis.com/.

Slung, Michele. "Scare Tactics." *New York Times* (May 10, 1981), sec. 7, p. 15, http://www.lexis-nexis.com/.

Spignesi, Stephen J. *The Essential Stephen King.* Franklin Lakes, NJ: New Page Books, 2003.

Stade, George. "His Alter Ego is a Killer." *New York Times* (October 29, 1989), sec. 7, p. 12, http://www.lexis-nexis.com/.

Staggs, Jeffrey. "*Sleepwalker* Trips over Its Horror." *Washington Times* (April 13, 1992), p. D4, http://www.lexis-nexis.com/.

Westlake, Donald E. "Richard Stark Introduced by Donald E. Westlake." *Payback* by Richard Stark (New York: Mysterious Press, 1999 [1962]).

Stein, Joel."Celebrity Bloggers? That's Stephen King-Scary." *Los Angeles Times* (May 15, 2005), p. M2, http://www.lexis-nexis.com/.

"Stephen King Meets *The X-Files*." *Portland Press Herald* (January 26, 1998), p. 2C, http://www.lexis-nexis.com/.

"Stephen King Penned Five Novels Under Pseudonym." United Press International (February 10, 1985), http://www.lexis-nexis.com/.

"Stephen King: The Roots of Terror." *Maclean's* (August 11, 1986), p. 6, http://www.lexis-nexis.com/.

Sterritt, David. "When Shivers Came from What You Didn't See." *Christian Science Monitor* (August 28, 1980), p. 18, http://www.lexis-nexis.com/.

Stickney, John. "The Latest Word on Word Processing." *Money* (September 1984), p. 129, http://www.lexis-nexis.com/.

Stone, Jay. "King Eyes Monsters Within." *Times Colonist* (November 24, 2007), p. D5, http://www.lexis-nexis.com/.

Streitfeld, David. "Stephen King's No. 1 Fans: The Author Gives His Readers a Lively Dose of *Misery*." *Washington Post* (May 8, 1987, Friday), p. D5, http://www.lexis-nexis.com/.

———. "'Strange' Fans Gave King Idea for Novel." *Toronto Star* (May 17, 1987), p. D7, http://www.lexis-nexis.com/.

———. "Ideal Genuine Man." *Washington Post* (February 7, 1988), p. X15, http://www.lexis-nexis.com/.

———. "Book Report." *Washington Post* (August 20, 1989), p. X15, http://www.lexis-nexis.com

———. "Book Report." *Washington Post* (November 13, 1994), p. X15, http://www.lexis-nexis.com/.

Stuewe, Paul. *Quill & Quire*, 46 (October 1980), p. 40, http://vnweb.hwwilsonweb.com/hww.

"Supernatural Meanderings." *Maclean's* (December 18, 1989), p. 57, http://vnweb.hwwilsonweb.com/hww.

Tabor, Mary B. W. "Stephen King on the Installment Plan." *New York Times* (November 11, 1995), sec. 1, p. 39, http://www.lexis-nexis.com/.

Terrell, Carroll F. *Stephen King: Man and Artist*. Orono, ME: Northern Lights, 1991.

Testa, Bart. "The Techniques of Children's Fiction and The Shaggy Dog Story." *Globe and Mail* (September 12, 1981), http://www.lexis-nexis.com/.

Testi, T. Michael. "DVD Review: *Nightmares & Dreamscapes from Stephen King*." Blogcritics.org Video (November 8, 2006), http://www.lexis-nexis.com/.

Trachtenberg, Jeffrey A. "Stephen King Tries to Ring up Sales through Text Messages." Associated Press Financial Wire (January 17, 2006), http://www.lexis-nexis.com/.

Tritel, Barbara. "What the Wicked Magician Did." *New York Times* (February 22, 1987), sec. 7, p. 12, http://www.lexis-nexis.com/.

Underwood, Tim, and Chuck Miller, eds. *Kingdom of Fear: The World of Stephen King*. New York: Signet, 1987.

———. *Bare Bones: Conversations on Terror with Stephen King*. New York: McGraw-Hill Book Company, 1988.

United Press International. (November 4, 1983), http://www.lexis-nexis.com/.

Van Rjndt, Phillipe. "The Other Woman Was a Car." *New York Times* (April 3, 1983), sec. 7, p. 12, http://www.lexis-nexis.com/.

Vernon, Scott. "King Takes Wheel on His Vehicle." *Chicago Tribune* (July 24, 1986), p. B15, http://www.lexis-nexis.com/.

Wager, Walter. "More Evil Than a 15-Foot Spider." *New York Times Book Review* (August 24, 1986), p. 9, http://www.nytimes.com/books/97/03/09/lifetimes/kin-r-it.html.

Washburn, Jim. "Writers Rock Around the Clock." *Los Angeles Times* (May 28, 1992), p. E7, http://www.lexis-nexis.com/.

Webb-Proctor, Gary. "The Little Fable *Eyes of the Dragon*." *Globe and Mail* (April 4, 1987), http://www.lexis-nexis.com/.

Weeks, Brigitte. "Stephen King Wields an Artist's Dark Palette." *Washington Post* (January 16, 2008), p. C1, http://www.lexis-nexis.com/.

Weingarten, Paul. "Meeting The Tiger: Stephen King's Books Keep America on Edge, But Oh, Those Frightful Films." *Chicago Tribune* (October 27, 1985), p. C10, http://www.lexis-nexis.com/.

Weinkauf, Gregory. "Instant Karma." *SF Weekly* (December 8, 1999), http://www.lexis-nexis.com/.

Werts, Diane. "Stephen King's Strongest Work." *New York Newsday* (May 8, 1994), p. 20, http://www.lexis-nexis.com/.

Westbrook, Bruce. "Endearing Characters Can't Save Crime Caper." *Houston Chronicle* (October 9, 2005), *Zest*, p. 19, http://www.lexis-nexis.com/.

———. "Man as Monster: Horror Still the Engine that Drives King's Novel." *Houston Chronicle* (November 15, 1992), *Zest*, p. 30, http://www.lexis-nexis.com/.

Wiater, Stanley et al. *The Complete King Universe: A Guide to the Worlds of the King of Horror*. New York: St. Martin's Griffin, 2006.

Williams, Stephen. "King Suspends E-Book Venture." (New York) *Newsday* (November 29, 2000), p. A66, http://www.lexis-nexis.com/.

Wilmington, Michael. "Deadly Intent: Kathy Bates Brings Humanity to Horrifying *Dolores Claiborne*." *Chicago Tribune* (March 24, 1995), p. C2, http://www.lexis-nexis.com/.

Wilonsky, Robert. "Stand by Them." *Dallas Observer* (September 27, 2001), http://www.lexis-nexis.com/.

Winter, Douglas E. *Faces of Fear: Encounters with the Creators of Modern Horror*. New York: Berkley Books, 1985.

———. "Venturing a Bit into the Magical." *Washington Times* (November 29, 1989), p. E2, http://www.lexis-nexis.com/.

"Woman Claims Stephen King's *Misery* as Her Own." United Press International (April 20, 1991), http://www.lexis-nexis.com/.

Wyss, Trudy. "Interview: Stephen King's Favored Child: The Dark Tower Series is Finally Finished." Borders Web site, http://www.bordersstores.com/features/feature.jsp? file = stephenking.

Yardley, Jonathan. "Stephen King's New Thriller: It's a Long, Deadly Road." *Washington Post* (March 23, 1983), p. B1, http://www.lexis-nexis.com/.

Zoglin, Richard. "Giving Hollywood the Chills." *Time* (January 9, 1984), p. 56, http://www.lexis-nexis.com/.

INDEX

About the Author

ALBERT ROLLS teaches at Touro College in New York City and has also taught at John Jay College, LaGuardia Community College, and other institutions in the City University of New York system. He coedited H. W. Wilson's *World Authors 2000–2005*, *Current Biography International Yearbook, 2006*, and *Current Biography International Yearbook, 2007*, and served as assistant editor of Wilson's *Current Biography* series.